THE URBAN SPECTATOR

INTERFACES

Studies in Visual Culture

Editors
Mark J. Williams
Adrian W. B. Randolph
DARTMOUTH COLLEGE

This series, sponsored by Dartmouth College Press, develops and promotes the study of visual culture from a variety of critical and methodological perspectives. Its impetus derives from the increasing importance of visual signs in everyday life, and from the rapid expansion of what are termed "new media." The broad cultural and social dynamics attendant to these developments present new challenges and opportunities across and within the disciplines. These have resulted in a trans-disciplinary fascination with all things visual, from "high" to "low," and from esoteric to popular. This series brings together approaches to visual culture — broadly conceived — that assess these dynamics critically and that break new ground in understanding their effects and implications.

For a complete list of books that are available in the series, visit www.upne.com

Erina Duganne, *The Self in Black and White: Race and Subjectivity in Postwar American Photography*
Eric Gordon, *The Urban Spectator: American Concept-Cities from Kodak to Google*
Barbara Larson and Fae Brauer, eds., *The Art of Evolution: Darwin, Darwinisms, and Visual Culture*
Jeffrey Middents, *Writing National Cinema: Film Journals and Film Culture in Peru*
Michael Golec, *The Brillo Box Archive: Aesthetics, Design, and Art*
Rob Kroes, *Photographic Memories: Private Pictures, Public Images, and American History*
Jonathan Beller, *The Cinematic Mode of Production: Attention Economy and the Society of the Spectacle*
Ann B. Shteir and Bernard Lightman, eds., *Figuring It Out: Science, Gender, and Visual Culture*
Anna Munster, *Materializing New Media: Body, Image, and Interface in Information Aesthetics*

The Urban Spectator

American Concept-Cities from Kodak to Google

ERIC GORDON

Dartmouth College Press
Hanover, New Hampshire
Published by University Press of New England
Hanover and London

DARTMOUTH COLLEGE PRESS
Published by University Press of New England, One Court Street, Lebanon, NH 03766
www.upne.com

Typeset in Sabon, Eagle, and Empire by Keystone Typesetting, Inc.
Designed by Eric M. Brooks
Printed in China
5 4 3 2 1

A different version of chapter 3 was originally published as "Toward a Networked Urbanism: Hugh Ferriss, Rockefeller Center, and the 'Invisible Empire of the Air'" in *Space and Culture: International Journal of Social Spaces,* 8.3 (2005): 248–268. Copyright © 2005 by Sage Publications.

Library of Congress Cataloging-in-Publication Data
Gordon, Eric.
The urban spectator: American concept-cities from Kodak to Google / Eric Gordon. — 1st ed.
p. cm. — (Interfaces: studies in visual culture)
Includes bibliographical references and index.
ISBN 978-1-58465-803-0 (pbk.: alk. paper)
1. Sociology, Urban — United States. 2. Photograpy — United States. I. Title. II. Title: American concept cities from Kodak to Google.
HT121.G67 2009
307.760973 — dc22 2009026507

For my brother, Adam

CONTENTS

ACKNOWLEDGMENTS

This book has been a long time in the making. I started the project in 1999 while a graduate student in the School of Cinematic Arts at the University of Southern California, and I have done little else but work on it ever since. Well, perhaps that's an exaggeration. But its big question (and it *is* a very big question) concerning the nature of the correspondence between the city and mediation has kept me occupied for years and I trust it will continue to do so.

Of course, my preoccupation with this question has not taken place in a vacuum. I had many accomplices. I received invaluable encouragement and inspiration from the faculty at USC. David James provided me with a model of scholarly discipline, Lynn Spigel provided the original inspiration for the project, and Marsha Kinder recognized the value in it when it was only starting to take shape. And then there are those friends, those very good friends, who put up with my lengthy pontifications and thought experimentations, and who volunteered to read chapters and even fragments of chapters as I was sorting everything out in my head. Specifically, I am referring to Sam Binkley, David Bogen, John (Craig) Freeman, Amy Murphy, and Christina Wilson. I should also mention Jason Young. Jason took an interest in this project for a series he was editing at a different press. He spent huge amounts of time reviewing the manuscript and offering amazingly insightful advice. The series never came to life, but Jason's ideas have. They have shaped this manuscript, and for that I owe him a heartfelt "thank you." There are others, too numerous to mention, who have provided inspiring ideas or suggestions over the years, each of whom has helped move this project from there to here.

Since 2004, I have been on the faculty in the Department of Visual and Media Arts at Emerson College. My colleagues and students have provided a stimulating environment in which to work and learn. And the college has provided needed financial support. I was lucky enough to get a faculty advancement grant to fund research trips and graduate research assistance. My graduate student Parvathy Venkatraman toiled away many hours in the Boston Public Library looking through photography and architectural magazines.

Her commitment to the project was exhilarating. Just when I was feeling discouraged, she would come to my office with piles of copies and ideas and encourage me to look at things in new ways.

But the two people to whom I owe the most gratitude are my wife, Justeen Hyde, and my son, Elliot. Justeen has served as the voice of reason to my sometimes emotionally heightened diatribes. Even though busy with her own work, she has read nearly everything I have written and provided sage advice, unafraid to ask hard questions or to simply tell me when I'm full of crap. She is my partner: always willing to listen to a new idea and always willing to explore a new place. Her strength and curiosity are an inspiration. And Elliot, even though only three years old, has taught me more about how we experience the world than any book ever could. Watching him watch the world is an education. He is truly a passionate person, continuously collecting perceptual tidbits of his environment and assembling them to produce his worldview. This is what I mean by spectatorship. And Elliot reminds me that spectatorship is rarely removed from experience and passion. I look forward to looking with him and learning from him as the American city changes over the next many years. Perhaps he will share my interest in these remarkable places and help me to evolve my own practices of looking.

THE URBAN SPECTATOR

INTRODUCTION

Linking the city to the concept never makes them identical, but it plays on their progressive symbiosis: to plan a city is both to think the very plurality of the real and to make that way of thinking the plural effective; it is to know how to articulate it and be able to do it.

MICHEL DE CERTEAU, "Walking in the City"

On the corner of Thirty-fourth Street and Fifth Avenue in Manhattan, there are dozens of people looking at little screens, typing on little keyboards, with plugs extending from their ears. Each of these people is having a different experience, customized through their personal media. The college student with his iPod selects his music to correspond with the weather and time of day; the businessman types an address into his GPS-enabled phone to find his next meeting; and the tourist stares through her mobile phone camera to capture the Empire State Building in the distance. Mediated by little devices, these people are shaping their experiences of the city. Nicholas Negroponte (1995) famously noted that the world of atoms (our bodies) would no longer need to correspond to the world of bits (data)—that physical proximity would cease to be necessary for public life. But as we can see on that street corner, the world of atoms and the world of bits come together in the city. There is little distinction between the practices of everyday life and the technologies that enable those practices. The soundtrack, the map, the photograph: these artifacts of the everyday are constructive of environments. The practices one adopts to navigate and comprehend any space can never be seen as separate from that space.

New technological practices introduce a profound complexity into everyday tasks, and perhaps challenge accepted notions of urban life, including the nature and scope of public interactions and the corresponding design of the built environment. Can one truly be engaged in public space if they are looking through a viewfinder or tapping sweet nothings with their thumbs on tiny

FIGURE I.1.
Spring in midtown Manhattan. Photograph by Elke Nominikat and Oliver Bouchard (2008) available under a Creative Commons Attribution-Noncommercial license

keyboards? Can the city, as an entity, continue to matter when digital networks enable public gathering without requiring the public to gather in physical space? The answer to these questions is a resounding "yes." The modern American city has never been bereft of these complications — from the handheld camera at the end of the nineteenth century to the mobile phone at the end of the twentieth, the city has always been a mediated construct. The city enters into the cultural imaginary as a hodgepodge of disconnected signifiers, often organized by the technologies that produce them. When Kodak introduced its handheld camera, or hand camera, in 1888, it provided a tool for people to record and retain experiences through visual reproduction. Photographers produced images and, even more importantly, possessed them and organized them to manage their memories. Likewise, when Google introduced its mapping software in 2004, it enabled people to record and retain experiences by marking places on a map, keeping notes, and connecting images. Google Maps has been implemented as both a way-finding tool and a personal organizing tool; through its simple interface, it serves to manage an individual's understanding of space. Communication technologies certainly produce new information about the world; but they also have the facility to organize that information through the literal or metaphorical storage capacity of databases or archives. They provide the spectator the unique opportunity to at once experience space and possess its traces.

These traces, and their inherent possibilities, have substantially altered the nature of media and urban practices in the twentieth century. I call the spectatorship structured around the desire for possessing these traces *possessive spectatorship*—a way of looking that incorporates immediate experience with the desire for subsequent possession. And while this phenomenon has had implications for the modern city in general, in this book I describe how it has been uniquely important for the American city. What's distinctive about the American context is the timing in which the city becomes central to the cultural imaginary. *The American city grew up in parallel to the technologies that enabled its possession.* Not until the late nineteenth century, corresponding to the introduction of the handheld camera and the cinematograph, did the American city take on a meaning outside of mere urban concentration. Prior to that time, while cities were of course present in America, they did not *present* themselves as unique constructs. The city did not become a legible concept until it appropriated the means of its representation into its form. I argue that emerging media practices transformed urban practices by naturalizing the notion that individual spectators could not only see the Concept-city but also possess it. And most importantly, I argue that this spectatorship altered the material shape of the city as urban plans were drafted to meet the expectations of a spectator eager to take control of the city's assembly.

Urban Practices/Concept-city

The concept of possessive spectatorship, on which this book focuses, places a decisive emphasis on visuality. But even as visuality is characterized as the dominant sense mechanism through which possession occurs, it is by no means exclusive, and rarely operates independently of other senses. Visuality is fundamentally embodied. To return to that fictional Manhattan street corner for a moment, the people standing around (with or without mobile devices) have appropriated certain expectations and practices into their everyday lives, integrating what they see into how they move and relate to their physical environment (Ito and Okabe 2006; Wellman and Haythornthwaite 2002). They expect the ability to locate and communicate with their social network in an instant; they expect the ability to query anything and retrieve an immediate answer; they expect the ability to record and archive thoughts and images. And they have, to varying degrees, internalized these expectations into their everyday engagement with urban space, subtly manifested through the direction of a glance, the instantaneous determination of acceptable social distances, and the interaction with streets and buildings.

The notion that visuality and its corresponding technologies might alter the way one engages with the urban environment is not particularly new. In a 1916 article in the photography magazine *Kodakery*, a journalist described how the camera had become naturalized into urban practices even without the presence of a camera. "The picture-thinking Kodaker has his eye out for 'likely' subjects wherever he happens to be. When he walks to and from his office, when he gets on the trolley, when he takes a trip to a neighboring city, he keeps his senses alert for the picture possibilities about him" (Snowden 1916, 9). Almost a century ago, it was not fantastical to imagine a world transformed by the cognitive and visceral transference of media practices. It was not fantastical to assume that expectations born of media practices did not necessarily depend on the technologies that gave them life.

Ever since the handheld camera prompted shifts in the framing of everyday vision, the process of collecting those visions has been framed through metaphor. According to Anne Friedberg, metaphors are necessary for the accessibility of new media, as they wrap "the newly strange in the familiar language of the past" (2006, 15). The practices of viewing a film, looking at a mobile phone screen, or listening to an iPod can easily seep into other practices through the connection of metaphor. The film becomes a means of travel to distant times and places, the tiny screen becomes a portal to information and other people, and the iPod becomes a soundtrack, connecting the urban landscape to cinematic scenery.

But while metaphor suggests important representational strategies, it alone can't provide much insight into practices. This book is concerned with how the dominant understandings of technologies, shaped through metaphors of one kind or another, collide with the consumptive practices of spectators. And ultimately how this collision serves to shape the city. Michel de Certeau introduces this relationship in his essay "Walking in the City." The piece begins with a spectator standing atop one of the 1,370-foot high towers of the old World Trade Center and looking down upon the streets below. That view "makes the complexity of the city readable," he argues, "and immobilizes its opaque mobility in a transparent text" (2002, 92). The view from on high is a fiction or facsimile of the city, like those drafted by planners or cartographers, but it does not provide access to the practices that actually compose the city.

Those are only accessible by the "practitioners" of the city that live "below the thresholds at which visibility begins." According to de Certeau, "These practitioners make use of spaces that cannot be seen; their knowledge of them is as blind as that of lovers in each other's arms . . . it is as though the practices organizing a bustling city were characterized by their blindness" (93).

Urban practices, themselves devoid of vision, always operate within what de Certeau calls the Concept-city, a space of total vision. Each of the people on that street corner is blindly interacting with their immediate urban spaces (despite their use of media devices), while their understanding of those spaces is framed by the evolving Concept-city (enhanced by those same devices). Whether directly mediated or not, each practice of the city is embedded within some articulation of the Concept-city. A man, brand new to New York, lifts up his arm to hail a passing taxi (an action he has seen again and again in movies); a woman photographs the Empire State Building contemplating the age of Art Deco that produced it; a tourist gets her bearings in the crowded city by calling up a map on her phone. In each of these examples, the concept of Manhattan (its logic and structure) influences the practice of its spaces. De Certeau aligns this phenomenon to Ferdinand de Saussure's characterization of langue and parole — the overall logic of any language (langue) is implicit in each individual speech act (parole). All urban experiences, he argues, comprise both the phenomenological encounter (the blind, embodied practices of the street) and the overarching logic of the Concept-city (the complete picture).

De Certeau demonstrates the interaction between urban practices and the Concept-city, but he doesn't address how each of the elements is composed. What shapes the concept? What organizes practice? This book begins from the dialectic he provides, and offers possessive spectatorship as an explanation of how practices and Concepts are structured around a complex assortment of media technologies and urban representations. How did the handheld camera change the way people walked through the city, while simultaneously changing the shape of the city walked through? How did film spectatorship influence the meaning of urban movement, and how did that new meaning get worked into the development of the Concept-city? Each chapter in this book explores these and similar questions in order to renegotiate de Certeau's urban dialectic in light of possessive spectatorship. Images, interfaces, and protocols shape urban experiences, structures of urban desires, and plans for urban spaces. Media practices mold de Certeau's walker into a historically contingent subject. So while there is a well-regarded tradition of aligning urban representation with totalizing spectacle—"everything that was directly lived has receded into a representation" (Debord 1994, 7)—I argue that spectacle, or Concept, is always directly lived, especially when mediated by screens and radio waves.

The Flaneur: Embodiment and Alienation

De Certeau claims that the "desire to see the city preceded the means of satisfying it" (2002, 92). As early as Renaissance painting, he points out, artists attempted to represent the city in various aerial views from which the human eye could never have directly experienced it. This desire is clearly demonstrated with the advent of urban panoramas in Paris and London in the late eighteenth century. Large-scale circular paintings gave the impression of an entire city being reduced to a single spectacle—surely, an impossible view, but one that captivated urban audiences by making the impossible seem obtainable. According to M. Christine Boyer, because of their immense scale and apparent totality, they had the effect of separating for the spectator the ideal city of the mind from the real city of physical space. They "revealed everything and said nothing. . . . The act of showing a city's image was becoming the spectacle itself. There was no need for narrative in this view, nor authentic collective experiences, for in the panorama the spectator was being isolated and her or his perspective privatized, trained to view the surrounding environment as a disciplined order of things" (1996, 253). The panorama opened up the possibility that the city could be consumed in a single glance as a fully contained representation. And as a result of this possibility, it disciplined viewers into cultivating a disinterested practice of looking. The city could be disentangled of its masses and presented as a spectacle available to the individual spectator. The panorama gave the spectator a sense of control over their urban surroundings by containing those surroundings in spectacle.

The impulse to manifest the city in a single glance or a collection of glances guided Baron G.-E. Haussmann's modernization of Paris in the 1850s (see figure I.2). Haussmann was commissioned by Napoleon III to redevelop the medieval city. His plan consisted of widening and straightening its circuitous streets and extending twelve grand avenues out from the Arc de Triomphe. From each boulevard, one could see the city's center. Regardless of the position of the spectator, the street plan created perspectives that reinforced the existence of the whole. On one hand Haussmann's design of Paris confirmed the helplessness of the individual spectator by so forcefully representing the

FIGURE I.2. Aerial view of Baron Haussmann's redesign of Paris. Photograph taken from balloon, showing the Arc de Triomphe at left center. Photographer Alphonse Liebert (1889). Courtesy Library of Congress

city's totality; but on the other, it demonstrated that the city was desirable because it was a product of an individual's visual desire. The paradox of the seemingly totalizing spectacle is that it could not exist without a spectator. For the first time, the city was seen as something to be seen.

Haussmann's Paris introduced the benefits of a rational street plan, but perhaps most importantly, it forced a redefinition of the urban subject. While the traditional European medieval city was constructed for God's point of view, the modern city was built for the spectator's point of view. Martin Heidegger suggests that this is indicative of a modern transformation in space more generally. While omniscience once guided spatial understandings, "embodiment" became the "organizing factor" of modern space (1984, 138). Space is the product of phenomena and sensations, a product that emerges from the process of being-in-the-world. Likewise, there was a growing awareness that the city was more than the sum total of its structures. The modern city was a barrage of sensations, a swirl of phenomena, and a collection of experiences that only came into being through embodied practices.

The instantiation of the Concept-city coincided with a reconceived urban subject who brought the city into focus through urban practices. However, it would quickly become clear that the Concept-city often obfuscated urban practices. Haussmann understood that the city was a product of the urban subject; but he didn't quite understand (or care) how the urban subject was a product of the city. Georg Simmel was one of the first commentators to state that the "metropolis" had a profound affect on "mental life" (1971). The conditions of the city, he argued, redefined subjectivity and dictated how individuals could, in turn, make sense of their conditions, even if the capacity to make sense was compromised by the mechanisms of the city (Allen 2000, 68). Each individual in the city is stricken with a, "one-sided type of achievement which, at its highest point, often permits his personality as a whole to fall into neglect. . . . [H]e is reduced to a negligible quantity. He becomes a single cog as over against the vast overwhelming organization of things and forces which gradually take out of his hands everything connected to progress, spirituality and value" (Simmel 1971, 337). Not only is perception fragmented in the city; as Simmel explained, the subject is fragmented. In what he described as the "blasé attitude," the urban subject develops "an indifference toward the distinction between things" (329). He can focus on individual fragments in the environment and in himself, but he is incapable of seeing how they all fit together. The inability to assemble one's environment into a unified meaning had considerable consequences: the individual spectator, while gaining significance in the larger scheme of urban life, loses significance to himself. As Simmel said, one's personality "fall[s] into neglect."

Simmel's metropolis was a rational place—formed from the "calculating exactness of practical life" (330). It was capable of turning human beings into parts of a machine. But Simmel also recognized the potentiality of urban life. He cautiously celebrated how the distance and anonymity of the metropolis offered freedom from the tyranny of opinions. "Today in an intellectualized and refined sense the citizen of the metropolis is 'free' in contrast with the trivialities and prejudices which bind the small town person" (334). Charles Baudelaire, who was living in Paris during the modernization, understood this as well. Removed from the intimacy of small town life, the urban subject could be a *flaneur*—someone who is integrated into crowds of people as part of some rational system of civic organization, while at the same time capable of seeing the crowd apart from himself. According to Baudelaire, the boulevards of Paris created a new primal scene—where lovers could display their affection to one another amidst the perpetual flux of strangers. They could be in private and public at the same time. As Marshall Berman explains, "They could weave veils of fantasy around the multitude of passers-by: who were these people, where did they come from and where were they going, what did they want, whom did they love? The more they saw of others and showed themselves to others—the more they participated in the extended 'family of eyes'—the richer became their vision of themselves" (1988, 152).

On the crowded boulevard, the self is bolstered by its becoming part of a crowd. In the crowd, the flaneur is blind. But being gazed upon by others enabled the modern spectator to see and himself gaze upon others. This dual perspective, of seeing and being seen, was the definition of the flaneur—a subject who stands midway between the man of leisure and the man of the crowd—alienated from both.

The flaneur, always outside looking in, enjoyed a unique form of autonomy within the modern city. But as Simmel pointed out, it was an autonomy manufactured from the rhythms of technology. It was for this reason, said Walter Benjamin, that Baudelaire eventually gave up on the mystique of the flaneur; he learned only to fight the crowd, not to be swayed by its perpetual motion (1986). Baudelaire grew increasingly uncomfortable with the near ubiquity of technology. His ideal urban subject was someone who could exercise complete freedom, alternating between the sighted and blind perspectives available in the city. Benjamin adapted the concept of the flaneur to accommodate the technological flows of the city. The flaneur did not coexist with technology; he was a product of technology. He was distinct from the urban drifter who aimlessly "cast[s] glances in all directions," Benjamin said. "Today's pedestrians are obliged to do so in order to keep abreast of traffic signals. Thus technology has subjected the human sensorium to a complex kind of training" (1985, 175). Urban spectatorship was guided by the disciplining qualities of all technological encounters. From traffic lights to streetcars to panoramas and film, what one was capable of seeing was dictated by the conditions in which seeing took place. The "experience which the passer-by has in the crowd," Benjamin asserted, "corresponds to what the worker 'experiences' at his machine" (1985, 176). He is carried away by the city—like Charlie Chaplin getting sucked into the factory machine in *Modern Times* (1936), the flaneur must necessarily give himself over to the structure and flow of technologies (see figure I.3).

The American Flaneur: Possession and Control

The flaneur, as defined by Simmel and Benjamin, had a limited amount of control against the forces of technology; he understood his alienation and could choose only to embrace it. By the end of the nineteenth century, how-

FIGURE I.3. Charlie Chaplin caught in a machine in *Modern Times* (1936).

ever, the philosophical discourse of American Pragmatism cultivated a rather distinct identity for the American version of the flaneur. This urban subject, while confronted with similar technological stimuli in the city, was perceived as having much more control in ascertaining meaning. The American flaneur, conceived through Pragmatism, earned self-sufficiency through the resolute possession and organization of perceptions.

Pragmatism became influential across a number of cultural and scientific disciplines in the late nineteenth century and served to distinguish a uniquely American perspective on the question of agency and experience. According to William James, "For rationalism, reality is ready-made and complete from all eternity, while for pragmatism it is still in the making" (1908, 123). Within this general framework, James described a cognitive process he termed "radical empiricism." If empiricism is the direct experience of reality, radical empiricism finds connections between experiences. "To be radical," James said, an "empiricism must neither admit into its construction any element that is not directly experienced, nor exclude from them any element that is directly experienced. For such a philosophy, the relations that connect experiences must themselves be experienced relations, and any kind of relation experienced must be accounted as 'real' as anything else in the system" (1996, 42). Reality, as determined through this formulation, is a combination of what would seem to be an infinite number of experienced parts. For all practical purposes, then, the individual part is subordinate to the whole of experience.

James denied that consciousness was composed of retrievable "ideas" subject to scientific scrutiny—that view, he said, sacrificed "the continuous flow of the mental stream" and substituted for it "an atomism, a brickbat plan of construction." Even before James adopted the term *Pragmatism* to describe his reclamation of experience as central to metaphysics, he was highly critical of a psychology that treated perception as a conglomeration of individual sensations. "We certainly ought not to say what usually is said by psychologists," James wrote, "and treat the perception as a sum of distinct psychic entities, the present sensation namely, *plus* a lot of images from the past, all 'integrated' together in a way impossible to describe. *The perception is one state of mind or nothing*" (1950, 80). What for Simmel and Benjamin was a constant struggle between self and perception for James was a necessary integration. Perception was a continuous flow of sensations, and any attempt to scrutinize a single sensation apart from the whole was meaningless. James referred to this "brickbat plan" as conceptual knowledge, and decried its inadequacy, saying that it couldn't achieve "the fullness of the reality to be known" (Morris 1950, 49).

By disregarding conceptual knowledge in the formulation of reality, James describes experience as fundamentally dependent on a self-aware subject. The perceptual flux, as he describes it, is a totality that depends on a certain amount of control from the subject to organize and process experience. While British empiricists such as Hume and Locke treated experience as just one element in a larger reality, James, and the radical empiricists saw no reality outside of experience. This would set in motion a trend in American philosophy that would rely on what many critics saw as the overly ambiguous "culture of experience." But as the philosopher John J. Stuhr commented, "What is American in philosophy is the use of the method of experience, not the endless cataloging of it independent of the context of its use, not the tedious formalization of its results in sacred categories. What is American is the emphasis on the continuity of belief and action in experience, not the mere assertion of this unity and continuity in theory alone" (qtd. in Jay 2005, 266). This reaction against intellectual abstraction went beyond the halls of academe; it was characteristic of an emerging American approach to popular culture. Increasingly suspicious of tradition and abstraction, Americans were much more eager to experience things firsthand as a method of constructing meaning. Indeed, as Catherine Cocks explains, "sensual experience had become the key to understanding both cities and America" (2001, 150).

James's Pragmatic subject position placed inordinate power with the individual to assemble experience from the perceptual flux. This ran counter to Benjamin's use of the flaneur and to Simmel's urban subject wherein experience was largely shaped by technological structures. And while their flaneur had some freedom to shift between the crowd and isolation, he was incapable of organizing the combination of perceptions into a meaningful whole. The popular manifestation of the modern American city was dependent on possessive spectatorship, or the belief in a Pragmatic subject with the flexibility to collect and assemble perceptions in the manner James described.

Possessive Spectatorship and the American City

Before the late nineteenth century, American cities were popularly understood as concentrations of people and structures, but not meaningful entities in their own right. Unlike European cities that had considerable historical interest to lure the traveler, American cities, according to one commentator, were "lacking in unity of purpose and harmony of design" (Zueblin 1903, 373). Alex Krieger points out that the nineteenth-century American city "engendered awe or fear, at times mistrust or disdain, but rarely genuine affection as in the case of, say, a Frenchman espousing a love for his Paris" (1987, 40). Overpopulated, polluting, and dangerous, the American city was understood as more of a folly than an accomplishment.

William Dean Howells, a popular novelist in the late nineteenth century, both perpetuated this understanding and helped to produce the framework from which it could be challenged. In several of his novels, Howells acknowledged the problems of the city while suggesting that they could be overcome through new ways of looking. The city was an ominous and chaotic formation, but it was poised for redemption. He wrote about the unseemly side of urban life, but only as it was consumed, often adoringly, by a distanced spectator. His characters have the uncanny power of transforming the poverty and blight of urban landscapes into the picturesque (Bramen 2000). Poverty becomes a romantic image of struggle; cluttered streets suggest attractive patterns of use; ethnic diversity is exotic. In his novel *A Hazard of New Fortunes* (1890), a traveler named Basil March explores New York's Little Italy, but he doesn't see the details of dilapidated tenements or human suffering, only the "familiar picturesque raggedness of southern Europe." He and his wife, Isabel, find beauty in poverty by reorienting the visual landscape into something distanced and familiar. Despite their fears of the menacing crowds and crime in the city, Basil and Isabel explain that "the chief pleasure of their life in New York was from the quality of foreignness" (Howells 1994, 255). In viewing New York as foreign, argues historian Amy Kaplan, Howell's characters experience the city as familiar: "The role of the tourist places them in a known relationship to the city and allows them to distance themselves from the surrounding poverty by framing it within the secure lines of the 'picturesque'" (1988, 49).

Howells reoriented the city from something that happens to people to something that the privileged onlooker can transform and ultimately possess. He made a claim on the Concept-city by removing himself from the blind urban practices that compose everyday life. In describing his own experiences of New York neighborhoods, Howells wrote: "I feel their picturesqueness, with a callous indifference to that ruin, or that defect, which must so largely constitute the charm of the picturesque. A street of tenement houses is always more picturesque than a street of brown-stone residences. . . . But to be in it, and not have the distance, is to inhale the stenches of the neglected street, and to catch that yet fouler and dread fuller poverty-smell which breathes from the open doorways" (Howells 1909, 186). To enjoy the experience of the city, according to Howells, one needed distance from its realities. The concept of the picturesque could essentially rescue the American city from the "poverty-smell" and "blotches of disease" by which it was plagued. Of course it could only rescue it for those given the privilege of distance, for those able, at least momentarily, to stand outside of the everydayness of life.

To stand outside was a practice not available to everyone. Even for a "refined" spectator like Howells, it was often the case that he would get too close, and became haunted by the sense of urban blight. He understood the precariousness of spectatorship. He acknowledged that the privileged position of his social class alone could not protect him from the realities of the city. The experience of the picturesque could easily transform into the experience of the everyday—where the individual is denied access to anything beyond his immediate surroundings. The wrong situation or the wrong place could force a dangerous proximity into the average urban experience. The picturesque could easily transform into the downtrodden and degraded.

Howells's New York was dangerous and sublime at the same time—a theme of contradiction that had been implicitly present in American urban life since Reconstruction. After the Civil War, the middle class and well-to-do desired urban spaces and practices that would allow them distance from the "dangerous masses"; however, they simultaneously desired urban spaces and practices that embodied the American ideal of democratic access. While perceptions of safety were surely desirable, democratic access became an essential psychological tool in the country's reconstruction. This living contradiction was clearly manifested in Frederick Law Olmstead's urban parks movement in the late 1860s. Olmstead's first major accomplishment, Central Park in New York City, was at once a socially exclusive space and steeped in the rhetoric of inclusiveness. In theory, Central Park was open to all; in practice, it was open only to those with commonly held aristocratic values. There were proper ways of behaving that served to weed out class diversity. Playing certain sports, and even running, was banned from its interior. Central Park was intended to be a space of leisure, a space for quiet reflection away from the bustle of urban life. It was intended to provide the necessary distance for refined spectators to transform the squalid images of the city into the picturesque. Howells described his experiences there as follows: "I plunge deep into the Park, and wash my consciousness clean of [the city] for awhile" (1909, 185). It was therapeutic both in its ability to grant distance from the city and its promise of democratic access from the safe position of de facto social exclusion.

The rhetoric of democratic accessibility, embodied in Olmstead's parks, set the tone for other public spaces as well. One of the most important transformations took place in the most unlikely of spaces—luxury passenger rail cars. George Pullman, one of the major manufacturers of luxury cars, created a system based on a surcharge, rather than explicit class distinctions. Unlike its equivalent in Europe, all that was required to obtain a seat in one of these cars was an expensive ticket. A writer for the Baltimore and Ohio Railroad claimed: "it is simply a question of cash, not of caste" (qtd. in Cocks 2001, 54). By letting the market resolve class distinctions, Pullman transformed the travel business by demonstrating that "democratic access" made good business sense. And he established a fairly straightforward principle that Americans still cling to today—the market doesn't discriminate. If everything in society is a commodity, even if the vast majority of people can't afford something, at least everyone is playing by the same rules. In short, Pullman's innovation was to convince the public that train travel was based on a universal *promise* of access.

But it wasn't just train travel that Pullman helped to transform into a commodity. The new accessibility of cities, coupled with the capacity to view them as distant images, served to reorient the urban landscape itself into a commodity (Kirby 1996). New technologies of vision, specifically the train and the park, produced a windowed perspective on the urban landscape that had never before been experienced. When the unremarkable architecture and industrial landscapes of American urbanism that once stopped Americans from desiring their own cities were framed as distant, picturesque images, they had the capability of coalescing into a cohesive city. And as the increased reach, comfort, and accessibility of the railroad in the United States made travel possible for people of moderate means, the potential throngs of short-term visitors to urban hubs motivated a significant growth in the urban tourism industry. Through urban tours and guidebooks, scores of new companies set out to produce a consumable image of American urban life. According to Catherine Cocks, the careful packaging of urban sights and events cultivated "a distinctive spatial practice that enabled tourists to perceive sprawling, divided, and often squalid cities as a series of lovely sites available to the cultured transient" (2001, 156). The efforts of the tourism industry pushed a transformation in the American public's relationship to its built environment. What was only implicit became an explicit desire to possess, through spectatorship, the rapidly expanding urban landscape, to turn it into something knowable, perhaps even something desirable.

The White City at the Chicago World's Fair in 1893 was the first instantiation of a city built to accommodate this emerging possessive spectatorship (see figure I.4). A writer for *Scribner's* described the White City, a 633-acre neoclassical, life-size model of a city that served as the fair's centerpiece, as follows: "It is far too big for any question of conscience to be allowed to enter in. Its bigness is beyond description. No words or pictures can tell the story of its size. Experience alone can teach it" (Mitchell 1893, 188).

The scale of the White City was no grander than the "gray" city that surrounded it. But unlike Chicago, which was known more for its unwieldy crowds and pollution than for its cohesive design, the White City was presented as a Concept-city.

It required participation from the fair's visitors. It was conceived as a complex puzzle of sorts with all of its parts meant to fit together in such a way that each visitor could come away with the impression of having experienced "the city as a whole"—not as it was presented, but as it was assembled. Daniel Burnham, its chief architect, said of his creation: "As a people we are beginning to see that in no architectural or landscape composition do many parts of themselves make a whole, unless by plan and design they are primarily laid out to have the reciprocal relations of a whole" (1902, 620). Burnham understood the White City as a new presentation of the whole, and he asserted that for the average American "the new has come, and he will possess it" (619). The White City established the character for the new American city as something obtainable through individual experiences. The American urban spectator could take control of the city's appearances and possess them through his own experience.

In some respects, possession was quite literal. The Eastman Kodak Company introduced its handheld camera in 1888. While photography had been around for a half century, the handheld camera introduced what is still today the most popular photographic genre: the snapshot. These portable cameras allowed people to walk around and capture images of landscapes and people for no other purpose than to collect images. The merging of the snapshot and urban design demonstrated in the White City set the stage for the modern American city—a construct that could only be manufactured through possessive spectatorship. Americans were uncomfortable with being a part of the

FIGURE I.4.
General view of the White City at the World's Columbian Exposition. From *Official Views of the World's Columbian Exposition Issued by the Department of Photography*, C. D. Arnold and H. D. Higinbotham, official photographers

urban masses, and they were even more uncomfortable with the inevitability of the masses. They believed that individuals could step outside of the crowd, that they could assemble fragmented experiences to compose the whole. They believed that they could take control of the Concept-city, consuming it like any other media object. The city didn't possess the individual; the individual possessed the city. The American city, therefore, achieved its modern identity as the product of individual consumption, while at the same time, it constructed the identity of individuals as actors capable of individually consuming.

The Map

This book is an attempt to map out specifically how possessive spectatorship in the United States, structured by architectural, urbanistic, and technological innovations, has influenced the shape of the American Concept-city. Each chapter describes a particular iteration of the Concept-city and the urban and media practices that developed alongside it. In the first chapter, I discuss the planning and implementation of the White City and investigate how handheld photography factored into its design and implementation. The Concept-city quite literally conformed to photographic renderings. The White City offers an ideal starting point for my discussion of urban spectatorship as it provides the model from which subsequent forms take shape. It was not simply a collection of buildings; it was an experiment in the presentation of the Concept-city wherein meaning was largely dependent on the possessive practices of spectators.

This came into clear relief as official practices of spectatorship, dictated by the fair's Department of Photography, butted heads with a growing population of amateur photographers. The conflict between a perfectly assembled city of images and a personally assembled city of images would, more than anything else, succeed in transporting possessive spectatorship to contexts outside of the White City. The American flaneur was defined by its populism and gestures toward democratic accessibility. This is the subject of chapter 2. As Kodak's hand camera soared in popularity, concerns emerged over the new populist spectatorship. Could the masses be trusted with framing experience? Could they be trusted with making history and defining beauty in such a playful manner? And could the Concept-city survive its own success as a commodity readily available to this unrefined spectator?

While these debates raged in amateur photography magazines, the practical knowledge of the city found its greatest transformation in the emerging medium of cinema. The aesthetics associated with "Kodaking," mobile and playful, got abstracted into new forms of media exhibition. In chapter 3, I look at the development of early cinema and its connections to "spectacular" advertising in Times Square. As the playful possession of urban imagery got transposed from the still photograph to larger-than-life displays, the intimate gaze of the spectator got transformed into a spectacle of mass consumption. In the early development of Times Square, from 1904 to about 1915, the spectator's desire to possess the city in the form of movement became quite apparent. Even though the spectator was not literally in possession of images, as he was with the hand camera, those same urban and media practices were appropriated in this new context.

But by the 1920s, this spectacle achieved yet a bigger scale. The early nickelodeon theater gave way to the movie palace, and as skyscrapers reached unprecedented heights in New York City and network radio connected distant spaces with invisible ether, the camera was no longer sufficient for capturing all the distant images of the city. Chapter 4 describes how the new scale of the Concept-city made each act of possession speculative — the vastness of the city was always greater than a visual perspective could capture. What I call "speculative architecture" was manifested in the artwork of the architectural renderer Hugh Ferriss, as well as the midtown Manhattan development Rockefeller Center. Each represented a Concept-city that could be assembled only through the speculation of the spectator.

After World War II, the culture of American cities was drastically altered. The 1950s transformed the spectatorial distance associated with speculation into a distance associated with alienation. Chapter 5 looks at how urban renewal projects sought to replace the speculative city with the operative city — a representation with no visual relationship to the thing it represents, only to its function. As the middle class rapidly left the city for the suburbs and was no longer interested in actively participating in the construction of the city, the government intervened to produce a Concept-city that could "compose" itself through machine intelligence. By looking closely at the renewal of Los Angeles's downtown, this chapter describes an unprecedented intervention into urban spectatorship where individual possession was sacrificed for the conveniences of machine intelligence. For the first time in the modern American city, urban practices were subordinated to the Concept-city.

But in the 1970s, the spectator was recentered through the popular negotiation of history and nostalgia. Chapter 6, by looking at the case of Boston's Faneuil Hall, describes how the preservation movement introduced historical proximity to remedy the geographical distance caused by renewal. The urban experience took on the character of television reruns — a continuous repetition of the familiar to evoke an intimacy and feeling of being at home. The "rerun city" would become the foundational principle for the neotraditional New Urbanism movement and help to shape practices of urban spectatorship that relied on the possession of space as well as time.

The basic tenets of the rerun city get reworked in the contemporary context, as historical proximity is reoriented to historical accessibility. The city remediates its previous iterations in order to present itself anew. But distinct from the logic of the rerun discussed in the previous chapter, the contemporary American city employs the logic of the database. Just as television was shifting from linear, broadcast television to Netflix, movies on demand, and file sharing, urban spaces were tasked with the job of presenting a platform from which the user could assemble historical and virtual references. In the book's final chapter, I describe the "database city" — a Concept-city that gives extraordinary freedom to the spectator to assemble her own experiences and urban imaginaries and organize them into something comprehensible, searchable, and exportable. This becomes particularly clear in the redevelopment of Hollywood Boulevard in Los Angeles. The functionality of the Concept-city corresponds with new digital aggregation tools from Facebook and Google Maps to smart phones. As possession and assembly of space, time, and social life are made quite literal by digital networks, the database city provides the platform for possessive spectatorship, a way of looking where individual spectators continually reinvent the city from their personal digital assembly lines.

Each chapter in this book describes an interaction between a Concept-city and its corresponding urban and media practices. And while these interactions influence the perception and manifestation of cities throughout the world, I focus on a particular element that is uniquely dominant in the United States — the cultural impulse to possess, control, and assemble the experience of the city. The consistently shifting shape of the American city in the twentieth century can be seen as a series of accommodations and reactions to the urban practices aligned with possessive spectatorship. As such, my goal is not to provide a comprehensive history of the twentieth-century American city; rather, it is to provide the reader with a new framework from which to view that history. And as media become ever more entrenched into the practices of everyday life, this framework becomes even more essential in shaping our understanding of the American city — not as a reflection, but as a hypothesis. The city, constantly emerging in a collision between practice and concept, has to be considered proactively by architects and planners. The challenge would seem to correspond with how Wyndham Lewis characterized the city of the immediate future in his modernist manifesto: the "first great modern building that arose in this city would soon carry everything before it; and hand in hand with the engineer, and his new problems, by force of circumstances so exactly modern ones, would make a new form-content for our everyday vision" (1986, 34). While this book is about the past, it is also about where we go from here, and how we settle on the processes that determine new directions. Seeing the city as both the subject and object of seeing will go a long way toward effectively designing a city that corresponds with the cultures that live within it.

MORE THAN THE SUM OF ITS PARTS

The White City and Amateur Photography

Thou shalt of all the cities of the world
Famed for their grandeur, even more endure
Imperishably and all alone impearled
In the world's living thought, the one most sure
Of love undying and of endless praise
For beauty only, — chief of all thy kind;
Immortal, even because of thy brief days;
Thou cloud-built, fairy city of the mind!
R. W. GILDER, "The Vanishing City"

The growth spurt in American urban tourism in the late nineteenth century coincided with the introduction of portable cameras, or hand cameras, into American life (West 2000). These new cameras, perhaps more than the very specific efforts of tourism boards, were responsible for the American obsession with "sights." Instead of simply receiving the "canned" thoughts of guidebooks, Americans were, by virtue of photographing the places they visited, involved in making them. The possibility that one could capture their own representations of urban space, that one could move through and document experience, allowed spectators to dissect the city into parts and comprehend a totality that would have otherwise been outside the possibilities of vision. By the 1890s, the increased popularity of Kodak's hand camera promoted the very kind of urban spectatorship that the tourism industry was attempting to sell — an urban unity constructed from the assemblage of multiple, disconnected parts.

The first conscious manifestation of this spectatorship took place in the White City at Chicago's Columbian Exposition in 1893. The White City was a photographic display of urbanism, meant to communicate the idea of the city through an assemblage of interconnected sights. The 633-acre development

FIGURE I.1.
Looking west from the Peristyle. From *Official Views of the World's Columbian Exposition Issued by the Department of Photography*, C. D. Arnold and H. D. Higinbotham, official photographers

was intended to display the grandeur of the American urban future. It was not a display of architecture per se; it was a picture of unified urban experience that was meant to outlive its temporary structures. Between May and October 1893, the World's Columbian Exposition attracted over one-tenth of the U.S. population and an estimated fourteen million visitors from around the world. During that time, more than four million guidebooks, viewbooks, and souvenir volumes were sold to extend the temporary exposition both spatially and temporally. The White City was a temporary exhibit that made the experience of the city exportable.

Notably, the Columbian Exposition marked the first use of picture postcards. According to a guide published by Rand, McNally & Company, in co-operation with the fair's Department of Photography: "This volume is published with two objects in view: First, to provide a fitting memento of the

World's Fair for those who made themselves familiar with its wonders and desire to keep its memories green; secondly, to supply the sixty odd million people in the United States, who have not seen the Fair, with a series of pictures that will convey, to the fullest extent made possible by art, a true and vivid idea of the sublimity of the great Exposition, and, as far as can be, minimize the loss they sustained through absence." These pictures served to expand the reach of the city and allow "visitors" well outside of its geographic space to experience it. Ultimately, the multiple perspectives and simultaneity promised by photographic representation would prove as important as the architecture in the composition of the city's material. As the subject of photography, the city was for sale—and not just representations of the objects and phenomena embedded within its geography; the city, in and of itself, as a symbol of social and cultural progress, was positioned as a productive *medium* capable of effecting change within its borders. The White City was presented as a Concept-city—an exposition of architecture meant to mobilize the concept of "city," outside of its material details, in order to evoke political and cultural change. Ultimately, the White City was a media exhibition, showing the world what the city could do to transform the conditions of modern life. "The possibility of quickly making or remaking other cities on a vast scale," notes William Wilson, "was present from the birth of the World Columbian Exposition" (1989, 62). The White City was not only the most photographed city in the world; even before the photographic representations of its buildings proliferated, the White City was designed within the conceptual framework of photography. It marked the distinctly modern possibility of packaging and marketing the experience of urban space for mass consumption.

The act of viewing or taking photographs was central to that experience. As such, the fair sparked a considerable controversy over who had the right to capture images. In addition to the official views, the White City attracted thousands of amateur photographers and motivated others to take up the hobby upon arrival. But this was seen as a direct affront to the fair's planners. In order to maintain control of the White City's official image, the Department of Photography placed restrictions on amateur photographers, making it cost-prohibitive to use hand cameras and banning tripods and large-format cameras all together. These policies proved to be incredibly unpopular and were eventually overturned because of the outcry from a growing number of amateur photographers eager to capture their own views of personal experience. The battle over amateur photography at the fair marked a significant move toward the development of a possessive spectatorship, wherein spectators took an increased level of personal control over immediate experience and memory.

Building the City

The White City was the realization of a Concept-city. With four hundred buildings covering over six hundred acres of land, the neoclassical building facades, sculptures, canals, lagoons, plazas, and promenades made up an indisputably extravagant experiment in American city building. No one lived in this city, but it was intended to serve as a model for urban residence.

Daniel Burnham, director of works for the White City, was charged with the task of creating an exposition that would symbolize America's significance on the four hundredth anniversary of Columbus's discovery of America. Not surprisingly, considering the importance of the commemoration, the decision to hold the fair in Chicago was somewhat controversial. For easterners, it seemed absurd that such a significant event would be held in Chicago, a city removed from the cultural affairs of the East Coast, and one that had still not fully recovered from the fire of 1871. And with the Parisian World's Fair of 1889 still fresh in everyone's mind, Chicago's fair was burdened with having to prove to the world it could compete with Paris. Incapable of matching the architectural innovations with steel and glass displayed at the Parisian exposition, the Chicago fair took advantage of its available resources—a large expanse of open space in the undeveloped Jackson Park. So in contrast to the Parisian fair, which displayed exhibit buildings in various architectural styles, the White City was conceived as a uniform neoclassical landscape, spread out across a great distance, that could cultivate a sense of urban unity and grandeur. As one commentator observed, "The most remarkable point about the Chicago Fair is its beauty as a whole" ("The World's Fair" 1893).

Less than thirty years after the Civil War, it was important for America to assert its unity and political stability to the world. Burnham envisioned the task of building the White City as consistent with the ongoing project of reconstruction: as more and more of the population resided in cities, a presentation of urban unity might inspire the resurrection of the war-torn national unity. John Nolen, writing for the magazine *The American City*, quoted the poet Henry Drummond in describing the role of the American city. "To make Cities—that is what we are here for. For the City is strategic. It makes the towns; the towns make the villages; the villages make the country. He who makes the City makes the world. After all, though men make Cities, it is Cities which make men. Whether our national life is great or mean, whether our social virtues are mature or stunted, whether our sons are moral or viscous, whether religion is possible or impossible, depends upon the City" (Nolen 1909, 15). For much of the nineteenth century, Americans preferred to distance their national identity from their cities. Therefore, Nolen's use of Drummond's proclamation was unique in the way it placed such significant stakes on the city. The very foundations of morality and civility, Drummond suggested, and Nolen echoed, were dependent upon and perhaps caused by the city. When Burnham, never wanting for confidence, set out to design the White City, he sought nothing less than a transformative experience for each visitor, and as a result, the entire nation.

And with his sight on achieving national prominence as an architect, Burnham set out to shift the ideal of urbanism westward, away from the established norms of Europe and the Northeast of the United States. If the city was to "make men," and define the "national life," then it should be centered in Chicago. An article in *Century Magazine* echoed this call: "As a civic marvel, therefore, Chicago will be the most significant exhibit at her own fair. . . . For if she may not claim to be the metropolis, she is at least the typical American city, the point of fusion of American ideas, the radial center of American tendencies" (Buel 1893, 615). The perception that Chicago was somehow more capable than New York of reflecting national values because of its status as the "typical American city" was important for the construction of the White City. The grand city to be built in Jackson Park could escape viewer perceptions of elitism and exceptionalism through its close association with the "averageness" of Chicago. Yet not everyone was convinced of this. Chicago wasn't the place one looked for architectural innovation or cultural progress. A commentator writing for *Cosmopolitan* put it this way: "They would have fought like the beasts at Ephesus to obtain ocean passages to visit Paris, London or Berlin, had it been at either of these capitals; but a World's Fair in the United States, and above all things at Chicago, must necessarily be an absurdity" (Grant 1893, 162–163).

Burnham's challenge was considerable: to design a city that would compensate for its less than impressive geographical location. He hired architects from all over the United States (primarily from the Northeast) to design the individual structures. To every architect and designer he mandated only a few specifications: location of the footprint, white facade, and a uniform cornice line. These specifications would ensure cohesiveness to the city and make certain that no individual structure would sound off beyond the group. "All those classic facades, roofs and porticos unite into a chord of delicious harmony," said a visitor to the fair. "Each edifice has its own individuality, accentuating its own note, as it were; but it is duly subordinate to the grand ensemble" (Boyesen 1893, 176).

The notion of the grand ensemble would appear again and again in comments about the fair. An article in *Scribner's* from July 1893 described the difficulty of achieving such a formation: "And how easily might such an assemblage of heroic structures such as these at Jackson Park, as in previous similar expositions, have been so disposed, with relation to each other and their environment, as to have completely lost not only their individual impressiveness but the infinite advantage of their imposing *ensemble*" (Gibson 1893, 29). The advantage the writer spoke of is the ability for architectural structures to have meaning beyond their material form. In this article, along with many others, there was a grasping for the language to describe how the relation between buildings opened up the possibilities for architectural meaning. In most cases, the resulting architectural meaning could only be described as *beauty*.

Urban beauty was something with which, before the Columbian Exposition, Americans were unfamiliar (Wilson 1989). According to one visitor, the fair was a world "in which ugliness and useless[ness] have been extirpated, and the beautiful and useful alone admitted" (Cocks 2001, 128). The profundity of the fair for so many visitors was to see the possibilities in the combination of beauty and urban life. That cities not be dirty, squalid centers of industry was an idea without much previous application. So when Burnham set out to design a city, he led with what was a fairly progressive idea in urban architecture—that the city be conceived prior to the individual design of buildings. "Everyone saw plainly that, though a pond be beautiful, a grassy lawn or bank beautiful, a building beautiful, all of these elements wrought into a harmonious design attain another and greater beauty, and that the beauty of the whole is superior to that of each of the several parts of the composition exploited separately" (Burnham 1902, 619).

In other words, he didn't want people leaving the fair commenting on the loveliness of a particular building; he wanted the experience of the whole city to be so overwhelming that the details would be inconsequential. In short, Burnham intended the White City to be a sublime experience. As it was popu-

FIGURE I.2.
Bird's-eye view looking northwest from Liberal Arts Building. From *Official Views of the World's Columbian Exposition Issued by the Department of Photography*, C. D. Arnold and H. D. Higinbotham, official photographers

larly understood in America, the sublime was any overwhelming site, any experience that seemed to surpass the ability of the senses to evaluate it. But distinct from its European origins, the American notion of the sublime was not an elitist notion; it required no special knowledge or cultivation; it was theoretically accessible to everyone. As David Nye points out, the American sublime was more closely associated with pleasure. And it needn't be solely dependent on serendipity. "The sublime soon became not the result of serendipity but rather a scheduled part of travel" (1994, 27). No sooner did people expect to find these sublime encounters with the natural world, in places like Niagra Falls and the Grand Canyon, than developers planned to construct these experiences for easy consumption. Burnham wanted the experience of the sublime to be available to everyone who visited the fair. He wanted it to be consumable, reproducible, and exportable. And it would start with the display of the beautiful.

He employed Frederick Law Olmstead to draw up the plans for the grounds. Olmstead, the best known landscape architect in the country, believed strongly in the power of democratically accessible beautiful landscapes. While Olmstead's involvement in the fair makes sense on a very practical level, Olmstead's conception of urbanism was quite different from Burnham's. Olmstead was not particularly fond of urban life, and he certainly did not believe in the redemptive qualities of urban form as Burnham did. For Olmstead, parks and urban landscapes were necessary alternatives to the urban surroundings; unlike the built environment, parks were democratizing spaces open to the full range of urban residents. Olmstead's designs for both Central Park in Manhattan and the Emerald Necklace in Boston were occasions for the democratic escape from the chaos of urban life. Olmstead said of Central Park: "The poor and the rich come together in . . . larger numbers than anywhere else, and enjoy what they find in it in more complete sympathy than they enjoy anything else together" (qtd. in Wilson 1989, 32). The classes could come together in the face of natural beauty, but only as it ran counter to the juxtaposed urban landscape. For Burnham, on the other hand, landscape was consistent with the urban form and he saw his design of the White City as perfectly blending architectural and natural beauty into a unified manifestation of urbanism. But Olmstead insisted that there be space in the city that was purely natural, removed from the potentially distracting presence of buildings. The result was the Wooded Island—a space that would satisfy both men's conceptions of beauty. The island was an oasis in the city's center into which the visitor could escape, and from which she could have a stunning view of the surrounding city. Indeed, the island could be the locus of the sublime experience.

The conceptual outcome of the partnership between Burnham and Olmstead is often considered the foundation of the City Beautiful Movement. City Beautiful, which was officially named in 1899, was an American urban design movement that sought to beautify cities through the implementation of pictorially consistent, neoclassically inspired, functional cityscapes.[1] While the White City was only a temporary exhibit, Burnham used it to establish a connection between beauty and usefulness. In his words, "The useful flowers only in the atmosphere of the beautiful" (1902, 620). For Burnham, it was the beautiful presentation of a city that could introduce a spectator to a city's function. Beauty makes the difference between order and chaos. The unbeautiful miles of American city streets are rapt with disorderly uses. But if one were to gaze upon a street and understand it as it connects with the overall city, the street and urban life in general would achieve a calm and gracefulness never before seen. "Beautiful and clean cities attract desirable citizens, and real estate values increase," said a supporter of the City Beautiful Movement. "Clothes don't make the man, but they come pretty near making the city" (Underwood 1910, 214). For Burnham, the beautiful, or the pictorial nature of urban environments, was the most functional means of grasping the city. It was not a distraction or simplification of urban process; it was rather a more efficient means of communicating complex or singular phenomena. Complex phenomena were the combined elements of urban life, and singular phenomena were the experiences of the whole city.[2]

Burnham's goal for the White City was to reduce the city's complexity to a singular phenomenon, with the intention of constructing an urban experience for each visitor that was both wholly new and fully comprehensible. That the city served the functional role of housing the fair's exhibits would only serve to heighten the singular effects of the neoclassical architecture. "To some," admitted the fair's historian Hubert Bancroft, "it may [have appeared] inconsistent to display modern industry in temples whose style of architecture carries the mind back to the days of Augustus Caesar and of Pericles, to place, for instance, hydraulic presses in a building into which one passes between classic columns of an order devised more than a thousand years before printing was invented" (*The Artistic Guide* 1892, 5). Each building contained exhibits that profiled the latest in American industry, technology, or fine arts. Burnham conceived the White City as the beautiful veil through which the spectator could access the possibilities of American innovation. And he would capitalize on these contradictions in order to better associate for the visitor the thrill of progress with the beautiful and democratic ideal of the city.

Insofar as the White City effectively communicated this sentiment, Burnham conceived of it as a pedagogical tool. It was a perceptual and intellectual training ground for urban comprehension. It was a Concept-city capable of teaching spectators how to view cities in general. Its facades and sculptures were not the main attraction; what was really magnificent to visitors of the fair was the chance to peer into the city itself, to experience an idealized urban unity that was utterly new to an American public. " 'I went to the fair at once and before I had walked for two minutes,' wrote Owen Wister, a visitor to the White City, 'a bewilderment at the gloriousness of everything seized me . . .

until my mind was dazzled to a stand-still. . . . *I studied nothing, looked at no detail, but merely go at the total consummate beauty and grandeur of the thing*' " (qtd. in Trachtenberg and Foner 1982, 218; italics added).

This reaction was precisely what Burnham had set out to create. He wanted to condition a spectator who was capable of experiencing the whole city through bypassing the mundane qualities of urban details. "Up to 1893," Burnham declared, "the American citizen, as a rule, had given little thought to the way that things generally looked about him. Not far had he then advanced in the development of a civic sense of the beautiful in the quality, quantity, and relation of the lands and buildings he works and plays in." Of course, after the fair, all of that had changed. He continued, "Here, studied on the spot by millions, and by millions more through the activities of the Bureau of Publicity and Promotion, a great truth, set forth by great artists, was taught to all our people. This truth is the supreme one of the need of design and plan for whole cities" (1902, 619). In the course of one summer, Americans had gone from not noticing their surroundings (not even the architectural detail in front of them) to consuming multiple details and then assembling those details into a whole experience. According to Alan Trachtenberg, Burnham's most important drive in the planning of the exhibition was to realize the "conception embodied in the total design of White City of how space might be ordered and life organized." This organization of space, not what filled it, was the most powerful meaning in the design. "Symmetry proclaimed the immediate message," says Trachtenberg, "the underlying spatial form speaking directly to the senses through the prestige of neoclassical monumentality. The message joined form to monument, each building and each vista serving as an image of the whole" (1982, 212).

For Burnham, the problem was not that the White City could be experienced in isolated instances (perhaps in photographs before even arriving at the fair), but that those instances might be mistaken for experience, thus disrupting the perception of the whole. This anxiety was anticipated in an article for *Scribner's*: "Superlative anticipation of our hopes is often disastrous to their full realization. But no such danger awaits the visitor to the Columbian fair. The most extreme glorification of this superb achievement at Chicago still leaves us the superlative of *actual experience*" (Gibson 1893, 37; italics added). In this writer's formulation, "actual experience" overshadows all other experiences and draws the authenticity of these subordinate experiences into question.

The architecture at the White City was lauded for making "actual experience" readily available to the average spectator. *The Artistic Guide to Chicago and the World's Columbian Exposition*, a promotional book published in 1892, advised visitors that "[a]ttention should be directed to the architectural grouping of these buildings. The principal difficulty consisted in grouping these huge buildings in such a manner that the *picture* they would present to the eye from any point of the grounds or outside might be one of perfect artistic beauty. . . . [T]o arrange all these various elements under a system that would combine beauty and usefulness was a task that had never confronted an architect before on such a stupendous scale" (10). Burnham set out to accomplish this task by building a system that could orchestrate the assemblage of multiple elements. Ultimately, he sought to build William James's "perceptual flux" into the form of the city. The White City should function as an aggregate of images—a personalized browser through which one can easily possess the necessary components to produce a complete experience.

This was certainly a higher order of comprehension than what was otherwise available to the masses. But according to several of the fair's contemporary critics, this "common" perception was difficult to avoid. "The rural American will be modified by the fair in manifold ways, and I think, to his advantage," said a writer for *Cosmopolitan*. "He will be a broader and better informed man, with a wider outlook on life. He will be less provincial, less narrowly parochial and Philistine" (Boyesen 1893, 186). And it would seem that only the most hopeless would not be positively affected. An article in *Scribner's* put it even more bluntly: "Unless the . . . 'Average American' is an undeserving barbarian who has made up his mind to prefer the wrong thing, these impressive monuments cannot fail to do him good" (Mitchell 1893, 188).

The White City was widely understood as a lesson in urban living. Visitors might stay for only a few days, or even hours, but they would leave understanding something profound about the structure and function of the city. One critic likened Burnham's approach to an Aristotelian formalism, wherein the city could only be properly understood as form. The goal was to create a city that was consumable and reproducible—where "form becomes formula" (Fojas 2005, 265). So while the structures were only temporary, the idea of the city, as manifested through the assemblage of beautiful images, could last forever.

The Department of Photography was charged with the task of producing this permanent vision of urban beauty. But immediately after the fair's open ing, it would find itself engaged in a heated conflict with the newly empowered amateur photographer. The conflict emerged when the department placed substantial restrictions on the type of camera that could be used by amateurs within the fairgrounds. The unpopular policy was eventually overturned, but it served to illustrate the stakes in urban spectatorship. The White City was constructed as a series of images to be assembled by the visitor; it was intended to democratize access to urban experience. Therefore, stripping the individual spectator of the power to create and assemble his own images was seen as an affront to the very foundation of the new city. The practice of photography opened up the possibility that individuals within a crowd (even without a camera) could each be made to believe that they could consume a common perception of the whole. It took the Department of Photography only a little time to realize that maintaining control of the White City's image required giving up control and adopting the populist rhetoric its planners espoused.

The Practice of Photography

Driven by the pursuit of progress, the designers and administrators of the White City were very much aware of the need for photography in the city's ability to communicate. The city's grandiose scale and dramatic vistas would have been mere isolated events if not for the mediating technology of the lens. According to Peter Bacon Hales, "the result of [the] densely layered combination of photographic depiction, exhibition, and dissemination was a city as real in photographs as it was in its physical form (perhaps more real, in fact), as permanent (or, again, more so) as that which it proposed to represent" (2005, 214).

From the fair's inception, photography was central to its design. Burnham appointed Charles Dudley Arnold, a Buffalo photographer known for his "architectural scenes," as the fair's official photographer. Arnold was hired in 1891 to manufacture controlled views of the fair and offer a complete course of vision from groundbreaking to closing. Taking the challenge very seriously, Arnold moved from Buffalo to Chicago in 1891, and took up residence there until 1894. During that time, he photographed the fair nearly everyday, creating an unprecedented record of a construction project. This meticulous documentation was important for Burnham so that he could justify expenses to the U.S. Congress, which had voted to hold the fair in Chicago over Washington, D.C., and New York. But he was also quite aware of the uses of images to drum up publicity for an exposition still many months away. In the summer of

1892, the Chicago-based Committee on Ways and Means, which regulated the fair's expenditures and contracts, would grant Arnold exclusive rights to make and sell photographs for public distribution. There was, at the time, surprisingly little opposition to Arnold's monopoly on imagery, as even the most eager fair watcher considered his work a service to them. Construction images appeared in many newspapers and magazines, and even after the fair's opening, there remained a persistent public fascination with seeing the fair in progress.

Arnold was quite adept at getting his images into the public eye: in guidebooks and newspapers and magazines. He was very aware that the promiscuity of photographs would build anticipation of the fair's opening and give people a sense of having already seen the White City, long before it was even possible to have done so. So when Arnold and his appointed apprentice H. D. Higinbotham released the *Official Views of the World's Columbian Exposition* in 1893, it would seem, for many eager visitors, to be the culmination of years of desirous image consumption. The official guidebook had views of buildings taken in a grand architectural style, with the carefully plotted vistas taking precedence over everything else in the image. The *Official Views* was such a carefully crafted vision of the fair that it was claimed to be all one needed to remember the fair, or even experience it for the first time. Yet the majority of pictures included were grand vistas of the White City, devoid of people. "These photographs were deliberately taken very early in the day when there were few visitors to interrupt or anecdotalize the majestic forms and spaces," writes Margaretta Lovell. "The intention, however, was not to exile people from this vision but to let the architectural forms stand in for the collective accomplishment of an artistic and technological vision" (1996, 46). This strategy of representation, widely cited as the best way to view the White City, would stand in stark contrast to the other side of the fair—the Midway Plaisance.

The Midway Plaisance, a long street paralleling the White City, was conceived as a collection of "exotic" cultures from around the world. It functioned as an important counterpoint to the majesty of the White City. For most commentators at the time, it had no lasting architectural interest, thus Arnold, concerned with developing a grand urban photography, downplayed its importance in his official photographic records. In the official views, only a few images of the Midway were included. According to Stanley Applebaum, "most of the Midway exhibits that were not merely temporary shacks were feeble imitations of buildings and places elsewhere" (1980, 95). Arnold felt that the Midway's lack of symmetry and chaotic display of cultures was beyond the scope of his photographic project. With exhibitions of reproduced streets in Cairo and China and almost every other "exotic" part of the world, the unordered collage of urban landscapes in the Midway lacked a cohesive vision, Arnold thought, and was thus rendered antithetical to the urban project of the White City. As one writer for *Scribner's Monthly* put it: "the Midway Plaisance is not far away with its turbaned, sandaled, greased, and befeathered inhabitants" (Low 1893, 512).

However, the contrast between the two was necessary for the White City's manufacture of symmetry—the Midway served as the "loose," "morally ambiguous" (read: racially other) space in opposition to the unified urban future conceptualized in the neoclassical (and white) cohesion of the White City. The ideology of unity in the White City was premised on racial, ethnic, and national exclusion. For example, in an issue of *Cosmopolitan* published in 1893, a writer warned the amateur photographer against photographing the Midway Plaisance: "The scene was all too comprehensive for him to grasp it in its entirety; there was no beginning or ending with anything like definition" (Markley 1893, 62). Per this article and many others like it, the Plaisance was considered a prephotographic, and premodern space. Because it could not be photographed in an orderly fashion, Arnold felt that it should not be considered on par with the modern phenomenon of the White City.

The Rise of the Amateur

All the controversy over photographing the fair was centered on preserving the order of the White City—a controversy almost entirely driven by the cultural wave of amateur photography that was just beginning to crest. The handheld camera had been around for many years, but when George Eastman introduced his new Kodak in 1888, the technology found a much more significant place in popular culture. Eastman made two noteworthy additions to the market: he made his cameras affordable, and he invested in a marketing campaign that forcefully situated the camera into everyday life and away from the rarefied domain of hobbyists. As Nancy Martha West points out, "the transformation of amateur photography into a commercialized leisure activity also meant its exile from a world (albeit a largely masculine one) characterized by commitment, exertion, erudition" (2000, 41). But for the Department of Photography, an independent department established in April 1893, this new breed of amateurs would be nothing more than a nuisance. Accordingly, the department put the heaviest restrictions on those amateurs who might be committed enough to produce "quality" images. Tripods, large-format negatives (four by five and larger), and stereocameras were expressly excluded from the fairgrounds. Handheld cameras were allowed in, but the department charged the outrageous fee of two dollars a day (which was four times the daily admission charge) to each visitor entering the fair with one. If a visitor wanted to bring in a camera, they were required to obtain a daily permit. To do this, they had to pay admission at the gate, then carry their camera, escorted by a Columbian Guard (the fair's police), to the Department of Photography office, pay the fee, and then return to the main gate where they could enter legally. If that weren't enough, once on the grounds, they couldn't buy film. Vendors were prohibited from selling film on the fairgrounds. Eastman responded forcefully to this policy by marketing the Kodak as "the world's fair camera" — boasting the fact that it came equipped with a 100-exposure roll of film. This way, visitors wouldn't need to buy film, because they could adequately capture the fair in 100 shots. Soon after this initial response, Kodak announced a new film called the "Columbian Spool," a 250-exposure roll designed specifically for the fair. An advertisement claimed that visitors could "bring home the fair experience on just one roll" (West 2000, 65). Kodak successfully capitalized on these restrictions to perpetuate the notion that the number of photographs taken is directly proportional to the level at which one's experience is secured in memory.

While Kodak struggled to convince visitors that they needed to take their own pictures, the Department of Photography continued their struggle to convince visitors that the official views were the only ones worth looking at. Arnold insisted that the new Kodak amateur wandered through the fair, carelessly capturing his surroundings, whereas the official photographs were thoughtfully planned and executed. But as Kodak's Columbian spool became more popular, it became increasingly unpopular for the department to maintain restrictions on camera use. Letters from disgruntled amateurs began appearing in newspapers and magazines. An article in *Cosmopolitan* quoted an "average" snapshotter after his camera was confiscated for not paying: "Guess they don't want no pictures took, they got so many photographs to sell" (Smith 1893, 154). Alfred Stieglitz, the newly appointed editor of *The American Amateur Photographer*, scaled up the magazine's criticism of what he deemed Arnold's elitist policies. After a number of critical editorials in various photography magazines, the Department of Photography began to yield to the cultural trends. Fair officials quickly came to realize that, despite its limitations, the camera-mediated gaze was a necessary component of urban spectatorship. As a result, they relaxed their restrictions on amateurs by reducing the permit fee and turning a blind eye to large-format cameras.

After relentless campaigning by George Eastman, on May 16 (weeks after the fair opened) Kodak was granted exclusive concession rights for its film on the fairgrounds. An advertisement published in June 1893 declared: "Having seen the superior work done on our new Kodak films, the World's Fair authorities have decided to sell no other film on the grounds" (West 2000, 64). Of course, this decision was not premised on the recognition of superior work; more likely, it was premised on the recognition of comfortably inferior work. The images that came from amateurs would pose no immediate threat to the Department of Photography's ability to sell "official views." And just maybe it would encourage people to purchase them, because watching people with cameras could be the best advertisement for photographs.

This dynamic was illustrated when one of the official photographers at the fair, F. Dundas Todd, wrote an article for *American Amateur Photographer* that outlined a photographic walking tour. Todd directed visitors to begin at eight in the morning (in order to make use of the best light) and proceed to make a sequence of a half dozen photographs of key buildings from a series of four points on a circular route around the Wooded Lagoon. It is telling that Todd's descriptions largely mapped out how to reproduce Arnold's "official views." The reproduction of Arnold's views became common practice in short time. Kodak's concession was right next to the Department of Photography's offices, so every person who applied for a permit was offered guidebooks with the best vantage points from which to photograph (in service of reproducing Arnold's images). One of these books offered an hour-by-hour guide for a complete day's photo tour.

These guides were very popular. Despite some anger at the department's policies, most amateurs didn't see their practice as exclusive from that of the Department of Photography. As the official photographs of the White City were most likely known to visitors long before they set foot on the grounds, amateurs wanted to find those already familiar views and recapture them. This was something of which Arnold was aware. In one of the more famous photographs from the fair, Arnold captured two amateurs photographing the Fisheries Building from precisely the spot he had captured the image that was

FIGURE I.3. Fisheries Building. From *Photographs of the World's Fair*

FIGURE I.4.
Arnold's photograph of two amateur photographers re-creating his view of the Fisheries Building. From *Official Views of the World's Columbian Exposition Issued by the Department of Photography*, C. D. Arnold and H. D. Higinbotham, official photographers

included in the "official views" (see figures 1.3 and 1.4). While Peter Bacon Hales wonders whether or not he "recognized that he was witnessing his own imminent supplanting by new forces in photography" (2005, 244), it seems more likely that he gloried in the power he had over the image-making practices of others.

The self-produced image allowed spectators to feel as though they could contain and control the modern metropolis. But it produced a considerable amount of anxiety as well. One writer focused on the inevitable conflict between the spectator's expectations and actual media practices:

> He had read and heard by word of mouth, potent descriptions of the marvelous beauties that would greet his eye, and he yearned for the time when it would be possible to stroll about in this land of enchantment and picture its marvels with the aid of the camera; but when he came to look upon it, he

> was moved and affected, and felt that descriptions failed because the vision was one that, in its magnificence, was beyond the scope of words, and presented a severe task for him to record pictorially with anything like justice. (Markley 1894, 61)

Another article in *Century Magazine* written just after the fair opened in May 1893, suggested that the aggregation function of the White City might cause frustration in some, more experienced, sightseers. "It is not easy to follow any plan in such sight-seeing if one has the usual American mind, as alive with mere curiosity as it is with a craving for instruction—pleased to look at anything, discontented only to think that other people are seeing things with which it cannot make acquaintance" (Renssalaer 1893, 6). The American wants to see and experience everything—but with the vastness of the White City as its subject, this might not be possible. The thought of not achieving a complete experience might, for some, prove reason enough to stay away. "But such people, if they are true *flaneurs*, will make a great mistake in keeping away from Chicago. Of course there are dawdlers of an inferior sort, people who are simply stupid, and can enjoy nothing but doing and thinking nothing; and it makes no difference whether these go to Chicago or stay at home" (Renssalaer 1893, 11). In other words, seeing the White City required a certain level of refinement—knowledge of how to see, which the author associated with personal freedom. With that freedom, assembling one's personal experience requires little effort. The city presents itself with perfect clarity. "If you go in perfect freedom," he declares, "you will find such an idler's paradise as was never dreamed of in America before, and is not equaled anywhere in Europe to-day" (12).

Cultivating the American Flaneur

One critic of the fair described the distinct qualities of the American flaneur as someone who wanders through the city "not like a painstaking draftsman, *but like a human kodak*, caring only for as many pleasing impressions as possible" (Renssalaer 1893, 12; italics added). The flaneur, or the human Kodak, can safely distance himself from the crowds by adopting certain practices of looking—the collection of sensory stimuli for the purpose of immediate experience. He needn't have a camera with him, he only need gaze as if he did. The Kodak, in this case, is the perfect metaphor through which to understand the ideal conditions of possessive spectatorship. The "kodaker," armed with hun-

FIGURE I.5.
The top of the Ferris Wheel extended 264 feet above the fair. From the *Official Views of the World's Columbian Exposition Issued by the Department of Photography*, C. D. Arnold and H. D. Higinbotham, official photographers

dreds of exposable images in a handheld photographic outfit, can simply snap pictures without thinking too deeply about frame and composition. The Kodak defined a way of looking that was deliberate, but not immediately reflective (in that it would often take days to get exposed images). Approaching the White City like a "human Kodak," the spectator assembles experiences without reflection, constantly implicating each experience with the impression of the whole. This concept of spectatorship within the American city offered unprecedented power to the individual consumer. Even without a camera, visitors came to view their movements through architectural space as a form of spectatorship mediated by the possibility of the camera. This way of looking, designed into the form of the White City, could be sustainable and reproducible even without the hardware that initially brought it to the attention of the American spectator.

A Reproducible, Mobile Vision

The correlation between photography and the reproducibility of the White City was made clear in the most modern of exhibitions — the Ferris Wheel (see figure 1.5). The wheel offered a mobile perspective from which to view the entire fair. Since the onset of the fair's planning, Burnham had been trying to figure out a way to "out-Eiffel Eiffel." He needed something taller, more extravagant, and more dramatic than the tower built for the 1889 Parisian exhibition. Hundreds of engineers submitted plans — some utterly fantastic, like the forty-story log cabin. But George W. Ferris, a bridge builder, tester of metal bridge elements, and contractor, submitted plans for a giant amusement wheel capable of carrying thousands of people at once. Immediately, Burnham took to this idea. Because it was commissioned very late in the fair's planning, the famous wheel didn't open until the middle of June, exactly fifty-one days after the opening of the fair. But this only added to the anticipation. People couldn't stop talking about the great wheel that was soon to open in the Midway (Larson 2003).

And there was good reason. The wheel's 45-foot-long axle was the largest single piece of steel ever made. It was 250 feet in diameter and the full height at the top was 264 feet. With thirty-six wood veneered cars with room for sixty people in each, the fifty-cent ride included two revolutions and lasted for twenty minutes. From the wheel, one could see the entire fair and parts of Chicago (see figure 1.6). Significantly, the Ferris Wheel was not a stationary observation deck with a single perspective; the wheel supplied a constantly moving viewpoint that allowed one to see the fair from all conceivable angles on a single plane. With a turn of the body (within the mechanical wheel), all other images are conditioned and made accessible to the spectator. It is significant that the American equivalent of the Eiffel Tower was a temporary, reproducible structure, now housed in amusement parks throughout the country. Without a mind to permanent monumentality, the Ferris Wheel, in accordance with Burnham's plans, was to enable a reproducible mobile vision rather than a permanent stationary perspective.

The White City defined the American city as a phenomenon that transcended time and space. It solidified for skeptical Americans that urban experience was something desirable and achievable. And it placed the condition and representation of urban America at the forefront of national consciousness — for the first time in the United States, the cohesive image of the city was

FIGURE 1.6.
The Ferris Wheel provided magnificent views of the White City. From the *Official Views of the World's Columbian Exposition Issued by the Department of Photography*, C. D. Arnold, and H. D. Higinbotham, official photographers

a marker of national health. Different from the grand, singular displays of European cities, the White City suggested the American urban landscape was more democratic in its construction. The Concept-city was organized through an assemblage of representations, and built as a commodity around the technological possibilities of the camera. The White City, widely understood as a "miniature of the ideal city" (Zueblin 1903, 374), set the standard for urban presentation and consumption. And more importantly, it demonstrated that American urbanism was uniquely aligned with its emerging consumer culture.

PICTURE THINKING

Kodaking and the Art of Nature

The "you press the button and we do the rest" class of amateurs can no more claim the credit of making the photographs they so proudly display than they could claim the credit, after starting a stone rolling down the hill, of creating the law of gravity which caused it to keep on moving.

W. S. DAVIS, "Photography's Worst Enemy"

As Kodak unveiled new, more accessible cameras after the fair, the qualities of possessive spectatorship began to change. The release of Eastman Kodak's one dollar Brownie camera in 1900 extended photography to a much wider population (by 1910, more than one-third of the U.S. population owned a camera). These new cameras were inexpensive and required no technical skill whatsoever. The new breed of photographers born from these cameras, commonly referred to as "kodakers" or "snapshotters," quickly altered the perception of photography, not to mention the perception of the world being photographed. Through the ambitious advertising campaigns of the Eastman Kodak Company, Kodaking became associated with the growing utility of possessive spectatorship in organizing the spaces of everyday life. These inexpensive cameras demonstrated that there were no barriers to visually possessing public spaces. One could simply point, shoot, and possess the surfaces around them. The "Kodak Girl," the carefree figure used repeatedly in Kodak advertisements, embodied this sentiment. She would take to the streets and countryside and capture the world as she saw it. She was the face of photography in the United States before World War I: playful, confident, and adventurous.

But this representation did not sit well with those who considered themselves true amateurs. What once was a craft that required the honing of technical and aesthetic skills had quickly become a seemingly frivolous part of mass culture. During the World's Fair, amateurs struggled to legitimize their practice in the face of the imposing Department of Photography. And Kodak's meteoric rise threatened to take that legitimacy away and replace it with the frivolousness of the snapshot. This anxiety was rehearsed repeatedly in the pages of amateur photography magazines, where "real" amateurs (who considered their work a serious engagement with technology and art) struggled to distance themselves by constructing a binary relationship between craft and play. The amateur produced art, while the kodaker played. The amateur mastered the technology, while the kodaker had no understanding of the apparatus. In fact, Kodak's user-friendly handcameras helped to disassociate photography from the technology altogether. This was characterized by the famous slogan "you take the picture—we do the rest." Kodak's campaigns attempted to manufacture the idea that photography was, like talking and breathing, a part of daily life. Or, as another ad suggested, photography was best when it was done "the simple, Kodak way." Kodaking changed the way people looked at and experienced their environment—with or without a camera. It at once facilitated spectatorship through the literal or metaphorical possession of snapshots, and at the same time transformed it into something playful and widely accessible.

Freedom and Possession

While most camera companies advertised solely in trade and hobby magazines, the George Eastman Company advertised in general interest and travel magazines. Eastman made the risky decision to market the Kodak camera to a general audience—the ads made little reference to technological specifications, and instead focused primarily on the experience and social benefits of Kodaking. During World War I, Kodak began marketing its cameras as a tool for family reunification—the camera could connect the soldier on the front line with his wife and kids at home. This trend would continue well after the war, with ad campaigns highlighting the domestic function of photography. But before the war, Kodak ads were predominantly focused on travel and adventure, touting the wonders of the apparatus to enhance the experience of the outdoors.[1] A popular ad from around 1903 featured a young woman walking in Washington, D.C., carrying a Kodak. The caption led with the imperative: "Take a KODAK with you." Other popular campaigns insisted: "Kodak, as you go" or "Put a Kodak in your pocket." Each emphasized the portability of the camera and the necessity of having it with you at all times. An advertisement for a "pocket camera" featured a businessman dropping his camera into his lapel pocket, with the small text suggesting that one should "have it ready for the unexpected that always happens" (see figure 2.3). The spontaneous, the adventurous, and the playful, so these ads suggest, never have to go unnoticed or unremembered again.

Eastman contextualized the practice of photography as having two equally important parts: play and possession. An ad implored its readers to "Make the most of the lure of the first soft days of spring. Picture the parks and the fields and the woods. Let Kodak be your companion on every out-of-door day—'twill give you fuller joy in the day itself—and afterward the joy of possessing pictures of the places and people that you are interested in."

Another ad further emphasized this point: "At the moment—the fun of picture taking—afterward the joy of possession. There's all this for those who keep the personal story of their outings with a Kodak." In ad after ad, the Kodak was positioned as excelling in these two primary functions and reinforcing their necessary connection. The freedom of play was only knowable through the security of possession. One ad claimed that "a Vacation without a Kodak is a vacation wasted."

Play, according to Eastman, was the spontaneous fun or adventure one could have while snapping pictures. Because the Kodak was so easy to use (remember: "you press the button—we do the rest"), users were free to enjoy the day, without the concerns of setting up their apparatus or developing their film. An article in *Camera and Darkroom* from 1904 put it clearly: "A few years ago, the photographer had to carry a camera turning the scale at several pounds, an awkward heavy tripod, at least half a dozen clumsy plate-holders and an assortment of glass plates as heavy as lead; this indeed was work. Under new and improved conditions, photography is play" (Voitier, 1904). For this author, play implied a freedom from restrictive equipment—a freedom that resulted in unrestricted access to landscape and subjects. But the freedom enabled by these new conditions was always accompanied by the orderly phenomenon of possession. According to the anthropologist Johan Huizinga, play has two important characteristics: it is always free, and it acts outside of "ordinary" or "real" life (1950, 8). Like children frolicking on a climbing gym, or adults playing a game of cards, play activities are removed from one's everyday life and placed within a unique and limited time and space. Because of the rules established for most acts of play, play does not lead to chaos; quite on the contrary, it leads to order. Huizinga says of play, "into an imperfect world and into the confusion of life it brings a temporary, a limit-

FIGURE 2.1.
This ad is from a Kodak campaign that emphasized the possibility of possessing one's personal vision of the world. Courtesy of George Eastman House, International Museum of Photography and Film

ed perfection. Play demands order absolute and supreme" (10). The Kodak camera encouraged the most deliberate sort of play. One could enjoy the serendipity of a moment; but one then had the capacity to order that moment into a comprehensible and reproducible object.

This connection was made quite clear in a few popular campaigns that privileged the concept of possession. A campaign starting around 1910 had a distinct emphasis on the personal control of a hectic world. The slogan "The World is mine—I own a KODAK" appeared on ads featuring women in various stages of travel. In one example, a woman is waiting outside a train, carrying her Kodak like a purse, as a porter drops her suitcase at her feet. The small print reads, "Take a Kodak with *you*, and picture, from your own viewpoint, not merely the places that interest you but also the companions who help to make your trip enjoyable" (see figure 2.1). The ad suggests the spectator can possess the *world* through the filtering device of the Kodak. The world can be reorganized from her viewpoint, and need not consist only of pictorial representations of places and things, but also of other people.

In another campaign, the theme of possession was taken to an even greater extreme: "There are no game laws for those who hunt with a KODAK." One ad in particular really embodied the spirit of this slogan. In an autumnal nature scene, a man is in the foreground holding a shotgun. Two women, one of whom has a Kodak dangling casually from her hand, are walking away and glancing back at the man as he stares despondently at a sign posted on a tree that reads "game laws." His play is hindered by the game laws, while the women are able to capture anything they like without having to abide by any rules. The ad suggests that the kodakers are equally as capable of capturing and possessing nature as the hunter; they, however, are the privileged spectators, as their play is unbridled by regulation (see figure 2.2).

This cavalier approach to possessing nature did not go without controversy. For many, the Kodaking of nature posed a substantial threat to the natural world and to public space. These kodakers were much maligned in the pages of photography magazines. Early hand cameras didn't even possess viewfinders, so kodakers would literally point the box at things and snap pictures. The results were often blurry, awkwardly framed, and poorly lit. "Of such photographs," wrote one commentator, "are probably 90 per cent of all the snapshots that are made, and those who make them, and even proudly carry their cameras wherever they go, are no more entitled to be called pho-

FIGURE 2.2.
This popular advertisement likened Kodaking to hunting. Courtesy of George Eastman House, International Museum of Photography and Film

tographers than is he who knows not the multiplication table to be called a mathematician" (Taylor 1899, 56).

For devoted amateurs, who took pride in the "work" of photography, the transformation of the landscape into a plaything was a devastating assault not only on the art of photography but on nature itself. Very soon after Kodak released its first camera, a writer from *The Photographic News* argued that "there are some people no more to be trusted with a camera than they are to be trusted with a six-shooter." And if that weren't criticism enough, he ventured to say that the photographer posed a greater danger. "He who misused the six-shooter and killed someone, would probably be sorry for it, but those who misuse cameras, and blaze away, pot-shotting . . . anything and everything that turns up, are hardened sinners, and usually very boastful of their enormities" (Newman 1890, 179). For this author, it was more than the amateur's willy-nilly approach to the craft; it was the lack of humility that he showed when doing it. This hapless snapshotter is persuaded by the temptations of the new technology. "For this reason," he continued, "I look — perhaps with suspicion — upon some recent inventions in photographic apparatus, as offering, by their extreme simplicity, premiums to this sort of people to commit something worse than homicide, for they kill their mother Nature, and glory in the crime" (179). The problem with the snapshotter, as opposed to say the sharpshooter, is that this picture-taking perpetrator is so naïve as to not recognize the life he's taking. The snapshotter is not capable of recognizing the sublimity of an unmediated landscape. Quite on the contrary: he breaks it apart with his camera, blind to the innate beauty of a scene, only so that he might possess proof of having been in its presence.

The "recent inventions" to which this angry writer referred included primarily the dry-plate developing process that enabled the hand camera. This, along with the point-and-shoot simplicity of Kodak's cameras, came to be called the "fatal facility." For at least a decade after this article in *The Photographic News* was published, several writers took the position that it was the technology, not the user, that was ultimately to blame for this assault on nature. In 1899, an editor's note in *The American Amateur Photographer* sought retribution for the misconduct of photography's innovators. "The man that first suggested the idea of the hand camera," the editor wrote, "and the men who have done so much to make it popular, have much to answer for; and still more is to be charged against the 'fatal facility' that has made the hand camera possible" (Ross 1899). This seemingly innocuous technological addition has created a spectator with little willingness to do any of the work once required to obtain decent images: "Before the advent of the easy, 'pre-digested breakfast-food' class of photography, any one who wished to use a camera had to learn something about the various processes necessary to produce a finished photograph, and as it required a little labor even to make an exposure, a beginner would look twice at a subject before exposing a plate, and if upon second thought the subject was considered worth taking, it would be examined from different standpoints with the idea of obtaining the best point of view" (Davis 1908, 139). This deliberateness of purpose, the thoughtfulness of seeing, was literally commandeered by the convenience of the technology. The victim in all of this, as stated again and again, was the innocence and integrity of nature.

The snapshotter was often placed in opposition to the concept of nature—which for most of these writers was defined as the perceptual integrity of the "world out there." In other words, nature was the thing that existed prior to the photograph—whether rural or urban. Accordingly, nature was something that needed preservation. But to do this required a finely honed artistic skill only the practiced amateur and professional could obtain. And even among their ranks, the artistic capability of photography was not universal. One writer asked, "how many possess this art sense which enables them to unerringly differentiate the good from the bad or choose from the maze of Nature the subject most worthy of being limned by the camera lens?" (Thompson 1911, 518). The implication is that the snapshotter, because of his unwillingness to slow down and perceive the complexity of the unmediated landscape, could only wreak havoc with his camera. Unlike a seasoned photographer, the snapshotter collected the scenery about him in a manner more similar to a garbage collector than a landscape painter. Without having to concern himself with the process of exposure or developing, he could rush through a scene, completely engaged by the game of collecting without even noticing the manner of the things collected.

Small handheld cameras were often called "detective cameras," and for a while, during the 1890s, they were called "body-snatchers." But Walter Welford, the author of an oft-reprinted handbook on the hand camera, described how these nicknames gave the hand camera a bad name. "What's in a name?" he asked. "Well, in this case, it conveys a distinctly wrong impression of what a hand camera is expected to be used for. The annoying part of it, too, is that the direction implied by the title is just the one photographers decry, viz., the seizing of incidents and scenes in which friends or others are portrayed awkwardly, or in positions that are very liable to lead to unpleasantness" (1897, 23).

While many people considered the hand camera to be a "public nuisance," Welford argued that the problem was not the technology, but how the public used it. Instead of turning their backs on the hand-camera, a technology not likely to go away, "serious" amateurs should appropriate it into their own refined practices. After all, the inability to view nature in a respectable manner was symptomatic of trends that extended well beyond the practice of photography.

Mobility and Gender

Americans were always in a rush. Even without a camera in hand, they hurried from one place to another without a mind to detail. Add a camera to that equation, and that hurried glance got represented and disseminated. An article in *Camera and Darkroom* explained that, "In the United States the rapidity with which its inhabitants accomplish everything, from eating their meals to making and spending money, is one of the first things a foreigner is apt to notice. We don't take our time and proceed leisurely even when sitting about to enjoy ourselves—picture making suffers severely through this disease and many's the good promissory piece of work that has died by the instantaneous process all on account of the desire to hurry up" (Newcomb 1900, 8). The Eastman Company deliberately molded the kodaker to this characterization of the hurried American lifestyle. The American was constantly on the move, and needed a camera that could accommodate the rapidity of life's pace. To emphasize this point, the Kodak was often represented alongside the automobile. An ad featuring a woman driving a car had the following caption: "Wherever the purr of your motor lures you, wherever the call of the road leads you, there you will find pictures, untaken pictures that invite your Kodak." The choice of words here is quite deliberate. The woman in the car is going to "find" untaken pictures. She doesn't have to stop and make them; she only has to collect them. In this case, the spontaneity of road travel need not be hindered by the labor of photography. Each could function at the same pace.

The juxtaposition of the camera and the automobile only increased the ire of "serious" amateurs. The automobile aggravated the disease of the hurried American lifestyle. One author for *The American Photographer* characterized it as an affliction called "go-itis." He suggested that photographing while in the car was difficult because of all the distractions. And when one was accompanied by friends, the proper ascertaining of nature was virtually impossible. "Yet if it were not for the others whom he takes with him in the car," he asserted, "I am sure that the motoring amateur would seize many more opportunities for pictures than he does. The lone driver is much more a creature of free choice, and he is not so continuously the victim of go-itis" ("Local Manipulation" 1920). While the automobile provided a mechanism for mobility, it introduced too many possibilities for distraction. Whether talking to friends, driving a car, or both, the "motoring amateur" could not give nature the attention it required.

Perhaps because of it being a solitary mode of transport, or simply a slower mode of transport, the bicycle was much more ardently associated with the Kodak, in both ads and magazine articles. In most cases, ads emphasized the inseparability of one technology from the other. An ad from 1895 declared that "A bicycle outfit is as incomplete without a Kodak as it would be without a pump." And another asserted, "nothing so fits into the pleasures of bicycling as photography." This sentiment was echoed in an article from the *American Journal of Photography*. Referring to hand cameras and bicycles, the author wrote, "The two fads . . . are destined to go together, and not antagonize each other. The devotees of the one will ever have a penchant for the other. Camera makers and wheel makers will have to come together and adapt themselves more or less, one to the wants of the other" (Sachse 1895, 436). Bicycles, more than automobiles, were represented in parallel with the use of hand cameras. At the time, bicycles were solely associated with leisure and play, so the correlation makes a good deal of sense. And like the Kodak, the bicycle was largely marketed to women. In the *American Journal of Photography*, the humorously pseudonymed writer J. Focus Snappschotte declared that "the new means of propulsion has found especial favor with the advanced and progressive femininity of the present age. No class of persons has taken more readily to the wheel than the new or strong-minded woman" (1896, 448).

The bicycle and the hand camera were repeatedly aligned with the figure of the woman so as to reinforce the playfulness of the individual technologies. Men were rarely featured in bicycle ads, as they would too readily appear to be on their way to work. The figure of the woman, on the other hand, either on a bike or taking snapshots (or both) was the ideal modern figure of playful mobility. She was strong minded, yet removed from the workaday world. An early article in *Cosmopolitan* put it thusly:

> Amateur photography is of special interest and importance to women. It has provided for them a peculiarly interesting field. It is ever an incentive to good health. Many a ruddy cheek there is whose hue has been won on long camera tramps, many an elastic step which would have been slow and halting, many a spirit dull and languid, but for the leading of the lens. There is something so fascinating to a woman when once she enters the field which stretches away before the lover of the camera, that she is drawn on and on, irresistibly, into the open. (Harwood 1893, 253)

The woman is drawn into the open, and the bike is a machine that expedites that process. Therefore, the woman on the bike with a Kodak was the perfect symbol of playfulness: she was most likely acting outside of everyday life and was capable of possessing and ordering the process through snapshots.

Accordingly, the "Kodak Girl" was the most popular figure in Eastman's ads through the beginning of World War I. For the reasons stated above, she best embodied what the technology stood for—leisure, adventure, play, and possession. But just as she symbolized the potential freedom of the medium for male and female photographers, she set the stage for a gendered criticism of the technology. Kodak Girl made it possible for "serious" amateur photographers to attack the figure of the snapshotter as weak, frivolous, and feminine. An author in the *American Journal of Photography* complained "to what ludicrous and ungainly positions it is possible for the human being to degenerate when strict propriety is cast off for comfortable freedom of action" (Crane 1895, 458). This sentiment is highly coded, in that it criticizes the careless snapshotter as socially deviant. Snapshotting is more than just an unflattering artistic practice; it is symbolic of a playful feminine spectator that ignores accepted standards of decency for the allure of freedom and mobility.

This symbolic association, more so than the questionable quality of the majority of snapshots, was seen as a threat to the medium. An article in *The American Amateur Photographer* entitled "The Degradation of Photography" lamented the feminine qualities of the snapshotter: "Several causes have led to this loss of respect for, and interest in, photographers; the almost universality of the little black box, the known want of a serious purpose in the great majority of those who carry it; the knowledge that many, if not most, of them merely 'press the button' and know nothing whatever about 'doing the rest'; and, perhaps, greatest of all, the miserable results of such pressing" (Hamilton 1902, 341). The lack of serious purpose was an identifying feature of the

Kodak Girl. She wandered aimlessly, snapping bits of nature without mind to the whole; she meandered on her bike, carelessly passing beautiful scenery with no inclination to pause. She was always hurried, always playful. In the Kodak ads that featured boys, the copy would emphasize the possibility of playing with the technology and even developing pictures on one's own. In contrast, those featuring Kodak Girl were solely focused on the ease of use, simplicity, and lack of serious purpose.

Work versus Play

While the editor of *The American Amateur Photographer* in 1899 declared that the Kodak was of little threat because it was "merely a pastime" (Editor's Note 1899), most of Kodak's critics found it necessary to wage a discursive war against the encroaching feminine figure of the kodaker. This was done through the constant assertion that "real" photography is work. According to one author, amateurs ought to "eschew the hand camera as they would the road to perdition, and have nothing to do with snap-shotting until they . . . know a good negative when they see it" (Taylor 1899, 56). Knowing a good negative from a poor one requires discipline and a commitment to detail—in other words, it marks the distinction between play and work. So while play might be acceptable in some contexts, it should be treated as a luxury only obtainable after the photographer achieved a sufficient mastery of the craft.

In response to this concern, many writers began arguing for the necessity of placing photography into the context of education. Between 1900 and 1902, about a dozen articles appeared in the magazine *Photo Era* that described the emerging practice of teaching with photographs. In most of these articles, the proper use and teaching of photography was described as being transformative—where uninspired students achieve remarkable results (Jollie 1902), and scientific disciplines are opened to a staggering new potential of discovery (Waugh 1902). But the ultimate justification for the institutionalization of photography was the redefinition of the practice as an art. The easiest way for people to understand this redefinition was to witness, firsthand, the transformation of a beginner. Before they've fallen too deeply into the trenches of snapshotting, they could be guided fairly quickly into a deep comprehension of the art. The best way "by which photography may be made to act as an educator is to place the camera in the hands of an amateur," said another article in *Photo Era*. "The amateur starts in at first on any old thing, snapping here and there at figures or groups just as the fancy takes him. But wait a year and see how he develops." There is a possibility that he won't ever change, "but may remain always a mere presser of the button." With a little guidance and hard work, however, "he may be able to rise above the making of mere photographs until he is able to produce pictures" (Johnston 1902, 68). As this article described, the best way to situate photography as an educator is to ensure that it uplifts both the teacher and the student. Photographic education adopts a model similar to that of Alcoholics Anonymous. Recovering from snapshotting is an iterative process — one benefits from the persistent witnessing of other recoveries. A writer for *The American Amateur Photographer* described a similar model. "Under a perfected system of education," he wrote, "amateur photography would be lifted from its present rut of worthless snapshotting to the plane of an artistic and entertaining pastime" (Miller 1900, 308–309). Education was an uncontroversial method by which photography could be wrested from its menial social position and placed squarely within the masculine realm of labor.

But just as soon as this method began gaining traction, other articles took a much more straightforward tactic. In a 1901 article in *The American Amateur Photographer* entitled "The Waning of the Popularity of the Camera," the author (identified only as "An Observer") simply claimed that the hand camera was losing favor because people were beginning to discover that photography was hard work. He claimed that if one intended to properly document an outing, it would inevitably interfere with the pleasure one expected from the outing. In regard to producing images, "he would find it very difficult to carry it out satisfactorily. It is hardly likely that he is going to succeed when in holiday mood. The same applies to the individual picture. If worth anything it must have meant thought and work. A holiday means just the opposite" (Observer 1901, 396). By negatively juxtaposing the play of holiday with the work of photography, the author hoped to appeal to a logical inconsistency in the Kodak mystique — the apparent freedom of the kodaker is, in fact, a lot of work. One had to think about and adapt to the apparatus when traveling with a Kodak, whereas complete freedom, as was typically associated with the kodaker, would seem to imply freedom from all material hindrances. The "Observer" continued,

> It is astonishing what a nuisance even a small hand-camera can become in a day's outing if the object with which it was taken was merely the hope of catching something. Full physical freedom is lost, and when the other mem-

> bers of the party are free to swing their sticks, climb rocks and jump across the brooks, he, with the camera in hand or slung across the back, must move more gently and warily. If anybody feels disposed to doubt it, the proof is easy. Let him take a camera with him to a picnic. And far more important, mental freedom is also lost, for he is eternally on the look out for a photographic scrap to justify his burden. (1901, 398)

While this article makes a compelling case for the burden of the camera, it is unusual in its approach. In most cases, the hand camera is positioned as the bad object precisely because the "fatal facility" compels the spectator to adopt a distracted and playful approach to nature. The "Observer," however, reverses that logic to suggest that, despite the perceived ease of the technology, it acts as a disruption to the otherwise free movement of a holiday. He makes specific note of how mental freedom is lost because of the nagging need for possession. What he calls the "photographic scrap," hardly a monumental representation, is the only fruit of one's labor. And even this pittance is merely compulsory, as it is only acquired to justify the labor of having participated in the fleeting fad of Kodaking.

So while the Kodak was most commonly disparaged for encouraging a reckless playfulness in the modern spectator, it was, as evidenced above, sometimes disparaged for disrupting that playfulness. But even the latter perspective stems from a reaction against the play of the kodaker. The writer begins from the assumption that most people associate Kodaking and play. He, therefore, reinforces the connection before he negates it. In this sense, it matters little how he frames his rhetorical argument; the main goal of his polemic is to disassociate the Kodak from the everyday experiences of public space.

The multiple and varied responses to the Kodak in popular and trade magazines shows just how penetrating the Kodak was in popular culture. The influence of play, as represented by the Kodak Girl, was powerfully linked with a desirable experience of public space—whether in the country (as the ads represented) or in the city. "Kodak-thinking," or the process by which a spectator frames nature even without a camera in hand, became the norm for a middle class spectator eager to consume a modern experience. And as urban populations exploded just as the majority of Americans were acquiring Kodaks, urban spectatorship was constructed from a Kodak view. This became especially obvious in New York City.

The Kodaker and the City

Regardless of whether someone had a Kodak or was merely in the sight lines of one, the presence of cameras in the city was unavoidable. Cameras were everywhere capturing the scenes of city streets and the expressions of people. "In a large and cosmopolitan city like New York," noted one writer in 1902, "the range of interesting subjects for the camera is almost unlimited" (Helm 1902, 107). Amateurs, both in the formality of camera clubs and the informality of snapshotting, took to the streets and pointed their lenses at everything from skyscrapers to crowds to the individual expressions of strangers. And, not surprisingly, this onslaught of novice photographers into the streets of New York sparked considerable controversy. Many felt their right to privacy was being violated by what seemed the ubiquitous "little black box." Surely one's likeness was one's own, and not simply some photographic scrap to amuse a kodaker. Angry editorials appeared in photography magazines, complaining of this new nuisance. "Something must be done, and will be done, soon," said one writer. "It is a mistake to imagine that the public is clamoring for a pictorial representation of all the events of the daily life of even prominent citizens." These "camera fiends," as they came to be called, posed a threat to the "proper" function of public space. They turned the virtue of outer appearance into a commodity, and they threatened to transform the deliberate leisure of the bourgeois into a chaotic and uncontainable form of play. The writer continued with this not-so-veiled threat: "A jury would not convict a man who violently destroyed the camera of an impudent photographer guilty of a constructive assault upon modest women" ("What Is to Be Done?" 1906, 103).

The figure of the "modest woman," innocent and servile, was akin to the figure of nature in the amateur photography debates. Each was a pure form susceptible to the antagonizing forces of the snapshotter, which of course was represented by a feminine figure. The discourse around photography was focused on two opposing views of women—the free, playful, chaotic figure of the Kodak Girl versus the fixed, stationary, and orderly figure of nature. Whether in the city or the country, these two opposing views of femininity framed the dialogue of photography, and by extension, the emerging practices of spectatorship.

But regardless of the distinctly rural theme of the majority of Kodak ads, the debates raging over the proper relationship between cameras and nature came to a head as that relationship applied to the city. In the city, people composed nature. And just as critics lamented the deconstruction of the natural world by the clumsy hand of the kodaker, so they felt threatened by the deconstruction of the social world. In addition to butchering the representation of a tree or pond, the camera fiend would, almost certainly, misrepresent people. The camera transformed each figure into surface and threatened to distort their meaning through dissemination. For many residents of the city, this led to a transformation in the way they conceived of the relationship between internal life and its outward manifestation. According to Robert Mensel, "bourgeois New Yorkers understood that they were responsible for the visible evidence of their feelings at every moment. If they were caught betraying an inappropriate or indelicate feeling, there was no escape from embarrassment, and if that moment were captured in a photograph, embarrassment could be perpetual" (1991, 32).

Wealthy New Yorkers became very concerned that too much about their lives could be communicated through an itinerant photograph. It was quite possible that an unpleasant image could end up in the newspaper or an advertisement without one knowing. The presence of "detective" cameras further aggravated these concerns. "The day has gone by when a well-concealed hand camera can be used with impunity," said Walter Welford. "Too much is now known of 'detectives' altogether, and it is only by quick use that shots can be secured without the knowledge of those figuring in the scene" (1897, 82). He continues in his chapter on "Street Scenes" to document precisely how best to make "quick work" out of the hand camera. "There are many little tricks that I resort to to keep away attention from the camera. Buttoning a top coat, loading up and lighting a pipe or cigar, earnest attention at something in a shop window, even if it be only a milliner's, asking a question of the latest *victim* . . . of course these are only necessary if it is imagined that the camera is detected" (85; italics added). Welford made no apologies for his practices, going so far as to refer to his subjects as victims. Aligning his rhetoric with the popular Kodak ads, Welford characterized the photographer as a hunter, complete with decoys and tactics. And once the game was captured, he boasted, the hunter could do with it whatever he pleased. The first edition of Welford's book was published two years before this issue was challenged in court.

In the case *Corliss v. Walker* (1894), the family members of the deceased inventor George H. Corliss opposed the use of his image in a magazine. According to the Massachusetts circuit court judge deciding the case, "the ques-

historical process," he argues, "can be determined more strikingly from an analysis of its inconspicuous surface-level expressions than from that epoch's judgments about itself" (1995a, 75). Surfaces gleaned by the snapshotter are not an affront to nature; rather, these hunted surfaces, however random, are the materials through which nature is composed. In his essay on photography, he claims that "the world has taken on a 'photographic face'; it can be photographed because it strives to be absorbed into the spatial continuum which yields to snapshots" (1995b, 59). In this sense, the assimilation of faces into pictures of crowds was not a symptom of nature falling from grace, or losing its purity. Instead, nature had become so entwined with the snapshot that it could no longer be conceived independently of it. "In photography," asserts Kracauer, "the spatial appearance of an object *is* its meaning" (1995, 52).

Establishing a New Urban Paradigm

The presence of cameras in cities altered both how people saw the city around them and how they saw themselves as part of the city. The spectator could collect artifacts of experience with his camera, and he could just as likely be collected as someone else's artifact. The concern continued to be that there was little control over what happened to those artifacts once collected. Torrents of images were being produced by snapshotters and used for a myriad of purposes outside of any official sanctions. The notion that photography should be used in the service of unified beauty was fast becoming fantasy. As the handheld camera entered into everyday life during the first decade of the twentieth century, the public began to assert more control over their own experiences and memories. But those who understood themselves as privileged benefactors of nature (serious amateurs who treated the subject of photography with respect), or architects and planners with a vested interest in the manufacture of holistic beauty, fought hard against this new populist vision. Frivolous amateurs capturing scenes in the White City were one thing. Indeed, that city was designed to be assembled into a comprehensible whole. But it was a different matter all together when careless snapshotters assaulted nature at large. Nature does not have the benefit of carefully plotted architectural cohesion. And surely the public could not be trusted with the task of capturing and assembling surfaces to manifest a whole experience. But there was no turning back. The handheld camera, with its initial showcase in the White City, shifted power away from the designers of spaces and toward those who consumed them. The central role of the urban spectator was established.

Julian Street, writing in 1914, declared that Americans do not like to be "'guests of chance.' We always go from one place to another with a definite purpose. We never amble . . . we rush about obsessed by 'sights,' seeing with the eyes of guides and thinking the 'canned' thoughts of guidebooks" (1914, 3–4). Thousands of images were produced each day from the peripatetic cameras of snapshotters, composing the raw material from which the spectator could assemble his vision of the city. The "picture thinking" kodaker no longer needed to sift through a finely crafted tourist manual—the picture possibilities about him were apparent even without a camera. While spectatorship in the White City was framed by an architectural cohesion, spectatorship in New York City at the turn of the twentieth century was framed by the very mobility that seemed to undermine the frame all together. To "see" New York was to see the act of seeing. The content of the surface captured hardly mattered; but *that* the surface was captured, or that it *could* be captured, was what mattered. The man with a camera would simply glean surfaces from the urban landscape without any recognition or care about their meaning. He would move through the city, recording its buildings, streets and people in motion. New York City became a product of individual possession, even outside of architectural cohesion. The handheld camera became the paradigm, not the tool, from which the American city could be known.

CITY IN MOTION

Early Cinema and Times Square

In the States a city is a moving landscape for its inhabitants.
JEAN PAUL SARTRE, "American Cities"

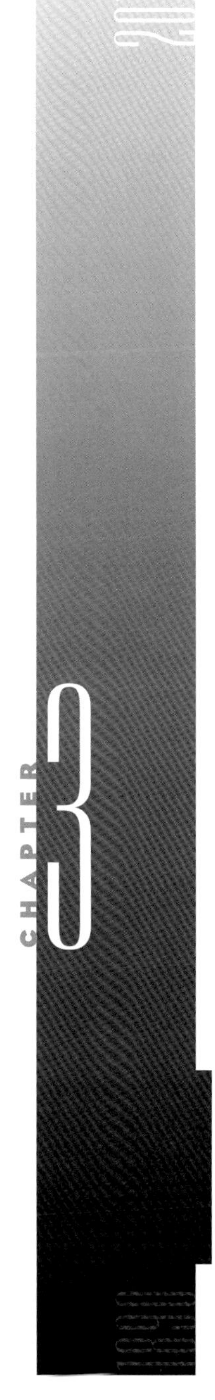

Unlike the European city, so forcefully grounded in its past, the American city contained streetscapes likely no older than its inhabitants. For the middle class, the city contained little permanency—it was doubtful that one would spend their entire life within the same cityscape. According to Jean Paul Sartre, American cities "are not oppressive, they do not close you in; nothing in them is definitive, nothing is arrested. You feel, from your first glance, that your contact with these places is a temporary one; either you will leave them or they will change around you" (1955, 117). Americans were moving, their landscapes changing. This phenomenon was captured in the figure of the snapshotter: constantly moving and recording without stopping to reflect. But as the cinema rose in prominence—a medium stemming from a technology capable of nothing less remarkable than automating the movement of pictures—a new Concept-city began to emerge in the United States.

Before 1906, films were mostly screened as part of variety acts in vaudeville houses, as transitions between stage performances or as warm-up gags for comedians. They were also found in penny arcades, inside moving-picture peep shows called kinetoscopes. Resembling the atmosphere of a saloon, these penny arcades were not family friendly. Women and children largely stayed away from these establishments, making cinema an almost exclusively male, working-class medium. And yet cinematic spectatorship, just like the kodaker, was commonly associated with the figure of a disorderly woman—a woman at play, a woman with little regard for the cohesion of nature and the beauty therein. Even though the actual person in the theater was typically a man; his gaze was often disapprovingly portrayed as feminine. As Jacques Derrida explains, "that which will not be pinned down by truth is, in truth,—*femi-*

nine" (1979, 55). The characterization of a feminine spectatorship stemmed from the anxiety that the spectator might be stripped of his power to document truth. Some middle-class reform groups expressed concern that male moviegoers would be stricken with feminine disorders. "A night at the variety theater," Tom Gunning writes, "was like a ride on a streetcar or an active day in a crowded city . . . stimulating an unhealthy nervousness" (1990, 60).

Cinema's correlation with the practice of Kodaking was not incidental. Despite the medium's current capacity for narrative complexity, from its beginning in the mid-1890s to about 1906, the vast majority of cinematic products reflected a concern for capturing the moving landscape. As Gunning notes, early cinema was a distinctly nonnarrative medium, which he characterizes as the "cinema of attractions." These films, quite simply, had the ability to show something. Narrative and story were more often afterthoughts than they were defining elements. For Gunning, the important qualities of this new medium were the movement of the frame and the movement of objects within the frame.

Film, during this period, was not considered an art form—much like the product of snapshotters, it was considered an unfortunate byproduct of modern life. It was an attraction, an amusement, but hardly a contemplative document of nature. Nonetheless, the demand for these "frivolous" documents was growing rapidly. The majority of films fell into one of two categories: travelogue or documentary. Of these, most could be described as "urban actualities," single-reel (or sometimes double-reel) films that documented some aspect of urban motion. While these films were made all over the world by traveling film crews, the most noteworthy of them were made in New York City as the urban motion and dramatic skyline of that city provided uniquely dynamic material. Several familiar styles of urban actuality emerged within a short time. The panorama was very popular. Capturing a viewpoint from a strategic locale, the panorama film was composed of a camera rotating upon its axis, from 200 to 360 degrees around. Other styles consisted of stationary cameras in front of busy urban scenes, or moving cameras attached to the front of a train or panning across a crowded sidewalk. But by 1908, the number of urban actualities had declined significantly (*The Life of a City* 1999). The rapid drop-off of these urban films can be associated with the medium's transition to longer format narrative and more established screening venues. But during the height of urban actuality production, film developed a uniquely visual language—it had its own unique mode of address that was more connected to photography than theater. As Giuliana Bruno suggests, "the language of cinema was born not out of static theatrical views but out of urban motions" (1997, 17). The photoplay (as film was popularly known) made photos play. The urban actuality in particular was a packaged articulation of the surface play of snapshotters. It codified the playful gaze embodied by the kodaker by abstracting the gaze from bodily practice, and making it easily consumable and reproducible.

The mechanical task of making pictures play was not unique to cinema. The qualities of cinema extended out into the urban landscape in a number of ways. But there was one way in particular that did more to extend cinematic spectatorship into the city than any other. They were public displays, first introduced in Times Square, known as "sky signs" or "spectacular ads." These giant signs, built high above the city street, were dazzling displays of moving and flashing lights that attracted huge crowds of people throughout the day and evening. Spectators would gather on street corners for minutes, pausing from their daily activities to watch a sign run its course. And while they were each advertisements for particular products, the exact content of the ads was overshadowed by the presentation of electric movement. Sky signs were the equivalent of urban actualities, distilled to their essential form and displayed within the city.

The possessive spectatorship emerging from the kodaker was on display in the moving image. In a *Century Magazine* article from 1893, the author predicted the possibilities of this happening: the "true *flaneur* feels a genuine interest in one thing—his own capacity for the reception of such new ideas and emotions as may be received without exertion of any kind. He does not care for facts or objects as such, or for what they teach, but he does care for their momentary effect upon his eyes and nerves. He does not crave knowledge, but he delights in impressions. He likes to idle in the city because, if he keeps himself purely receptive, the city prints each instant a fresh picture on his brain" (Renssalaer 1893, 11). The abstraction of urban movement into an easily consumable form could allow the spectator to receive new ideas and emotions without any exertion. In this sense, urban experience, while still premised on possession, could be preassembled. And as the spectator stood on the corner of Forty-fourth and Broadway, the city could print each instant "a fresh picture on his brain." The White City and the Kodak opened up possibilities for this distinctly American form of spectatorship—the ability to possess images of a city designed to communicate itself at every instant. But the projection and display of moving images of and within the city made the individual apprehension of a city a reproducible product. In simple terms: the moving image transformed the city into a mass medium.

Cinema and the Kodaker

Why do men prefer the photoplay to the drinking place?
For no pious reason, surely. Now they have fire pouring into
their eyes instead of into their bellies. Blood is drawn from
the guts to the brain.

VACHEL LINDSAY, *The Art of the Moving Picture*

In his description of early cinema, Gilles Deleuze writes: "The essence of the cinematographic movement-image lies in extracting from vehicles or moving bodies the movement which is their common substance, or extracting from movements the mobility which is their essence" (1986, 23). For Deleuze, the power of the early cinema was far greater than its ability to tell a story or represent an object. It was its ability, better than anything else, to produce and to communicate the very mobility that came to define modern life.[1] As such, cinematic images were not simply representations of people, places, and things in the world. They were *presentations* of the world, in its immediate, rather than mediate, condition. Representations were distancing; presentations were immersive. According to Henri Bergson, "Representation is there, but always virtual, being neutralized, at the very moment when it might become actual, by the obligation to continue itself and lose itself in something else" (1988, 28). In other words, representations are always deflected onto the thing they are representing. If I were to ask someone holding a picture of a dog, "What do you see in this picture?" they would likely respond with, "I see a dog." In fact, what that person actually sees is an *image* of a dog. But the image is not seen because it is in service to the thing itself. Early cinema, according to Deleuze, did not have such a problem. The concept of the movement-image makes it possible to imagine a cinematic image that is not tethered to the spectator's identification with objects outside of it. The early cinema is one "that displays its visibility," Gunning writes, "willing to rupture a self-enclosed fictional world for a chance to solicit the attention of the spectator" (1990, 57). It does not solicit its audience by representing a familiar object with which a spectator can identify, but rather the cinematic image presents itself as an end-in-itself. The practical implications of this would suggest that early spectators understood a film of a busy street corner to be about movement, rather than the specific spatial qualities of the represented corner.

However, representation did play some role in early film spectatorship, especially in travelogue films, where the appeal was to view an "exotic" city or place. But most of the films exhibited during this period were demonstrations of modern life more than they were representations of anything in particular. People packed into theaters to view the spectacle of film, to gaze upon modern life in ways never before possible. The novelty of cinema was not simply the thrill of gawking at a new technology; the novelty of cinema was the promise of seeing the world as form, of seeing space reduced to its most basic element of movement, or play. Leo Charney and Vanessa Schwartz argue that film technology grew out of a cultural impulse in modernity that was compelled to replicate itself: "The emergence of cinema might be characterized as both inevitable and redundant. The culture of modernity rendered inevitable something like cinema, since cinema's characteristics evolved from the traits that defined modern life in general" (1995, 1–2). In this sense, cinema was not an escape from reality; it was presented more as an extension of lived experience. Encounters with film were never far removed from encounters with urban space. Mike Featherstone sees any conceptual separation of these encounters as artificial. Urban experience does not only "rely upon physical mobility, but could equally depend upon the mobility of the gaze, which could be equally well stimulated by movement on a screen" (1998, 916).

On the screen, one could see the product of the moving body, or the flaneur, without having to move at all. Objects and people were transformed into the moving surfaces of urban scenes. "The movements of photographed people," notes historian Dai Vaughan, "were accepted without demur because they were perceived as performance, as simply a new mode of self-projection; but that the inanimate should participate in self-projection was astonishing" (1990, 65). From the earliest films, like *L'Arrivée d'un train à La Ciotat* (1895), there is careful attention paid to the movement of inanimate objects within the frame. As the legend goes, the angle in which the train approaches the camera created quite a stir with early audiences, making crowds jump from their seats for fear of the train bursting through the screen. The view of the train pulling into the station at a screening in New York, wrote a reviewer for the *Boston Herald*, was "so realistic as to give those in the front seats a genuine start" (Bottomore, 186). The camera doesn't move at all; it is strategically placed to achieve the most dramatic effect of the moving train along the *y*-axis

FIGURE 3.1.
Louis Lumière's *L'Arrivée d'un train à La Ciotat* (1895).

of the frame. When the train finally comes to a complete stop, people pour out of each of its cars. The crowd begins to move, creating an interesting movement of shapes perpendicular to the movement of the train (see figure 3.1).

Companies in the emerging film business sought to deliver on these promises, as they struggled to build associations between film and modern life. Raff and Gammon, the company that in 1896 designed the projection system known as the Vitascope, claimed in their prospectus, "When the machine is started by the operator, the bare canvas before the audience instantly becomes a stage, upon which living beings move about, and go through their respective acts, movements, gestures and changing expressions, surrounded by appropriate settings and accessories—the very counterpart of the stage, the field, the city, the country—yes, more, for these reproductions are in some respects more satisfactory, pleasing and interesting than the originals" (qtd. in Musser 1990, 118). The canvas becomes a stage: a place for performance, for play. Within that play, not people but acts, movements, gestures, and expressions are positioned upstage. And of course the most compelling feature of this document is the claim that the reproductions are somehow better than the originals. Film projection, the company claimed, infused new life in the merely alive. Living beings typically move about, but when they move about as projections on a "stage," that movement becomes something entirely more interesting.

This theme would be repeated again and again in advertisements and commentaries throughout the period. And the usefulness of this characterization went well beyond the self-serving prognostications of marketers. It became a substantive aesthetic through which to imagine modern life. According to Vachel Lindsay, the author of a 1915 book on the photoplay entitled *The Art of the Moving Picture*, "by the law of compensation, while the motion picture is shallow in showing private passion, it is powerful in conveying the passions of masses of men" (1915, 40). In what he called "the picture of crowd splendor" the motion picture is perfectly suited to communicate the life of the crowd. It gives life to what the photograph had rendered surface. In his words: "I have said that it is a quality, not a defect, of the photoplays that while the actors tend to become types and hieroglyphics and dolls, on the other hand, dolls and hieroglyphics and mechanisms tend to become human. By an extension of this principle, non-human tones, textures, lines and spaces take on a vitality almost like that of flesh and blood" (133). For Lindsay, the ornament was vital. It is not only indicative of a modern American culture—it is worthy of celebration. The photoplay brings the inanimate to life through mobility.

Objects move on the screen, like flesh and blood. The crowd splendor to which Lindsay referred did not discriminate between people and things. On screen, all moving objects were the same. All were distilled to the communicative capacity of the movement-image. All were capable of being possessed.

Strategies for Containing Movement

If we look at urban actualities prior to 1907, this phenomenon is almost without exception. Cutting through crowds or gliding atop boats or trains, the camera captured mobile surfaces on simultaneous and distinct trajectories. These films captured for the spectator the experience of movement without having to move. They represented the playfulness of the photographic apparatus, without any of the danger, or dirty looks, with which it was typically associated. They represented the practice of Kodak thinking—the experience of playing with a camera distilled into a hundred feet of film.

One of the most remarkable examples of this is American Mutoscope and Biograph's (AM&B) *At the Foot of the Flatiron* (1903), where the camera is positioned across the street from the Flatiron Building on a very windy day. Crowds of pedestrians cross in front of the camera, holding their hats to their heads and pressing down on their skirts to keep them from flaring up. The corner of Twenty-third and Broadway was notoriously the windiest corner in the city, so the location was deliberate. But outside of a few slapstick moments—a man's hat flies from his head off screen, and a woman's skirt blows dangerously high—the moving people, seemingly propelled by the wind, are no more than moving objects. The film is a cacophony of visual images, drawing the viewer's attention to lines and angles more than the specificity of human form.

Another AM&B film, entitled *Broadway and Union Square* (1903), extends the presented movement from people to things. In this film, also composed with a stationary camera, the main bit of action derives from two streetcars, facing in opposite directions, diagonally bisecting the screen. The film begins with each moving away from the other toward opposing corners. Within seconds, the cars come to a stop and people stream out creating two additional moving lines set off approximately thirty degrees from the diagonals of the trains (see figure 3.2). *Lower Broadway* (AM&B, 1903) is a film where crowds of people stream upward on the right side of the screen, adjacent to an intersection of streetcars, horses, and people that converges in the screen's center. Whether of streetcars, people, or horses, the movements of objects on screen

FIGURE 3.2. *Broadway and Union Square* (AM&B, 1903) represented a bustling Manhattan street corner.

command focus. The people are stripped of their life, as Lindsay said, transformed into hieroglyphs and dolls. And at the same time, objects (including those people stripped of life) are given life, infused with the vitality of moving bodies in the city.

The panorama film featured a different kind of movement. Typically, the camera was placed in a prominent location and rotated to achieve a view of the skyline, or some element of the urban landscape. *Panorama from the Tower of the Brooklyn Bridge* (AM&B, 1899) was taken from the tower on the Brooklyn side. The camera starts out facing southwest toward the southern tip of Manhattan and makes a complete rotation around. Reminiscent of the spectator's view from the Ferris Wheel discussed in chapter 1, the panorama film highlights the kaleidoscopic view of the snapshotter. It creates movement by putting the landscape in motion to connote a totalizing view. The camera becomes like a surrogate body, assisting in the assemblage of views. This is an instantiation of William James's perceptual flux. But Henri Bergson even more explicitly addressed the experience of the panorama: "At each of its movements everything changes, as though by a turn of a kaleidoscope" (1988, 12).

Bergson's metaphor of the kaleidoscope illuminates how the whole view of the city could come into perspective. Within the single viewfinder of a kaleidoscope, the viewer is able to see light refracting from many angles on a singular plane. By turning the viewfinder, the image is altered, but always connected to the previous image. While we think it has passed from one state to another, it is actually just a continuation. "Just because we close our eyes to the unceasing variation of every psychical state, we are obliged, when the change has become so considerable as to force itself on our attention, to speak as if a new state were placed alongside the previous one. Of this new state we assume that it remains unvarying in its turn, and so on endlessly. . . . Discontinuous though they appear, however, in point of fact they stand out against the continuity of a background on which they are designed" (Bergson 1998, 3). The panoramic film combats the appearance of discontinuity by connoting totality. No image in the panorama presents itself as entirely new — because each is connected to the overall presentation. Any slight change of location or movement would alter the whole thing — not simply a single image. Panoramas, more than other city views, highlighted the centrality of the spectator in assembling "total" views of the city. Viewing the panorama, like walking in the streets, created a spectator akin to what Charles Baudelaire called a "kaleidoscope equipped with consciousness" (Benjamin 1985, 175).

Panorama from the Times Building (AM&B, 1905) highlights this spectatorship by combining two motions. The film begins with the camera pointing down from the top of the newly completed Times Building; the lens slowly moves up to capture the distant cityscape. The film then cuts to a horizontal pan across the city and comes to a close by looking down on Times Square. *Panorama of the Flatiron Building* (1903), on the other hand, is a pan from the ground level. The film begins, like a standard static view, with the movement of people and objects on the street. But then the camera slowly begins to pan up the side of the Flatiron, creating a grand unveiling of the street corner. The movement of objects gives way to the movement of the camera — with the latter putting the former into a larger, spectator-controlled, context.

Hundreds of panorama films were made from various perspectives, each placing the spectator in a new, previously unimaginable position. The camera became a kind of technological prosthesis — extending the possibilities of vision beyond what was possible with the naked eye or even with a hand camera. But even more popular than the panorama film was the track film. These films involved mounting a camera to the front of a trolley or train as it made its way through the city or countryside (Uricchio 1982). The possibilities of vision were further enhanced by mechanization — as the railroad track gave

FIGURE 3.3.
Interboro Subway (AM&B, 1905) was shot at the opening of the Times Square station.

the camera its own prosthetic enhancement. One of the earliest examples was Edison's *New Brooklyn to New York via the Brooklyn Bridge* (1898), where a train-mounted camera crosses the trestle bridge toward the looming Manhattan skyline. *Elevated Railway* (1903) is a later example that explores some other visual tricks. With a camera mounted to the front of a train traveling along an elevated track in Manhattan, the majority of the film shows buildings streaming backward across the frame. But the most compelling moment is at the film's beginning. A train heading the opposite way crosses dramatically in front of the camera, obscuring the distant buildings into a blur of steel and glass. As the train passes off screen, the view continues to meander along the circuitous path of the tracks.

On the occasion of the opening of the Times Square subway station, the two-reel film *Interboro Subway* (1905) was made (see figure 3.3). This film adopts a mix of methods to achieve its effect—combining the track film with the static crowd shot. The camera follows the rear of a subway car as it travels from Fourteenth Street to Times Square. Despite the simple premise, this film had quite an elaborate setup. It was highly produced to achieve a very deliberate effect. A special car ran on an adjacent track with carbon arc lights shining upon the rear of a moving train as it traveled through the recently opened New York subway system. When the car arrives at the new Times Square station, people flood out of the cars, moving in every direction, toward and away from the camera. An interesting thing about this film is that the station scene was entirely staged. It is clear that people are being told in what direction to walk. If you watch closely, it is possible to see two men walk back and forth in front of the camera three times. The orchestration of this movement suggests that

urban actualities were not matters of chance at all; filmmakers were self-conscious of the movements that made for a compelling scene. Whether by choosing a location or completely orchestrating a crowd, they were packaging an encounter with the city that needed to correspond with existing audience expectations.

Actuality films, whether screened in a peep show or at the tail end of a variety act, or even within a nickelodeon, needed to approximate an aesthetic of mobility that was tied to existing practices of spectatorship. In other words, the cinema did not yet have much of an internal formal logic. It relied heavily on the formal attributes of existing media practices. Lynn Kirby (1996) argues that film spectatorship grew out of the viewing practices of the railroad passenger. Seeing landscapes rush by in rapid motion from behind the window of a passenger car was a brand new perspective in the nineteenth century. The train window served as a screen of sorts to observe the moving landscape. The perceptual paradigm of the railroad, as Kirby describes it, "prepared a path for the institutionalization of a certain kind of subject or spectator that cinema would claim as its own, a subject molded in relation to new forms of perception, leisure, temporality, and modern technology" (1996, 24). Kirby argues that this cinematic spectatorship, assembled from the familiar experience of rail travel, created a touristic subject called the spectator-passenger — a way of seeing that rendered the visual consumption of movement into an act of travel. The result of this conflation was a shrinkage of perceived space, which, as told by Kirby, "was to convert space into time, to turn the distance between two cities into a matter of days or hours and, in film, to turn the visual passage from Tokyo to Lyons into a matter of seconds" (1996, 50). The spectator-passenger is part of the larger phenomenon of possessive spectatorship. Indeed, as it became more common for people to possess space as a collection of moving surfaces — landscapes rushing across a train window, machines and people migrating across screens, physical bodies moving behind camera lenses — space was better measured in increments of time. What Kirby doesn't consider is that the attraction of these new perspectives was not just the immediate experience but the ability to possess, collect, assemble, and reflect on those experiences. So just as technologies like the cinema, the handheld camera, the train, and the park shrank space, regulatory measures and practices were formed to systemize that shrinkage or to turn it into an aesthetic. Railroad companies compelled the government to establish standard time zones to rationalize their operations and cinema rationalized the operations of the kodaker. Each structured time to accommodate the assemblage of distant views of space.

Building a Platform for Spectatorship

At the 1904 World's Fair in St. Louis, a fireman and mechanical engineer named George C. Hale unveiled his cinematic amusement ride called "Hale's Tours and Scenes of the World." Hale sought to reproduce the experience of being in a moving train by placing "passengers" in a stationary railway car along with a cinematic projection shot from the perspective of a moving train. It was a carefully crafted illusion. The front of the car was replaced with a slightly inclined screen upon which films shot from the cowcatcher of a moving train were projected. The size of the screen, the placement of the projector, the size of the image were all orchestrated so the image would appear life-size to every passenger in the car. In addition to the visual effect, several environmental enhancements were included. A mechanical belt with projecting lugs that moved over rollers and shafts simulated the sound of motion. The lugs would strike a metal piece under the car to make the clickety-clack noise of a train. To assure that the sound corresponded with the image, the "conductor" could accommodate changes in the speed of the film by adjusting the speed of the belt. In addition to this, air jets would occasionally release a gust into the car to simulate wind. Passengers often found this to be such a realistic experience that, according to trade papers, when trolley rides through cities were shown, they would sometimes yell at pedestrians to get out of their way or be run down (Fielding 1970).

Its first commercial location after the World's Fair was at the Electric Park in Kansas City in 1905. But it did not receive national press attention until later in that same year when film producer Adolph Zukor opened it in New York City at 64 Union Square (Fourteenth Street and Broadway). Hale's Tours was, for a brief time, a sensation. Zukor and his partner, William Brady, quickly acquired the rights for Hale's Tours in Pittsburgh, Newark, Coney Island, and Boston. At this point, dozens of other entrepreneurs entered the business. At the height of its popularity between 1905 and 1907, there were over five hundred installations throughout the United States. But the Tours quickly lost appeal, largely because the production could not meet the demand. The films were hard to come by and couldn't be changed often enough to keep people coming back. Only a limited number of titles were available, so the variety of content at any given time was unsatisfactory.

Despite this, Hale's Tours is evidence of Kirby's assertion that the view from a moving train was formative in how film audiences built expectations of the new medium. By explicitly referencing an existing mode of spectatorship, it provided the necessary memory aid for spectators to comprehend the moving picture. In making this deep-seated relationship explicit, it functioned as an important bridge between the early exhibition of cinema and the nickelodeon era (Fielding 1970). It was the first uniquely designated space for the projection of actualities. For many people, including film producer Carl Laemmle and actress Mary Pickford, it was their first experience seeing projected film. Even though it was framed by the theme of the train, Hale's Tours demonstrated for them that film could be an attraction in its own right.

By the summer of 1907, Hale's Tours could scarcely be found; that same summer, the dominant mode of film production had shifted from the single-reel actuality film to the multireel narrative. The need to remediate film through the explicit metaphors of existing media was subsiding. The train passenger, and the kodaker, each constructive of the early cinematic spectator, ceased to be a necessary adjunct to the act of viewing film. Likewise, as film manufactured its own formal logics, the movement-image was no longer able to easily migrate between forms.

Regardless of these formal shifts, the aesthetic of possessive spectatorship had sufficiently established itself in the American vernacular. This is no place more evident than in Vachel Lindsay's declaration that the physical landscape needs to be consciously reshaped to match this aesthetic: "The photoplay can speak the language of the man who has a mind World's Fair size. . . . After duly weighing all the world's fairs, let our architects set about making the whole of the United States into a permanent one. Supposing the date to begin the erection is 1930. Till that time there should be tireless if indirect propaganda that will further the architectural state of mind, and later bring about the elucidation of the plans while they are being perfected. For many years this America . . . will be evolving" (Lindsay 1915, 246). For Lindsay, the cinema reflected the American state of mind—the model from which the whole of America could be reconstituted as an exposition. Lindsay premised this assumption on the work of Gerald Stanley Lee, who, one year prior to the publication of *The Art of the Moving Picture*, published his book *Crowds: A Moving Picture of Democracy* (1914). In this lengthy volume about the metaphor of crowds in American life, Lee directed special attention to the moving picture; it was the "moving picture, a portrait of the human race, that shall reveal man's heart to himself" (15). Lindsay adopted this position that the moving picture is illustrative of a changing American culture. He wrote that in the age of the moving picture, "America is in the state of mind where she must visualize herself again" (1915, 248). In other words, the moving picture is both the source and the product of a new American culture. It informs what exists—for instance, by pushing up against the boundaries of nature; and it is the only viable form in which to represent what exists, in that it captures the perpetual movement of the culture.

In proposing that the whole of the United States was in the process of becoming a World's Fair, Lindsay made the argument that, even outside of the material medium of film, the moving picture (in any form) could distill the culture of cities for individualized possession. And Lindsay was not alone in making this observation. Years later, the same sentiment would be popularized by Lewis Mumford in his *Culture of Cities*. "The metropolis itself," Mumford suggested, "may be described as a World's Fair in continuous operation" (1938, 265). This would become abundantly clear when a little place called Longacre Square in Manhattan's midtown got a name change in 1904.

Times Square as Cinematic Presentation

What the moving picture presented to an American public was a possessable experience of modern urban life. It took the experience of the Kodak and made it available for quick and easy consumption. The moving picture was, quite literally, a picture of movement; in its varied forms, it was a presentation of the potential of modern life. Lindsay relied on this metaphor to explain how America could compete in a world cultural economy. "It is time for the American craftsman and artist to grasp the fact that we must be men enough to construct a to-morrow that grows rich in forecastings in the same way that the past of Europe grows rich in sweet or terrible legends as men go back into it" (1915, 288). The moving image was distinctly American: and, for Lindsay, it was the best way to quickly and completely communicate the potentiality of American culture. Accordingly, without so much as erecting another building, neighborhoods could fundamentally alter their structure through displaying a moving picture. This is not simply referring to the exhibition of films in city spaces (although that is certainly part of it); any presentation of movement within the city adopted the qualities of the moving picture.

By New Year's Eve 1904, when the *New York Times* officially relocated from its downtown offices to the newly constructed Times Building in what was then called Longacre Square (Forty-second Street at the intersection of Broadway and Seventh Avenue was thereafter known as Times Square), significant changes in urban form were already under way. In the years leading up to this move, midtown Manhattan had become the transportation nexus of New York City. Grand Central Station and Pennsylvania Station brought the major railroad lines directly into the center of Manhattan while in 1904, the opening of New York's subway system further established Times Square as the new center of commerce. Largely because of this transportation cluster around the square, many industries began moving up from lower Manhattan. The garment district relocated factories from their old location in the Lower East Side. Entertainment companies, seeking inexpensive rent, gravitated toward this underdeveloped part of town. In 1895, Oscar Hammerstein purchased his first theater on Forty-second Street and began the remarkable migration of live theater uptown. In the 1890s, "New York's theater district had been scattered along Second Avenue, the Bowery, East Fourteenth Street, on 125th Street in Harlem, and along Broadway from Union Square to 42nd Street" (Hammack 1991, 45). In the next twenty-five years many of these theaters closed, and almost eighty new theaters were built in and around Times Square.

Unlike other major cities with prominent theater districts, New York's cluster of theaters had a particularly spectacular aesthetic. Historian David C. Hammack observes that "because New York lacked the subsidized state theaters of the great cities of Europe, these buildings were designed to the specifications of entrepreneurs driven by the market" (1991, 45). As one walked down Forty-second Street or Broadway, one couldn't help but be affronted by the moving lights of theater displays and signs. It was a new kind of kinetic urban aesthetic facilitated by the extreme clustering of entertainment businesses in the area. People traveled from all over America and the world to see what advertising entrepreneur O. J. Gude called "the phantasmagoria of the lights and electric signs" (Leach 1991). In 1905, a writer for the *New York Times* described it thusly: "For a mile or more north or south of the New York Times Building, Broadway, when the electric lights are ablaze, is the spinal column of the midnight pleasureland of the town. Broadway is in many respects the most wonderful thoroughfare in the world . . . [b]rilliantly illuminated with electric lights in all the colors of the rainbow, some as steady as the stars and others that are ingeniously arranged to flash at intervals" ("By Night as by Day" 1905).

Electric lights were introduced to Americans at the 1893 Chicago World's

Fair, but the lights of Broadway solidified a commercial aesthetic. As businesses fought hard to compete for the crowd's attention, new forms of advertising developed, specifically, the sky sign. Studded with lamps, illuminated signboards, and the floodlighting and outlining of exteriors, these "spectaculars," as they came to be called in the industry, dominated the view of the area. What's more, they placed within the context of the city the practices of spectatorship normally associated with the kodaker and cinemagoer. According to David Henkin, "Despite changes and variety in size, function, and discursive style, the explosive growth of New York's commercial signage tended toward the development of a monumental architecture of the written word, providing new maps of city space suitable for the silent circulation of strangers, a new semi-official public discourse, and the seeds of new public authority in what has been called (for many good reasons) the private city" (1998, 50).

The "private city" to which Henkin refers is one in which the spectator's primary method of interaction with the city is in the consumption of image and text. The practice of being behind the camera and hunting for photographic "fragments," or sitting in a theater and watching the play of images, begins to manifest itself outside of photographic technology — most notably in the signs of Times Square.

In a 1913 visit to Times Square, the poet Ezra Pound had this to say of his experience: is New York "the most beautiful city in the world? It is not far from it. . . . Electricity has made for [people] the seeing of visions superfluous. . . . Squares upon squares of flames, set and cut into one another. Here is our poetry, for we have pulled down the stars to our will" (Pound 1950). Marveling at the celestial grandeur of the lights of Times Square, Pound made clear the connection between the "seeing of visions" and the spectacular use of electricity in public spaces. Both, as Pound explained, are visual experiences shaped to our will — again, a private assertion of authority. For Pound, the experience of seeing was exteriorized by the public display of electric lights, by the dancing of illuminated objects on the cinema screen, by the privileging of the movement-image in the modern spectacle.

But Pound's reaction was not unique. Another visitor, author Arnold Bennett, upon visiting the square in 1912, described it as "an enfevered phantasmagoria. . . . Above the layer of darkness enormous moving images of things in electricity — a mastodon kitten playing with a ball of thread, an umbrella in a shower of rain, siphons of soda-water being emptied and filled, gigantic horses galloping at full speed, and an incredible heraldry of chewing gum . . .

Sky signs!" (qtd. in Starr and Hayman 1998, 61). Far more than just involving the spectacular use of electric lights, the signs in and around Times Square from the turn of the century to the beginning of World War I materialized the aesthetic of the moving image within urban space. This movement, already established in the culture as signifying a certain play, insinuated a future-looking American city. While people understood they were consuming advertisements for products, these moving images were immediately integrated into the semiotics of the American city. Advertisers didn't spend sometimes upwards of $100,000 to publicize a product in Times Square simply for the purpose of catching a little attention; they paid for these signs perched high above the street to emphasize the movement of the street itself. They "wish to make the name of their product as nearly standard as possible," said an editorial in the *Times*, "so that when you think of that particular drink you will think at once of their electric scream" ("Lighting 'The Great White Way' " 1907). Ultimately, spectaculars were more about the street they loomed over than about the products. The goal, of course, was that the person walking along the street would associate that experience with the name of the product advertised.

O. J. Gude, the man the press called "the creator of the Great White Way" and the "Napoleon of Advertising," was probably the most significant figure in developing the Times Square aesthetic. Gude formed his own company in 1889 and began making modest electronic signs as early as 1898. But it was in 1905 that Gude's company created what would become the first significant spectacular in Times Square: Miss Heatherbloom, the Petticoat Girl. At a staggering cost of about $45,000, this multiple-story sign depicted an incandescent Miss Heatherbloom walking through a driving rain (Starr and Hayman 1998, 187). The rain-effect was created by the movement of slashing diagonal lines of lamps concealed by a shelllike umbrella. The gale behind her whipped at her dress, revealing this immense electronic figure's shapely outline. Her skirt, with her ("Insist Upon the Label") petticoat peeking out, fluttered before her as twinkling lamps (see figure 3.4).

Because of the immense popularity of this sign, it remained in Times Square well into the teens before being replaced. Crowds of tourists and residents would gather below the spectacular sign and nightly gawk at the bright lights and movement of the pouring rain and fluttering skirt. The walk through Times Square, once Miss Heatherbloom moved in, was nothing like it used to be; now the spectacular movement of the skies surpassed the motion and speed of the street.

From this point on, the moving spectacular continued to pepper the skyline of Times Square. In 1912, the famous ad for Corticelli Spool Silk, a brand of sewing thread, went up on the roof of the Albany Hotel at Broadway and Fortieth Street. This sign showed a kitten persistently tugging at a spool of thread, all the while becoming hopelessly entangled in it. A sewing machine on wheels whirred by the top with a revolving belt that fed the smooth running Corticelli thread through the needle bar. The kitten, avoiding the moving needle, would jump down to the roof and stop the machine. This, of course, would repeat every thirty seconds or so, but it continued to fascinate spectators because it was packed with complex movements. The kitten's tail wagged, its ears twitched, and its paws batted at the turning spool in a blur. As with the phenomenon of repeated viewings of actualities, spectators would marvel for several minutes at the same ad, continually delighting in the movement of light and shape with each successive viewing.

While O. J. Gude was the dominant force in the market for these signs, he had several competitors who attempted to nudge their way into the business in one form or another. Elwood Rice, an ad salesman from the Midwest, moved to New York in 1909 to break into the Times Square business. In June 1910, he lit the biggest sign to hit Broadway. This sign, supported by a sixty-ton superstructure and measuring seventy-two feet high and ninety feet wide, rested high above Herald Square on Thirty-eighth and Broadway on the roof of the Hotel Normandie. "It entirely dwarfs every other sign along the famous 'Great White Way,'" said a writer for *Strand Magazine*. "Overlooking the busiest business section of the American metropolis, it is probably seen by a greater number of people during an evening than any other 'free show' of the kind in the world" (Jones 1911, 443). The show was basically a message billboard couched within a moving panorama of a Roman chariot race. But it was not like all the other signs that spotted Broadway. Instead of being one of those "ordinary signs which must be changed every few weeks in order to retain the attention of the public," this sign was to have "permanent value" (Jones 1911, 446). It was equipped with a space for fifty-four four-foot letters to advertise different products. The idea was that it function like a rotating ad slot, with companies buying a month at a time.

(opposite)

FIGURE 3.4.

Miss Heatherbloom, the Petticoat Girl, was one of the most popular ads in Times Square before World War I. Outdoor Advertising Association of America Records, courtesy of Duke University Rare Book, Manuscript, and Special Collections Library

The sign garnered a significant cultural response. The public was generally pleased with the magnificence of its light and movement. Crowds, gazing up at the endlessly repeated thirty-second illuminated chariot races, packed into the streets for weeks after the sign was turned on in June 1910. At first, the "crowds that collected to stare became so great that a special squad of New York's brawniest police had to be told off to handle them. Vehicular traffic was considerably impeded, chains of electric cars were held up, and the 'rubber neck' wagons with their tiers of sight-seers were brought to a standstill" (Jones 1911, 443). People couldn't help but look up at the grandiose spectacle: it towered over the Normandie hotel, was illuminated with over twenty thousand electric bulbs, and each horse was thirty-five feet long. The whole scene was animated—even down to the details of the horses' hooves, manes, and tails. Everything flapped in the illuminated distance. Again, from *Strand*: "It is more perfect and natural in its movement than the finest coloured cinematograph picture, and must be seen to be appreciated. The photographs reproduced are striking, but from them one can obtain no adequate idea of the perfection of illusion, which, after all, is the real triumph of a mechanical electric display" (Jones 1911, 444). Cinema was often characterized as more "perfect" than the object in life. Now, this spectacular sign was referred to as "more perfect" than cinema. Accordingly, this sign was not conceived as a representation of objects in the world, it was conceived as a representation of the movement-image. To stand in a crowd on Broadway and gaze up at the massive sign was the experience of the street.

Reproducing the Modern American City

If New York was established as the "crossroads of the world," Times Square was establishing itself as the "crossroads of the crossroads." More than any other space in New York City, Times Square, and much of Broadway, came to represent urban experience in general. One foreign visitor noted, "Perhaps Broadway outshines Piccadilly Circus and its other rivals in Paris, Port Said, and Vienna in that it has the essential features of every one of these. London's Village Street is most English, that of Paris is very French, while the Pike of Port Said is a Tenderloin still innocent of a 'lid'; but Broadway has the best of the these features and a great many others, all tempered by a 'native hue of resolution'" ("Impressions of a Scotsman" 1904). Broadway was, for this visitor, a perfect exposition of urban centers. It represented with complete clarity what other city spaces could not. "This atmosphere," continued the visitor, "is peculiar to cosmopolitan America, and, as New York's main artery is the greatest city artery in the United States, we will grant for the one-millionth time that Broadway is the greatest thoroughfare in the world, for you would smile at anyone who said it was not."

This "greatest thoroughfare," with that "native hue of resolution," was reproduced time and again in cities throughout the United States. Many "White Ways" cropped up around the country from cities as diverse as Wichita, Kansas, to Redondo, California. The phenomenon of having a central business district illuminated and mobilized with electric streetlights and billboards be-

FIGURE 3.5.
Irving Underhill, "Times Square North: night illumination," 1921. Courtesy of New York Public Library

came the most efficient way of communicating the experience of the modern American city.

Like the White City before it, Times Square harnessed cultural attitudes about urban experience to package and sell city space. Sign builders, and later urban planners, used recognizable codes from Kodaking and early cinema to communicate the "experience of modern life" to urban spectators. The playful gaze that sparked controversy among amateur photographers became the representation that best captured the modern city. The opposing view of urbanism, characterized by the "modest woman" or the staid presence of nature was certainly still present in New York City. But it was the presentation of play in cinema and in the streets that succeeded in creating a comprehensible and distinct American urban scene — one that was bigger, more easily consumable, and more readily reproducible.

Gude saw the city as a theater and built on its stage the attractions he knew his audience loved. Times Square marked the beginning of a trend in American urban development wherein the experience of play was built into the city in order to attract an audience, further enforcing the public's conception of itself as urban spectators. This is not to suggest that urban space was suddenly no longer "authentic," that spectatorship somehow connoted a false, distanced engagement. Rather, the commercial reproduction of play into urban space actually opened up perceptions of access. The modern urban space of Times Square served to democratize urban space and extend the rhetoric of populism already existent in the American city. Times Square, as urban experience, was accessible to a far more diverse public than, say, the parlors of Fifth Avenue. Certainly, other social forces, including overt discrimination, continued to deny access to public space for many people, but it is clear that the shifting nature of urban form made the street more accessible to a greater number. Access to the space wasn't prefaced by one's historical and social connection to the city. Historical reference was no longer the main determinant of urban meaning; in Times Square, the moving image flashing high above the city's structures was designed to contain all that the spectator might desire. Walter Benjamin described this transformation as it applied to the work of art. "For the first time in world history," he said, "mechanical reproduction emancipates the work of art from its parasitical dependence on ritual" (1986, 226). The city, like the work of art, was no longer accessible only to those who could claim a ritualistic attachment to its culture. The American City was made available to anyone willing and able to look at it.

SCALING UP

The "Speculative Architecture" of 1930s New York

In his 1925 drawing "The Lure of the City," the architectural renderer Hugh Ferriss depicts the future metropolis towering boldly in front of an intrepid spectator (see figure 4.1). Standing atop what appears to be a grassy hilltop, a lone figure stares upward at a group of skyscrapers. Each of the tall buildings is drawn with enough detail to distinguish it from the others, but not enough to stop one's eye from washing over the scene all at once, from seeing what Ferriss called "the unformulated, yet gleaming metropolis" (Leich 1980). In Ferriss's rendering of the city, the spectator is decidedly separate from the spectacle; he stands at a distance and optimistically gazes upon the grand scale of structures emerging in the new city. The city, grand and accessible, is presented in clear view, away from the crowd and other threatening signifiers of the industrialized landscape. Ferriss is able to achieve this simultaneous distance and proximity by rendering the city within the act of spectatorship. There is no illusion of an unmediated landscape; the lone spectator is privy to the urban landscape only as an object of speculation.

After World War I, the American city underwent considerable changes. The population of New York City expanded by more than 1.5 million people between 1918 and 1930. And as most of this population was crowded on the island of Manhattan, the city was engaged in a race to the sky. In these boom years, skyscrapers went from a novelty to the norm. As the streets transformed into crowded urban valleys lined with brick and terra cotta, the possibility of a spectator achieving a cohesive view of New York grew ever more remote. The playfulness of the moving image, as a medium and symbol of urban experience, was limited in scope. As the size of the metropolis grew, the means by which the spectator could possess and reproduce the experience of it changed. The street gave way to the sky, proximity to distance, and movement to network.

As a result, the character of possessive spectatorship was transformed. The

FIGURE 4.1.
Hugh Ferriss, *The Lure of the City*, from his 1929 book, *The Metropolis of Tomorrow*.

distance produced by the camera lens was augmented by a much more significant distance—a temporal distance of speculation. Jean Paul Sartre, writing in 1945, said the American city "is mainly a future; what [Americans] like in the city is everything it has not yet become and everything it can be" (1955, 112). As buildings grew skyward, as moving pictures moved from the peep show and nickelodeon to the picture palace, and as radio became a broadcast medium, the city that housed them became a "projection," a spectacle removed from the embodied experience of the camera in motion. By examining speculative architecture in the 1920s and 1930s—skyscrapers, movie palaces, and radio networks—we can locate a shift in urban spectatorship. No longer characterized solely by the immediately visible and mobile, spectatorship comprises the projection of place into far-off spaces. While it is still presented as a form of play, the definition of playfulness is significantly altered in the popular discourse. Now, more aligned with the play of the imagination than the play of the body, the American city is placed firmly in the future. In 1925, the architect Harvey Corbett predicted that in fifty years automobiles would have completely disappeared from New York's streets and pedestrians will be shot across vast distances "like parcels. . . . New York will be vast and the growth of all our large cities will probably be such that they will extend for 50 or 75 miles. New York will be a Titanic city half a mile high, probably tiered in gigantic terraces; a Gargantuan pyramidal conception, fit for a race of giants; 60 miles across, and conducting its traffic through tubes and on moveable platforms and escalating galleries" ("Sees City Traffic" 1925). Increasingly, the everyday experience of the city was associated with speculation. Corbett saw speculation as necessary to accommodate the individual in the crowding city. "The herding instinct of man to congregate in cities grows stronger. . . . [T]he evolution of the city is pointing toward more astounding developments every day. We have already seen the city take shapes that a few years ago were characterized as 'absurd, fantastical, impossible' when architectural drawings of them were made public" ("Sees City Traffic" 1925). Corbett and others considered Hugh Ferriss to be an urban soothsayer. His drawings of New York, "absurd, fantastical, impossible," were predictive of the shape of the city to come. Ferriss became the best-known artist of this new speculative architecture. His drawings of skyscrapers and cityscapes brushed over detail in favor of fantasy. They insinuated the deep connections between the city and the acts of projection and broadcast. While the move toward speculation in the framing of urban spectatorship is much more complex and expansive than Ferriss alone depicts, his work serves as a connection between the architectural discourse of modernity and the emerging desire for speculation. Skyscrapers, cinema and its palaces, radio broadcasting, the construction of Rockefeller Center, and the culminating speculations of the 1939 World's Fair all contributed to transforming urban spectatorship from something proximate to something far off.

City of the Imagination

The rise of the modern skyscraper in New York was an essential element in the changing urban landscape of the 1920s. These buildings, grand in scale and utopian by design, looked unimpeded toward the future. They were architectural displays of a particular vision of America—sturdy, immobile, and theoretically unaffected by the changing world around them. The skyscraper was built to alter the sky, not the street; only the first two or three floors were designed for the local pedestrian. The larger structure was for the benefit of the skyline—it existed only in the imagination for those at street level. Skyscrapers demanded speculation from urban spectators, a certain faith in the beauty and strength of the structure.

Whereas these tall buildings began dotting the urban landscape as early as the nineteenth century,[1] most notably in Chicago, it wasn't until after World War I that the sheer display of scale in the form of the skyscraper became the primary means through which New York communicated the idea of the American city. New York, as Le Corbusier famously put it, was the "vertical city." The skyscraper shifted its dimensions, affecting both urbanism and the literal shape of urban space. Le Corbusier described this transformation in his New York travel journal: "A thousand feet of height looked at from the streets, or appearing as an ineffable spectacle from the plains of New Jersey, above the Palisades—the cliffs along the Hudson River—that is the *scale* of the new times" (1947, 45; italics added). As the architect W. A. Starrett wrote in his autobiography in 1928, the skyscraper is "essentially and completely American, so far surpassing anything ever before undertaken in its vastness, swiftness, utility, and economy that it epitomizes American life and American civilization, and, indeed, has become the cornerstone and abode of our national progress" (qtd. in Leeuwen 1986, 4).

Starrett was one of many who celebrated the skyscraper as the essential icon of the new American city. Throughout the 1920s (a decade often referred to as the "age of the skyscraper"), tall buildings were overwhelmingly heralded as the unique contribution of American architecture. In 1926, an exhibition devoted exclusively to the skyscraper opened at the Corona Mundi International Art Centre in Manhattan. According to an account in the *New York Times*, the exhibit was the first of its kind where "the public was invited to attend to judge for itself whether the skyscraper was of the detriments to our growing life, as recently alleged, or a phase of art comparable to the Pyramids or the architectural creations of Greece and Rome" ("Skyscraper City" 1926). The tone of the exhibit, featuring Hugh Ferriss and many of New York's prominent architects, was decidedly geared toward the latter option. The skyscraper was a form to be celebrated as distinctly American, with its most ambitious manifestation in New York.

We might assume that the public had already made up its mind. Hugh Ferriss's drawings had by that time became iconic representations of the urban future. The first images of the Empire State Building, published years before the building was complete, were Ferris's fantastical representations. Utopian and yet possible, expressive and yet realist, Ferriss's pencil-drawn renderings were displayed in museums and published in popular magazines throughout the 1920s and '30s. His prescriptive drawings made sense of the potential shape of the American city in ways much more powerful than written commentary or even actual examples of finished buildings. Ferriss intended the texture of his drawings, with their heavy shadows and dramatic lighting, to soften the technological aesthetic of modernity. The catalog of his 1932 exhibit at the Roerich Museum stated his doctrine as the "recognition, preservation and encouragement of human values in an age increasingly mechanistic" ("Architectural Design Show" 1932). By emphasizing spectatorship in the representation of skyscrapers, Ferriss managed to exhibit the grandiose on a human scale. In his depiction of the Empire State Building that appeared in the *New York Times* (Poore 1930), the perspective originates from a pedestrian's position at street level and is directed upward. The dramatic lighting starts low and fades away as it approaches the top of the building shrouded by the night sky. The result is a picture of a grand building of unprecedented scale, softened and made comprehensible by the humble texture and perspective of the drawing.

Even those skeptical of the potentially dehumanizing scale of the skyscraper city concluded it to be inevitable and consequently took comfort in Ferriss's work. According to one critic, "That Mr. Ferriss' metropolis or something less lovely, is in store for us, can hardly be denied. Monster cities and buildings are already here. They are being built by forces not yet under control. The task is to subdue them . . . [and] Mr. Ferriss has contributed something to the fulfillment of that goal" (Duffus 1929). Ferriss rendered the skyscraper a functional aspect of continued urban centralization and successfully articulated the popular desire to embrace the American skyscraper as a vision of the future. While some viewed skyscrapers as excessive symbols of capitalism, most wanted to believe that this peculiarly American form could be a lasting contribution to modern life. One critic referred to Ferriss's drawings as "a gorgeous feast . . . appealing as a work of art, [and] magically stirring as a prophecy" (Guerard 1930). From these prophetic works, Ferriss managed to distill the skeptical American desire for a skyscraper future into a palatable aesthetic style.

But representations of the skyscraper future were already familiar to most spectators through cinema. Ferriss's aesthetic was reminiscent of the foreboding urban landscapes of Fritz Lang's *Metropolis* (1927) and King Vidor's *The Crowd* (1928). In each of these films, the city's immensity and its resulting claustrophobia are highlighted through darkly lit, expressionist design. Distinct from Ferris's optimism, the metaphor of verticality in *Metropolis* encompasses the themes of social inequality and mechanization. High above the city, the leisure class basks in the sun, while down below the laborers toil. In *The Crowd* also, the relentless ant's eye views of the skyscrapers are part of the titular crowd that serves to alienate the protagonist, John Sims. The skyscraper is the visual reminder of Sims's insignificance. Its towering form preexists, and thus actively negates, the act of spectatorship. Instead of each building emerging out of an anticipatory gaze, the buildings crowd in and overwhelm the senses to communicate a future that has already arrived.

But not all cinematic representations of skyscrapers were so bleak. Musical representations often highlighted the speculative qualities of the city. In most New York musicals, skyscrapers were heralded as an ecstatic monument to progress, or what Scott Bukatman calls a "delirious urban celebration" (2003). For example, in Lloyd Bacon's *42nd Street* (1933), skyscrapers literally dance to their own success. In Mervyn Leroy's *Gold Diggers of '33* (1933) and Busby Berkeley's *Dames* (1934) and *Bright Lights* (1935), the tall buildings figure prominently in musical numbers and serve to metaphorically couch the success of the stage stars. Bukatman makes the argument that the musical numbers featuring New York's skyline create a unique relationship between the city and spectatorship: "As with Times Square, Broadway, or the movies themselves, the numbers represent an oasis within which spectacle can be indulged, consumed, and played with" (2003, 158). Emerging in the midst of the depression, these cinematic spectacles compelled viewers to look beyond the present city and toward the city of the future—one that could dance and sing with potential. This was a city in play. Bukatman describes this musical city as having a "creative geography," wherein the characters could enter "into an integrated, syncopated, and carefully synchronized environment in which work is either replaced by play or transformed into a kind of play" (2003, 162). Different than the spectator described in the last chapter, who desired an immediate engagement in the rhythms of the city, the spectator the musical constructed could watch play unfold within a speculative landscape. The play discovered in the musical film was in watching the city transform from a spatial to a temporal distance. Similar to what R. L. Duffus, writing for the *New York Times*, called "a better city to live in," the "syncopated city" was in the future tense. "It is too late to plan the city that is," said Duffus. "The more glorious city of the future," he declared, "is within our grasp if we wish to reach out for it" (1928).

The best example of "reaching out" for this city of the future within cinema can be found in the 1930 musical *Just Imagine!* (see figure 4.2). In what the *New York Times* called "a beautiful production," this little known musical version of Lang's *Metropolis* represents New York City fifty years in the future (Hall 1930). In this version, a man falls asleep in 1930 and wakes up fifty years later only to discover a place where names are replaced with numbers and babies are "born" from vending machines. And the city has become a familiar futuristic vision (based on Hugh Ferriss's drawings) where traffic is split into nine vertical levels, buildings extend miles into the sky, and airplanes are more popular than cars. But the city is more reminiscent of *42nd Street* than *Metropolis*. James Sanders argues, "Where *Metropolis* seems inspired by Lower Manhattan, with its angular streets and closely packed towers, *Just Imagine!*'s city suggests midtown, its layout of buildings and avenues more regular and widely spaced" (2001). Indeed, the skyscrapers in this elaborately designed set (which was nominated for an academy award for "Interior Decoration") appear always to be at a distance from the characters. They have been explicitly removed from the characters and appear to be behind a proscenium so as to draw attention to the practice of viewing.

This was a practice with which most urban spectators were familiar. As movie theaters transformed from nickelodeons to palaces in the 1920s, the containment of the cinematic spectacle became part and parcel of the urban fabric. In many ways, the movie palace was the architectural equivalent of the musical. It was celebratory and speculative, and it transformed urban play from the mobile gaze of the body and lens to the stationary practice of the imagination. These fantasy structures built in exaggerated scale were grandiose containers for the cinematic image. Roxy Rothafel, the man known as the high priest of New York's movie palaces, helped design one of the largest movie theaters in the city, the Roxy (1927). This theater, which he dubbed the "Cathedral of the Motion Pictures," included a "set of tower chimes, a grand dome encircled by a spotlight gallery, and pulpits alongside the stage, reached by curving golden stairways suspended below them" (Naylor 1981, 109). The majority of these structures were premised on anachronistic designs, ironically, built to house the very symbol of modernity. With their grand cathedral-like architecture, movie palaces employed the cinematic image in the service of the city image. In other words, they were not solely built to enhance the cinema; in very important ways, these structures allowed the cinema to directly enhance the city. Movie palaces were more about the city that housed them than the spectacles they housed. And they provided the spectator the necessary architectural artifact—properly contained and controlled—with which to possess the city.

The City's Invisible Foundation

Just as spectators were introduced to the grandeur of the distant spectacle in movie palaces, they were comforted by the intimacy of the surrounding empty space. After the 1912 *Titanic* disaster, radio made the transition from a little noticed amateur's hobby to a clear necessity in the modern landscape. An article in the *New York Times* published on April 26, 1912, pointed out that

> Night and day all the year round the millions upon the earth and the thousands upon the sea now reach out and grasp the thin air and use it as a thing more potent for human aid than any strand of wire or cable that was ever spun or woven. Last week 745 [*sic*] human lives were saved from perishing by the wireless. But for the almost magic use of the air the *Titanic* tragedy would have been shrouded in the secrecy that not so long ago was the power of the sea. . . . Few New Yorkers realize that all through the roar of the big city there are constantly speeding messages between people separated by vast distances, and that over housetops and even through the walls of buildings and in the very air one breathes are words written by electricity. (qtd. in Kern 1983, 67)

Living among the invisible whirring of electrical messages was part of the parlance of modern life. Unlike other elements of the urban environment, like crowds of people and the congestion of buildings that were increasingly associated with crime and danger in the popular press, the crowding of invisible messages on radio waves carried redemptive possibilities.

Radio's emergence as a popular medium brought the invisible to the forefront of everyday life and significantly altered how the city could be imagined. Many developers and planners began to conceive of the city as a network—placing less importance on the center and more on the hubs surrounding it in a radial fashion. As early as 1896, immediately following Guglielmo Marconi's transatlantic wireless transmission, "hams" or amateurs began filling the newly discovered ether with information. But it wasn't until Lee Deforest's

FIGURE 4.2.
David Butler's *Just Imagine!* (1930) was conceived as a musical rendition of *Metropolis*.

1907 invention of the Audion tube (the first radio receiver) that this two-way communication device was reconceptualized as a broadcast technology. DeForest immediately began broadcasting from New York City and Paris even though very few people actually possessed the technology to receive the signals. Years later, after broadcasting caught on, DeForest recalled that through his accomplishment he had "unwittingly . . . discovered an invisible Empire of the Air" (qtd. in Barnouw 1990, 15). An absolute mania pervaded America: people rushed to buy receivers as transmitter towers cropped up throughout the country (Douglas 1986). Broadcasts, originating primarily in New York, redefined the physical limits of the American city by adding the invisible ether to its potential landscape.

Utopian discourses surrounding radio broadcasting forcefully emerged in the 1920s. An article in *Collier's* claimed that radio would become "a tremendous civilizer" bringing "mutual understanding to all sections of the country, unifying our thoughts, ideals, and purposes, making us a strong and well-knit people" (qtd. in Douglas 1986, 54). A writer for *Radio News* recounted her experience living in a farmhouse hundreds of miles from New York City: "But out under the old gnarled apple trees . . . we sat one evening and listened to the New York Philharmonic orchestra play the Beethoven Fifth Symphony; and we heard Roxy and his gang put on a good show at the Capitol Theatre. The thorny hands of the farm women, used to all labor and no amusement for the last half century, were still and awed. It was as though the Magic Carpet of Baghdad had come to life and transported them to Gotham" (Frederick 1926). Radio was considered the great conqueror of space with promise to unite a city, a nation, and perhaps even the world. However, there was still no viable way to create a national broadcast. Stations were not powerful enough, and it was unclear how to strengthen or even to connect them. Despite what some feared was a technological impossibility, the battle for national radio raged throughout the 1920s.

Local stations, broadcasting to individual cities throughout America, had been in existence for some time when the practical steps toward establishing national radio began. After World War I, there was no centralized control of the radio business. Privately owned stations existed all throughout the country, with large companies like General Electric (GE), Westinghouse, and AT&T controlling most of them. Yet there was not a real leader in the industry. However, because the British Marconi Company then controlled the largest segment of wireless-related patents, the American government felt it necessary to intervene in the emerging industry. In 1919 it urged the establishment of the patent pool Radio Corporation of American (RCA) in order to ensure that American firms could control wireless technology.

A series of conferences was held to establish legislative proposals for the future of wireless. While the first two, held in 1922 and 1923, were unsuccessful in providing practical focus, by the third, the issue of "interconnection" became central. The possibility of establishing "super-power" broadcasting towers that reached across states and perhaps the entire country was quickly deemed technologically impossible and ultimately undesirable. But by supplying "quality" programs to rural locations through networks, radio could bring "high" urban culture to the country without erasing the geographical distinctiveness of rural areas. One of the subcommittees of the Third National Radio Conference reported that "improvements in programs is [*sic*] essential." Such improvements would result from interconnecting "broadcasting stations, bringing the programs of the larger centers of art, music, and events of public interest to the more remote broadcasting stations" (Smulyan 1994, 39).

The promise of connectivity without centralization was the single most influential factor in determining the shape of radio broadcasting in the United States. Accordingly, this promise was equally influential in the framing of urban experience. Hugh Ferriss exemplified this utopian imagination. In his drawings of the "Metropolis of Tomorrow," the city is divided into multiple centers. These "centers" function as broadcasting stations, each emanating out to its proximate cluster of buildings, and each connected through a singular network. Ferriss's drawings reflected the distinctly American push away from the "super-power" centralization of European cities.[2] The American city was being built on a networking model that deemphasized the center while placing attention onto the circulation of information.

The social scientists Paul Lazarsfeld and Patricia Kendall, in their 1948 study conducted at the University of Chicago's National Opinion Research Center, concluded about the impact of radio: it "is not a single, isolated experience such as seeing a Broadway play or taking a vacation. It is woven into the daily pattern of our lives year in and year out" (1948, 44). The "Metropolis of Tomorrow," like the new medium of radio, is everywhere and nowhere at the same time. While Ferriss's city can be partially viewed from a distant parapet, the bridges between the centers remain invisible. And while radio could be experienced in a single instant, its origin and perpetual stream of information remained inconceivable. In each instance, space itself, or the invisible material that composes it, is central to the form of the medium. By the late 1920s, ether, and by extension the concept of the network, was an important building block in the popular imaginings of the American city.

An "Imaginary" Metropolis

(*opposite*)
FIGURE 4.3.
Hugh Ferriss, *Bird's Eye View, The City at Dawn*, from *The Metropolis of Tomorrow*.

> A First Impression of the contemporary city—let us say, the view of New York from the work-room in which most of these drawings were made—is not unlike [this] sketch. This, indeed, is to the author the familiar morning scene. But there are occasional mornings when, with an early fog not yet dispersed, one finds oneself, on stepping onto the parapet, the spectator of an even more nebulous panorama. Literally, there is nothing to be seen but mist; not a tower has yet been revealed below, and except for the immediate parapet rail (dark and wet as an ocean liner's) there is not a suggestion of either locality or solidity for the coming scene. To an imaginative spectator, it might seem that he is perched in some elevated box to witness some gigantic spectacle, some cyclopean drama of forms; and that the curtain has not yet risen. (Ferriss 1986, 15)

In this dramatic opening passage from *Metropolis of Tomorrow*, Hugh Ferriss describes the experience of looking out over New York City through the early morning mist (see figure 4.3). Like a theatrical spectacle, the city from afar is a "nebulous panorama," a scene yet to take form. But when the curtain rises, what is uncovered is a sea of towers, a mass equivalent to the most dramatic stage set or cinematic projection. In the drawing shown here, Ferriss represents the act of viewing the city, as if to suggest the city, like the stage set, exists primarily in the context of spectatorship. The act of spectatorship is highlighted by the easel and canvas in the foreground, implying that the city exists to be represented, that the city is composed in the process of viewing. The "imaginative spectator," Ferriss writes, is watching from an "elevated box"—a metaphor suggestive of a movie palace as he awaits the start of the "gigantic spectacle."

This process-oriented approach to the built environment can be seen in a great deal of Ferriss's work, perhaps explaining why he chose to draw buildings instead of build them. While trained as an architect, he worked only as an architectural renderer, a job title he created when he wrote *The Encyclopedia Britannica* entry in 1929 entitled "Rendering, Architectural" (14th ed.).[3] Even though Ferriss never actually designed a building, he was a significant figure in the development of American cities and architecture. Soon after graduating with an architecture degree from Washington University, Ferriss took a job in the New York office of Cass Gilbert in 1912 drawing details of the Woolworth

Building, then under construction. Fancying himself more a draftsman than an architect, Ferriss began working freelance making drawings of New York street life. In August 1914, his sketch entitled "The *Vie de Boheme* in Washington Square" was published in *Vanity Fair*. A self-proclaimed visionary, Ferriss was more concerned with imagining the city in drawings than he was with designing one of its individual elements in space. According to Carol Willis, Ferriss "sees mass and outline rather than fussy detail. He sees the play of light and shadow and feels, perhaps more than any other artist in America, the sense of bigness, the vast strength and size of America's modern architecture" (1986, 151). Precisely through working with pencil and paper and not brick and mortar, Ferriss found his niche in New York's world of architecture. He saw himself as more than just the producer of blueprints for future buildings. His drawings were intended to be a combination of the actual and the imaginary, a representation whereby mass is in dialogue with space. The underlying truth of a building, Ferriss wrote in 1926, "is that it is a Mass in Space." "He conceptualized buildings as a solid mass from which details slowly surfaced," said Willis. "Whereas another artist might first sketch lines and then shade individual areas, Ferriss usually darkened the general form, and then, working like a sculptor carving from a block, would create highlights and details with an eraser. He likened the process to observing a building emerge through a lifting fog" (1986, 151).

The architectural critic Douglas Haskell observed in 1930 that American urban architecture is preoccupied with the study of the "mass" (Willis 1986, 149). Ferriss's city was not composed through the accumulation of disparate structures, but it was instead composed of individual structures carved from a singular space. Like a sculpture, Ferriss's city began as one solid mass, its empty spaces intentionally carved away by the artist. Just as radio proved the existence of invisible mass called ether, Ferriss's city promoted the invisible materiality that connected its structures. This was the stability of the future-looking American city. *The Metropolis of Tomorrow*, Ferriss's best-known publication, was devoted to communicating this idea.

Metropolis of Tomorrow

Metropolis of Tomorrow is divided into three parts: "Cities of Today," "Projected Trends," and "An Imaginary Metropolis." It is in the last part where Ferriss fully explores the possibilities of new technologies for the future city. He theorizes scale and invisibility in the image of the city. It is here that the act of imagining the city to come develops into a necessary element in imagining the city that is.

In the opening passage of this final part Ferriss revisits the theme of the theater curtain: "Let us return to the parapet which provided us with our original bird's eye view of the existing city. It is again dawn, with an early mist completely enveloping the scene. Again, there lies beneath us, curtained by the mist, a Metropolis—and the curtain, again, is about to rise. But, in this case, let us have it rise, not on the existing city, but on a city of the imagination" (1986, 109). Looking down upon the city once again, after describing the face of the present city in previous parts of the book, Ferriss asks the reader to envision the "city of the imagination"—the face of the future city (see figure 4.4). In the center of this planned metropolis lies the "Civic Circle"—"which, with its parks, playgrounds and areas for open-air gatherings and exhibitions, is the focal point to which the radial avenues lead" (1986, 138). Along the circumference of the circle, there are three main hubs, each with a very specific purpose. The Business Center, the Art Center, and the Science Center are skyscraper clusters that house each of their titular activities and functions. To Ferriss, "Each of these tower-buildings houses all the facilities for the day's work; containing, in addition to the offices themselves, the necessary post office, bank, shops, restaurants, gymnasiums and so on. Each is, so to speak, a city in itself" (1986, 128). However, the ideal urban dweller Ferriss envisions in his city would, as a matter of necessity, frequent all of these spaces in order to fully realize the potential of urban life. The three centers are not meant to be separate; they are, for Ferriss, complimentary parts of a whole.

Ferriss's city was not intended to be experienced in a singular take. The experience of the city was premised on the connectivity of its parts. While each center remained separate, in that it was functional and self-sustaining, only in the correspondence of centers did the metropolis emerge. This multi-nucleated city was different from the dominant strains in urban planning at the time. Patrick Geddes's work and much of the Chicago School's emphasis on the concentric circle model was concerned with outward growth from an existing center. Spatial proximity was necessary for a functional city. While eventually this model changed to allow for the growth of individual hubs to exist within the larger metropolis, at all times the hubs needed to overlap or coincide.

In Ferriss's metropolis, it was the distance between centers that rendered the whole functional. Therefore, as none of the individual centers could, in

FIGURE 4.4.
Hugh Ferriss, *Return to the Parapet*, from *The Metropolis of Tomorrow*.

isolation, compose the city, it was the space between centers that took priority. It is in these "empty" spaces where one could obtain the unobstructed view of the individual centers. Ferriss envisioned the space between centers as a significant aspect of the future city's material. On the surface, Ferriss's position was quite similar to that held by other prominent architects, such as Le Corbusier. However, Le Corbusier's contention that cities were in need of open space was premised on the assumption that empty space was, in fact, empty. "WE MUST BUILD ON A CLEAR SITE!" he exclaimed in *The City of Tomorrow and Its Planning*. "The city of today is dying because it is not constructed geometrically" (1929, 232). While Ferriss shared certain of Le Corbusier's inclinations toward modern planning, Le Corbusier continually emphasized the top-down approach to the urban form. The geometry, rather than the perspective, is what mattered to him. Ferriss's city, on the other hand, was immersive and distant at the same time—the empty space was a tactile material through which each spectator viewed the world.

The assimilation of "empty space" into the structural mass of the city was premised on a long social and scientific debate concerning the existence of ether. In 1898, the American philosopher Hirom M. Stanley pondered the significance of space itself, concluding that space is "not full of things, but things are spaceful" (qtd. in Kern 1983, 154). From the advent of radio transmission in the late nineteenth century, vibrant scientific and philosophical dialogues emerged around the topic of space. Stanley's adjectival form of the word opposed predominant thinking on the subject; most nineteenth century physicists couldn't concede that space is itself a dynamic substance, with properties capable of altering the objects around it. The notion of ether, a medium that exists within space, then emerged as the dominant explanation for the mysterious potential of the invisible environment. For Ferriss, the space between things, the space across which spectatorship happens, is necessary to the experience of objects (see figure 4.5). Elements of the city are composed of the space that surrounds them, in that elements of urbanism (buildings, streets, and people) are unrealizable outside of the ability to view them. This is why Ferriss felt so strongly about maintaining open space in the city. Currently, he argued, there was not enough airspace for the pedestrian to actually view his environment:

> The fact is that in the general run of cities, the tall individual skyscraper, however well designed, can very seldom be individually seen. That is to say,

> juxtaposition is so close that only bits of the structure can be seen at one time by the pedestrian. Only by craning the neck does one see the whole of the tower; and then, of course, one sees only a ridiculous distortion. But in the city, now before us, each great mass is surrounded by a great spaciousness; here, we may assume, the citizen's habitual prospects are ample vistas. Without altering his upright posture, his glance may serenely traverse the vista and find at its end a dominating and upright pinnacle. (1986, 110)

(opposite)

FIGURE 4.5.

Hugh Ferriss, *Verticals on Wide Avenues*, from *The Metropolis of Tomorrow*.

Spaciousness allows vision. The structuring metaphor of radio, the redemptive possibilities of invisible material, ironically, created a paradigm wherein the city could be rendered visible and possessable—ultimately setting the stage for a more humane, "complete" access to the city.

Ferriss's future city did not have a centralized locus of power. It was the combinatory effect of the networked hubs that allowed the city to emerge. This is made clear in the epilogue to *The Metropolis of Tomorrow*, where Ferriss discloses that his ideas of the networked city were influenced by a "curious inscription" he discovered. "The manuscript was partly mutilated," explains Ferriss, "it may have been of quite ancient origin. Was it simply a curio? Or did it contain a clue? The author did not actually comprehend . . . yet he secured the copy which he now, at the last moment, includes—leaving it to whatever attention the chance reader may be inclined to give" (1986, 142).

The manuscript in question, entitled "Clue," includes the following text: "The CITY could be made in the image of MAN who is made in the image of" (see figure 4.6). Interspersed between the words there are two small images, each composed of a triangle embedded within a circle. Corresponding with the tips of the top triangle (which relates to the city) are the words "its sciences," "its arts," "its business." The bottom triangle (which references man) refers to "his thoughts," "his feelings," "his senses." There are a couple of noteworthy elements in this simple diagram that Ferriss places in the epilogue of his book. The design of the phrase suggests that the viewer read this text in a loop, implying that man is made in the image of the city, and so on. Man is composed within a triangle of qualities, none taking precedence over the other. The essence of man is his thoughts, feelings, and senses. This combinatory image of man runs contrary to the Cartesian grid plan favored by so many urban planners at the time—a plan whose hyperrational layout reinforced the distinction between mind and body. Yet Ferriss then suggests that man is "made," not in the image of God, but in the image of the city—that man and his environment

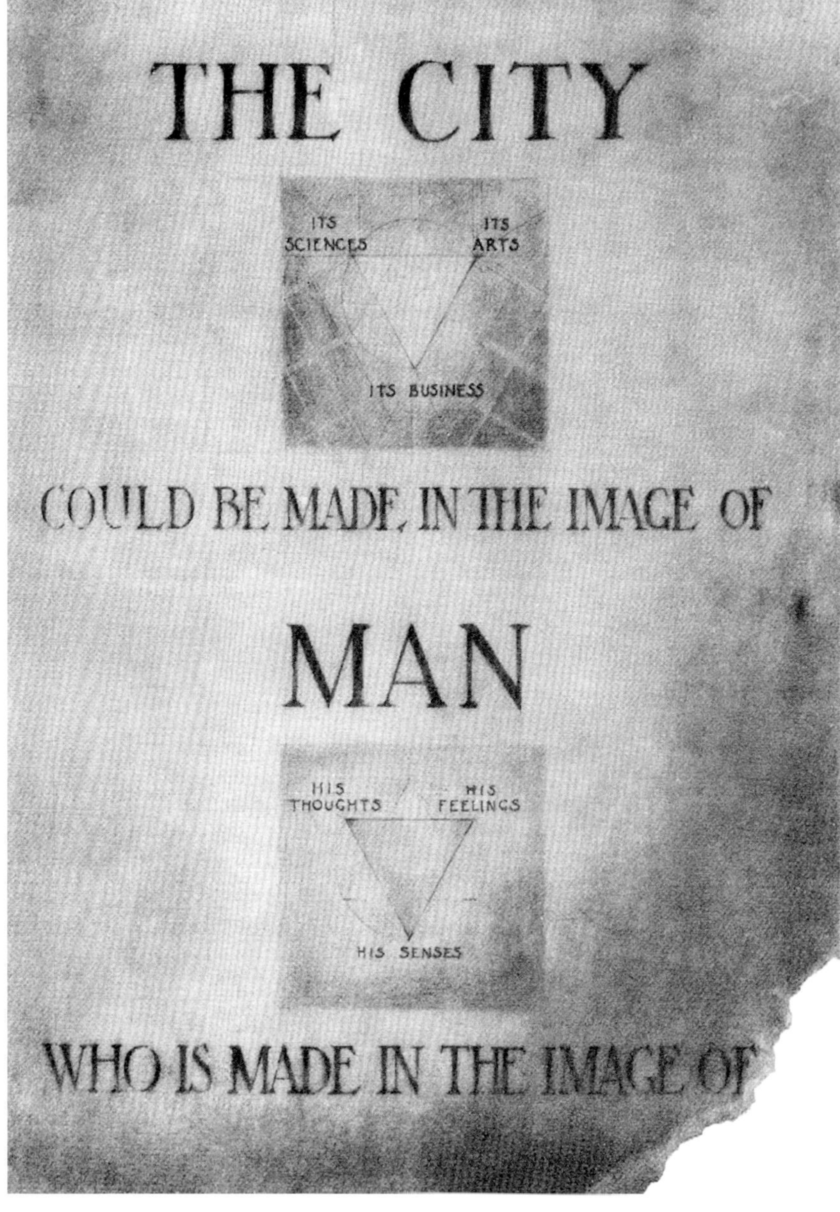

FIGURE 4.6.
Hugh Ferriss, *Clue*, from *The Metropolis of Tomorrow*.

are engaged in a continuous feedback loop, each mediating the other. It is useful to quote Ferriss at length:

> Architecture influences the lives of human beings. City dwellers react to the architectural forms and spaces which they encounter: specific consequences may be looked for in their thoughts, feelings and actions. Their response to Architecture is usually subconscious. Designers themselves are usually unconscious of the effects which their creations will produce. . . . Our criterion for judging this self-conscious Architecture will be its effect on human values: its net contribution to the harmonious development of man. We hope that eventually it will not only adequately meet the demands of our physical welfare, but will also serve in actualizing whatever may be man's potentialities of emotional and mental well-being. (1986, 142)

After asserting the responsibility architects should bear, he presents the following questions: "Who, indeed, can specifically define these potentialities—and what architects can prepare contributory or evocative designs? It may well be that at the present moment there are none; nor will there be, until architects have begun to call into their draughting rooms the scientist, the psychologist, the philosopher" (1986, 142). By metaphorically inviting "experts" to participate in the production of the city, the city might reflect a human face, ultimately creating the feedback loop for which Ferriss longed. In the "Metropolis of Tomorrow," there is a necessary correspondence between the qualities of man and the qualities of the city, each organically constructed to meet the needs of the other.

Ferriss asks how one can define the human potentialities of the city. And he succeeds in answering his own question by assimilating the metaphor of the new medium of radio into his design. Whenever a new medium is introduced into the culture, it is shaped to meet the desires of those who would use it. This is particularly true of radio. Implicit in that medium are the traces of the triangular qualities of man Ferriss is so eager to integrate into the design of the city. Ferriss's city has the same formal logic as network radio. The network of centers (or stations) that serve to define the whole is precisely the model that radio struggled with as it entered the broadcast era in the late 1920s. The issue of networking, how to connect large geographical distances, had become a question not only of technological advancement but also of human interaction. The fate of the future city, destined to become a chaotic megalopolis unless the newly discovered ether was utilized to connect people across space, was fundamentally indebted to the parallel technological advancements in radio broadcasting.

A "Real" Metropolis

Like Ferriss's dream of absolute connectivity within the city, the lead architect of Rockefeller Center, Raymond Hood, understood the new development as "a city within a city": freestanding hubs connected by invisible ether to manifest a whole (Hood 1932, 1).[4] According to a promotional book, "As each individual structure will harmonize with the architecture of the group, so also will the decorations fit into an inclusive ornamentative plan to tell, in the symbolic language of the arts, a connected, understandable story" (*Rockefeller Center* 1932, 5). Rockefeller Center, or what was until 1932 called "Radio City," was conceived as a single narrative, connected through a complex network of buildings and spectacles.

(opposite)
FIGURE 4.7.
Samuel H. Gottscho, "30 Rockefeller Plaza, from Fifth Avenue." Courtesy of Museum of the City of New York, Gottscho-Schleisner Collection

At a ceremony marking the completion of Rockefeller Center on November 1, 1939, the master of ceremonies declared that they were "dedicating a self-contained city whose structural form [had] finally emerged" (*The Last Rivet* 1940, 45). Rockefeller Center, a project spanning eleven years from groundbreaking to completion, is the most elaborate production of a permanent networked city ever attempted (see figure 4.7). This combination of offices and entertainment establishments marked the first structural implementation of radio form to urban space. To the architect Rem Koolhaas, Rockefeller Center embodied the essence of what he called Manhattanism—New York's propensity toward unscripted urban montage. "Rockefeller Center is the most mature demonstration of Manhattanism's unspoken theory of the simultaneous existence of different programs on a single site, connected only by the common data of elevators, service cores, columns and external envelope" (1978, 170). Lacking a traditional center, this mélange of skyscrapers, theaters, and shops avoids blending into the surrounding urban setting through a loosely conceived network that unites its individual structures. Koolhaas describes this paradox as "the maximum of congestion combined with the maximum of light and space" (1978, 173). Through the accessibility of "empty" spaces within the confines of the larger development, the spectator in the Center views individual buildings while at once maintaining an orientation toward the networked whole.

The significance of Rockefeller Center for American urbanism cannot be ascertained simply by viewing its final form; rather, the site's relevance rests in

the long development process that led to its current structure. Throughout the many years of its design and construction, the physical plans of the site seemed in constant flux. But the concept of the development remained unchanged from the beginning—its essential debt to an existing cultural form.

John D. Rockefeller, Jr., leased several blocks of land in midtown Manhattan from Columbia University for the explicit purpose of relocating the existing opera house to "an ideal city unit in the midst of New York" ("Architects Picked" 1929).[5] He dreamt of an opera complex that would reinvigorate the art form. Not surprisingly, Rockefeller's idea generated an underwhelming amount of corporate and public support, and he was forced to reconsider the plan. Eventually, after months of negotiating, Rockefeller chose to realign the project with a medium decidedly more modern. With the enthusiastic support of RCA, the project turned toward radio. During a radio broadcast, his son, Nelson Rockefeller, said the decision to highlight radio in the design of the Center was significant: "Since he had the property, there was only one thing for Father to do—develop it. The opera was 'out' as a nucleus for development, and the question was left—was there anything that could take its place? The answer was—radio. Opera was the great old art; radio the new—the latest thing in this contemporary world of ours, the newest miracle of this scientific era, young and expanding" (*The Last Rivet* 1940, 17–18). For Rockefeller, radio best embodied the cultural and technological potential of America. In addition to the economic promise of the new industry, radio provided the structuring metaphor for the complex—self-contained urban structures networked around a central square. Rockefeller Center was the first high-profile development, outside of the White City, that self-consciously integrated an existing medium—not just as part of its content (businesses, shops) but as part of its physical design. One might look to the Times Building (1904) as an example of another structure tied to an exterior media format, but the extent to which the Times Building was constructed with the newspaper in mind is quite different. The Times Building was built to house a company, not reproduce the form of the newspaper. Another relevant project might be the Chrysler Building (1930). The top of the building was a literal representation of an automobile's grill. Whereas the building was an explicit reference to an external cultural phenomenon, it was only a superficial representation. Rockefeller Center, throughout its extended planning and building process, more closely resembled the media it invoked.

As noted earlier, what is known today as Rockefeller Center was originally to be called "Radio City." For Rockefeller and his team of architects and developers, this was exactly what was required to infuse the space with popular appeal: "Here, in midtown New York, would be the headquarters of modern technology and the new home of radio, the common man's friend. Science, Progress, and Democracy — such were the powerful symbols which RCA's Radio City bestowed upon Rockefeller's projects" (Karp 1982, 27). Once the idea of a radio city was introduced to the public, speculative musings in newspapers and magazines proliferated.

Raymond Hood, the most prominent architect on the Rockefeller Center team, set the tone for the public's speculation. In a 1929 interview, "A City Under a Single Roof," he explained that the future city was to embrace the skyscraper as the primary method of interconnection in the urban network: "The central organization [of the city] entails a form of amalgamation such as occurs every day in the business world. . . . Certainly some such remedy must be applied to prevent New York from strangling itself by its own growth" (208). Essentially, Hood wanted to create, in a fashion represented in Ferriss's "Imaginary Metropolis," skyscraper clusters perfectly spaced throughout Manhattan. In his plan "Manhattan 1950," Hood rendered this scheme in a series of models and drawings. It consisted of thirty-eight "mountains" (or skyscrapers) positioned every ten streets on a grid. This "New Scale" of the city, as Hood called it, was the perfect combination of pragmatism and idealism needed to realize the networked city of the future. His plans for Radio City consisted of constructing one of these "mountains" as a prototype for his grand design.

Because of Rockefeller's reputation for philanthropy and Hood's increasingly high profile in the project, many expected Radio City to be an exciting representation of the media's future. But when the initial plans were unveiled on March 5, 1931, the public was shocked by how corporate (and soulless) the project appeared. The *New York Herald Tribune* condemned the plans: "The crux of the business is that Radio City is ugly. Its exterior is revolting and dreary" (qtd. in Karp 1982, 27). The public generally met the project with scorn — Rockefeller's project became fodder for cartoonists and Broadway plays. For example, in 1933, the Broadway comedy *As Thousands Cheer* made fun of Rockefeller with a skit depicting him attempting to sell the property to his father. Throughout the remainder of the project's development it endured constant scrutiny from the mainstream press — newspaper stories appeared detailing the project's financial troubles. After one major radio com-

FIGURE 4.8.
Wilbur Sawyer, view of New York City from an office in the RCA Building, 1936.

pany, Radio-Keith-Orpheum (RKO) filed for bankruptcy insurance in 1933, and RCA appeared to be in the throes of financial turmoil, the ideological foundation of the development seemed to be collapsing.

With brewing economic troubles, much had changed in the project's planning by the end of 1931. Rockefeller began looking outside the United States for investors and found quite a bit of interest. British and French syndicates played a huge role in reinvigorating the project, each of them leasing buildings and instilling the project with the international appeal needed to boost domestic confidence ("Rockefeller City" 1932). It was not that foreign companies were eager merely to have a presence in New York; they wanted specifically to be involved in New York's entertainment center. Having a presence in the radio nexus of America was an attractive selling point for entertainment companies wanting to compete with the U.S. stronghold. This international interest drastically boosted domestic confidence in the development ("Rockefeller Name" 1932).[6]

But while wrangling over financial backing was in progress, construction on the overall project continued. In February 1932, as the new British Empire Building was going up, the name of the project was officially changed to Rockefeller Center. However, the name Radio City was not entirely abandoned. The most spectacular of the project's buildings maintained the titular connection to the medium. On December 27, 1932, Radio City Music Hall opened its doors. A project headed by Roxy Rothafel, Radio City Music Hall was intended to be the largest theater in the world. Rothafel boasted of his theater in a promotional flier: "In grandeur of conception, in glory of planning, in perfection of fulfillment nothing like Radio City has ever been dreamed" (qtd. in Koolhaas 1978, 180). Its stage was to measure 110 feet across with a 50-foot revolving section in the middle. Electrical elevators on either side of the stage were to transport actors and animals to and from the wings in the quickest time possible. Its auditorium was to seat over six thousand people. Everything about the Music Hall was hyperbole. Even its design was supposed to represent the most grandiose of landscapes — a sunset. This motif is described nicely by Koolhaas: "The sunset theme is established through a series of consecutive plaster semicircles that diminish toward the stage to create a vaguely uterine hemisphere whose only exit is the stage itself" (1978, 179). Unlike the very literal Beaux Arts style of most of New York's movie palaces, the Music Hall, through its relative abstraction, redefined the architecture of fantasy. Without resorting to representationalism, the designers built the fantasy image directly into the structure of the grand auditorium. The most sublime of natural landscapes was now possible in New York's new mediated environments. According to Rothafel, "a visit to Radio City Music Hall is as good as a month in the Country" ("Debut of a City" 1933).

The essential element to the theater's interior design was its invocation of radio, or "visual jazz" as one critic called it. The semicircles radiating from the stage formed an architectural display of the technology that defined the complex. A promotional book describes the interior this way: "It is a space that seems to pulsate and throb, the feeling of life and motion intensified by the ceiling's unique design: eight enormous arching bands that seem to radiate from the stage like waves from a giant source of light" (qtd. in Karp 1982, 85).

Ultimately, Radio City Music Hall was based on a machine aesthetic, consistent with radio. The interior designer Donald Deskey had set out to make the space "completely and uncompromisingly modern in effect" (Karp 1982). He used industrial materials, aluminum statues, designed gunmetal mirrors, and lighting fixtures made from steel, chrome, and Bakelite. Every aspect of the theater was designed based on its relationship to modern technology. "America was the first country," notes Pierre Francastel, "to devise a new architecture based on the technological imperatives of the machine" (2000,

110). The Music Hall was conceptualized as the culmination of this American machine fetish. It was built to display the potential of the city as manifested in the new media.

Rothafel's futuristic conception of Radio City Music Hall was challenged only by his nostalgia for the old theatrical tradition. He had made a name for himself in the New York theater world by establishing the movie-plus-stage-show format wherein silent films were coupled with vaudeville acts to compose the evening's entertainment. This formula led him to become the most successful movie theater manager in the country. But when Rothafel was asked to take charge of the new theater in Rockefeller Center, he saw it as a return to the old-style theater. He believed that the movie-plus-stage-show format he had invented was doomed because of the coming of sound pictures. "Talkies" would be able to sustain themselves without assistance from live performances, he thought. His new innovation was to establish a "super variety show" to fit within his "super theater." "Talkies" would be relegated to the smaller, thirty-five-hundred-seat "New Roxy Theater" that was located just a block south on Sixth Avenue, but still part of the complex.

The opening night gala at Radio City Music Hall would quickly reverse Rothafel's dream of a pure variety theater. On December 27, 1932, six thousand people showed up to witness the six-hour live stage extravaganza that included choral singing, skits, dramatic vignettes, comic routines, and of course the "Rockettes."[7] The "super-vaudeville" to which Rothafel aspired was a total flop — the audience didn't have the patience for the saccharine nostalgia of the long-winded performance. Within two weeks the production had lost $180,000. In desperation, RKO (which controlled the theater) switched back to the movie-plus-stage-show format, essentially condemning the New Roxy Theater to a long twilight existence until its demolition in 1954. The movies had won out. Despite Rothafel's nostalgic desire to reinvigorate vaudeville, the spectacle of the motion pictures could not be removed from the spectacle of the Music Hall. Its size and grand design, cinematic from its inception, was consistent with the cinema's connection to speculative architecture. The Music Hall was to be a national symbol of the kind of architecture capable of containing the cinematic image. This was, from the beginning, part of the logic of the development — to use the mass media contained within its borders to communicate the promise of the space.

And this is precisely how radio functioned within the complex as a whole. By May 1933, the "Radio City" portion of the project was completed. Of this, the seventy-story RCA Building was its centerpiece. According to one commentator, the RCA Building was "the dominating vertical note of the development. The open spaces provided by the promenade and the Forum will allow passersby on Fifth Avenue to have an unobstructed view of the imposing tower and the great eastern entrance at street level" (*Rockefeller Center* 1932, 16). As in Ferriss's metropolis, the spectator gazes upon the main structure from the surrounding open space. The RCA Building is equivalent to one of Ferriss's "centers"—the slender vertical tower broadcasts the idea of the city within a city.

Indeed, the RCA Building became the literal origin of most national radio broadcasts. Another promotional book described plans for the building: "The Radio Corporation of America and the National Broadcasting Company will occupy more than one-third of the office and studio space in the RCA Building. Twenty-six broadcasting studios in this building will be supplemented by six audition rooms. One studio, the largest in the world, will be more than three stories high. The others will have a height of two stories. All the studios will be electrically shielded and provided with suitable lighting facilities for television. Many of them will have observation galleries for visitors" (Rockefeller Center 1932, 16). From the inside, the building functioned as New York's predominant origin of radio (and later television) waves. Audiences could gather around the studios and watch as the broadcasts originated. From the outside, it served as the central antenna-like tower, figuratively allowing for the surrounding buildings to communicate through the ether. As Koolhaas famously observed: "Rockefeller Center is the first architecture that can be broadcast" (1978, 172).

This quality permeates every facade of the RCA Building. Art objects celebrating the connections between the new development and new media were sprinkled throughout the space. On the east facade of the RCA Building, Lee Lawrie's sculpture is a grandiose salute to the industry. Entitled *Genius, Which Interprets to the Human Race the Laws and Cycles of the Cosmic Forces of the Universe, Making the Cycles of Light and Sound*, the long-bearded Zeus-like character is shown transmitting what can only be construed as light and sound from his fingertips. In a curiously classical celebration of the modern, Lawrie intends RCA to be the genius—the only conduit between the ether and the infinite information stream that travels within it.

Another sculpture over the Forty-ninth Street entrance of the RCA Building attempts to visually represent the inchoate technology of television. Leo Friedlander's work, entitled *Transmission Receiving an Image of Dancers and Flashing It Through the Ether by Means of Television to Reception, Symbolized by Mother Earth and Her Child, Man*, is actually composed of two sculptures, separated by three windows. On the left, a goddess figure (Transmission) holds her right hand up to a dancer in motion. On the right, a similar goddess figure (Reception) is presenting a miniature version of the dancer to a woman and her child (as the title suggests, mother earth and man). Transmission is a female figure that, in a sense, give birth to the image. The work ultimately suggests that the image, until RCA benevolently delivered it to mankind, was inaccessible. As one approaches the entrance on Forty-ninth Street, the sculptures are positioned to each side of the entrance. Centered over the door are three nondescript windows. The sculptures frame them and draw attention to the empty space in the middle. The sculptures highlight the invisible space where the image is being flashed through the ether. The ether then is linked to the building's unremarkable fenestration, ultimately suggesting that even the most banal spaces are packed with invisible images in transit.

The art ornamenting the facades throughout the complex is anything but subtle. Even Rockefeller himself found most of the art in Radio City "gross and unbeautiful" (Okrent 2003, 295). But the public, overwhelmed by the grand development, liked Rockefeller Center art work and all (Krinsky 1978). Despite the cultural derision only a short time before the opening, Rockefeller Center was for most New Yorkers a welcome celebration of a lucrative medium, and the "unbeautiful" art was warmly received as a kind of victory stele — in celebration of architecture's domination of media. The historian Kenneth Frampton summarizes this well when he refers to the Center as "the new Babylon born of euphoria" (Frampton 1992, 222).

Rockefeller Center, Inc., described the complex, without irony, in equally elevated terms: "Rockefeller Center is not Greek, but it suggests the balance of Greek architecture. It is not Babylonian, but it retains the flavor of Babylon's magnificence. It is not Roman, yet it has Rome's enduring qualities of mass and strength. Nor is it of the Taj-Mahal, which it resembles in mass composition, though in it has been caught the spirit of the Taj — aloof, generous in space, quieting in its serenity" (Rockefeller Center 1932, 38). Through this hyperbolic language, the passage makes clear the earnest, yet grandiose, intentions of the Center. By comparing it to classical architectural monuments, the promotional book has this new monument of corporate consequence embody the cultural significance of the past, done not through the mediation of history, as all the examples imply, but through the mediation of corporate mass media. Radio was to take the place of history; in the design of Rockefeller Center, the medium was indeed the message—the theoretical and real radio waves within the complex were at the core of the development's urbanism. Among the tall buildings and entertainment complexes, Rockefeller Center ultimately put radio broadcasting on display. According to the promotional book, "Rockefeller Center will be a beautiful entity in the swirling life of a great metropolis—its cool heights standing out against an agitated man-made skyline" (*Rockefeller Center* 1932, 38). As the sinking of the *Titantic* in 1912 demonstrated, the notion of electrical messages swirling through the invisible spaces of the city at a constant rate was a promise of the future's stability. The secrets of the sea were conquered; the distances between people were made insignificant. Within the perpetual motion of radio technology, the city could be quieted, slowed to the point where it was accessible to the spectator. Rockefeller Center, through the logic of the network, attempted to do just that—it "promise[d] a significant contribution to the city planning of an unfolding future" (*Rockefeller Center* 1932, 38). And most importantly, it condensed that future, complete with the invisible traces of space, into a containable format easily possessed by the spectator.

Within the Unfolding Future

Opening just before the completion of Rockefeller Center, the 1939 New York World's Fair amplified the formal trends attempted in that development. Conceived during the height of America's Depression, the fair's theme, "Building the World of Tomorrow," was pointedly directed toward reconfiguring the sight line of the American urban spectator away from the immediately proximate in such a way that Grover Whalen, the president of the World's Fair Corporation, referred to as "project[ing] the average man into the World of Tomorrow" (U.S. House 1937, 13). The fair was meant to be a burst of optimism at a time when most people were feeling disenchanted and disengaged from the country's future. From the first announcement of the fair's theme in 1936, Whalen's goal was to give the future over to the "average person" by making its vision simple, streamlined, and possessable through consumption. In the fair's official guidebook, Whalen wrote "this is your fair, built for you, and dedicated to you" (qtd. in Susman 1980, 18). Historian Warren Susman says that no previous fair had developed such rhetoric of popular appeal. The fair's planners wanted "the World of Tomorrow" to be void of pretense and abstractions. The future was to be presented entirely from the raw material of the familiar.

(opposite)
FIGURE 4.9.
Perisphere and Trylon at 1939 World's Fair. Courtesy of New York Public Library

As a means of achieving this familiarity, the fair showed particular emphasis on process over product. Even though the future at the fair was reducible to consumer products, each of the technological displays emphasized the familiarity of the machine so as to make the social ramifications of the technology less frightening. In all cases, the technology was in service to the human: from the highway that could rescue the urban dweller from congestion to Elektro, the Westinghouse robot who could perform everyday menial tasks. The world of tomorrow was not on display as an object of curiosity; it was a consumer intervention in a very real world of today. It was simple and easy to understand. In fact, the future was far less complex than the present. To Whalen, "simplicity must be the keynote for a perfectly ordered mechanical civilization" ("Floating Sphere" 1937).

Distinct from Chicago's 1933 Century of Progress exposition, the New York fair was not intended to be a far-off fantasyland; the world of tomorrow was possible with the technology of today. "The world of tomorrow," whispered the announcer in the popular Futurama exhibit, "seen from the world of today." Henry Dreyfuss, the designer of the fair's "Theme Center," said the city presented at the fair was "not some dream city of the future, but a dream city of tomorrow morning, a place to live and work that uses only materials and devices that are at our command today" ("Magic Carpet" 1938). Speculations were only as powerful as they were grounded. The familiar position of the spectator (we learned from Ferriss) was essential to imagining the future. So the "materials and devices" to which Dreyfus referred surely included technologies of commerce and industry, but they also included technologies of spectatorship. It is the case that organizing the conditions through which one looked at (and ultimately possessed) the future was central to the speculative architecture at the fair.

This was demonstrated in a number of ways. The most immediate was the fair's general layout. The centerpiece consisted of three central structures: the Perisphere, the Trylon, and the Helicline; or, in other words, a sphere, an obelisk, and a spiral staircase connecting them. The combination of these structures, known as the "Theme Center," became the literal and symbolic center of the fair (see figure 4.9). All of the other buildings and exhibits radiated outward from it, creating an orderly distribution and circulation of buildings and people (Santomasso 1980). Whalen sought to communicate order,

unity, and a comprehensive urban experience through the unifying force of consumer technology. "The visitor to the Fair was to be thrust into the full-blown Age of Consumerism and Age of the Machine" (Santomasso 1980, 29). In some ways, little had changed since Burnham tried to build an experience of a whole city into architectural form. But in New York, the parts were not meant to collide into a singular experience of the city; rather, each sector was to be a unique and compartmentalized manifestation of urbanism, always networked to a distant symbol of the whole. The 610-foot Trylon became the literal and figurative manifestation of this. Dreyfus called the Trylon the

FIGURE 4.10.
Democracity, New York World's Fair, 1939. From Architectural Forum, courtesy of Museum of the City of New York, The Wurts Collection

"voice of the fair." It was the tallest structure on the grounds and it housed a broadcast station and radio antenna—making it visible and audible from every location.

As television broadcasting was introduced at the fair, the promise of radio waves undoubtedly rested with each visitor. The first public television event took place at the fair on April 30, 1939, with a telecast of President Franklin Roosevelt delivering the opening remarks. The prospect of pictures traveling through invisible space made the presence of radio waves in the city that much more apparent. The Trylon served as a constant reminder to the fair's visitors that the surrounding space was not empty.

These themes became explicit in the fair's two most popular exhibits, both of which were immersive representations of the city of tomorrow: Democracity and Futurama. Democracity was housed inside of the 160-foot Perisphere and was a vast representation of a clean, perfectly organized city of sectors (set in the year 2039), where industry, commerce and housing were spatially separated and connected by vast highways (see figure 4.10). The writer David Gelernter observes, "in the future you would no longer have to live in a city just because you worked in one. You would live in the countryside or in 'garden apartments' around the city's rim. Factory workers would live in green towns just like everybody else. You would drive to work, or to sprawling green parks in the countryside, not on packed city streets but on landscaped highways." Gelernter concludes that "Democracity's utopian World of Tomorrow amounts, in essence, to the modern suburbs" (Gelernter 1995, 71). But while there are obvious similarities to what would become suburban sprawl, there exist important differences as well. Every "sector" of Democracity had a direct and essential tie to the city. Modern suburbs require no speculation from the spectator; in fact, we might say that suburban form actively resists it. Modern suburbs are increasingly self-contained, and their dependence on the central city increasingly disparaged. In Democracity, however, like in Rockefeller Center and in Ferriss's "City of Tomorrow," the spectator, regardless of how remote her position, is reliably referred back to the "city" through projection or broadcast.

This practice of spectatorship was present not only in Democracity's diegetic abstraction, but in the exhibit as well. As spectators entered the Perisphere, they were guided over the city on what the *New York Times* called "a magic carpet." "The traveler on the magic carpet will lose all sense of size and shape," reported the *Times*; "he will be flying in space. Above him will be the heavens and firmament. Below him on either side is a city—Democracity, the city of tomorrow morning" ("Magic Carpet" 1938). Dreyfus likened the experience of being inside of the Perisphere to the experience of floating through the ether, with no conception of space and time. In this sense, Democracity was to be seen from the perspective of radio waves. The city of the future was presented to spectators as something accessible through the fantastic, yet familiar experience of the ether.

Futurama, the fair's most popular exhibit, was presented in a similar manner. Only this time, spectators "flew" over the world of tomorrow in moving chairs. For the centerpiece of the General Motors exhibit, Norman Bel Geddes designed the world of 1960 that, not surprisingly, was organized around vast highways and the precipitous growth of the automobile's popularity. In 1960, Bel Geddes predicted, the city "has been designed for communal use and for the means of transportation which the community uses above all others—the automobile" (Bel Geddes 1940, 219). While the exhibit covered a vast world beyond the city, it had a distinct rhetorical focus on urban life. When spectators first entered the Futurama exhibit, they were thrust into moveable chairs that "flew" them over pastoral landscapes to the city of tomorrow. At the ride's conclusion, the chairs entered into open air where spectators found themselves in the midst of the fairgrounds. They were, according to the *New York Times*, "at an intersection of the metropolis of tomorrow, life size" ("Fair Visitors" 1939). Immersed within the city, the spectator was meant to conclude that this form of urbanism was the culmination of technological progress. Returning to the familiar pedestrian perspective, the spectator was invited to consider the vast scale of this 1960s city.

The city is spread out over a much larger geographic area than other models of the networked city, including Democracity and Ferriss's "City of Tomorrow." Highways, instead of radio waves, facilitated the separation of sectors. According to the promotional film *To New Horizons* released by General Motors in 1940, "residential, commercial, and industrial areas, all have been separated for greater efficiency and convenience," with each city block "a complete unit in itself." Like Raymond Hood's "city within a city," the city in Futurama was modular. Each unit was entirely self-contained, yet dependent on the whole. The actual position of the specific parts was of little consequence, because the urban highways would render proximate even the most distant regions.

The depiction of the city in Futurama complicated previously held assumptions about the city. No longer tied to a pedestrian scale, urban boundaries could spread well outside the traditional urban/rural lines. It was difficult to ascertain where the city ended and the country began. Bel Geddes proposed that "one must take into account the great popular impetus from the center outward. Great possibilities for the city lie in the land beyond it; the problem is to make that land accessible, to preserve it from exploitation that defeats its own purpose—in other words, to find a fruitful relation between city and country. Such a relation is a problem of approaches—a problem of communication" (Bel Geddes 1940, 207). The Futurama exhibit featured in miniature an entire American landscape, including farms, small towns, industrial centers, and amusement parks, networked together with an intricate superhighway system. This highway, promising travel from the East to West coast in twenty-four hours (wherein the speed and distance between cars was regulated by radio waves), could render the entire nation into a kind of urban network. Every city and town, every forest, and every river could be another functional aspect of a well-planned network of sites and resources. The narrator in *To New Horizons* boasts: "over space, man has begun to win victory." Now, from the safety of his vehicle, he could ride in the ether across the vast expanses once available only to the invisible messages of radio. The speculative architecture of projection and broadcast could become "actual" through the new highway system. Instead of a visual or aural connection to the spectacle at a distance, the city and nation could congeal into a consumable experience for the spectator through physical travel and presence. Bel Geddes noted:

> Already the automobile has done great things for people. It has taken man out beyond the small confines of the world in which he used to live. Distant communities have been brought closer together. Throughout all recorded history, man has made repeated efforts to reach out farther and to communicate with other men more easily and quickly, and these efforts have reached the climax of their success in the twentieth century. The increasing freedom of movement makes possible a magnificently full, rich life for the people of our time. A free-flowing movement of people and goods across our nation is a requirement of modern living and prosperity. (Bel Geddes 1940, 10)

For Bel Geddes, the automobile was the functional manifestation of radio waves. Free-flowing people along highways, like the orderly transportation of messages through the ether, became his practical model for the city of tomorrow.

Despite the success of Futurama, the 1939 World's Fair turned out to be a financial failure. Whalen was removed from his position as president at the close of the season because he failed to bring in the crowds he promised. The board decided to extend the fair another season as means of recouping some costs. The banker Harvey Dow Gibson was appointed as Whalen's replacement and was given the charge of saving the corporation from bankruptcy and returning a profit during the coming season. He failed on the first count, but nonetheless was able to make the fair profitable in 1940 by rearranging the message to appeal to rapidly changing American culture.

As the war in Europe began in earnest, Americans grew increasingly concerned over their involvement. And even though the managers decided not to broadcast news of the war at the fair, it was certainly on people's minds. Gibson responded to this perceived change in the culture by radically altering the fair's theme. "The World of Tomorrow" became "For Peace and Freedom." The social issues, international in scope, that were highlighted during the first season were replaced by pure entertainment and a folksy celebration of the American way of life. Gibson believed that America wanted to escape into fantasy, not speculate about reality. As a result, there were few things that stayed the same between 1939 and 1940. The Soviet Pavilion became the "American Common," and the Consumers Building became the "World of Fashion." In one of the most telling changes, the fair's entertainment area was renamed "The Great White Way"—an obvious reference to Broadway. Gibson sought to realign the fair with a kind of urban playfulness that was more visceral than cerebral. The speculative architecture at the fair would seem to have been recast as a celebration of the here and now; the eager longing for the City of Tomorrow was giving way to the demand for the city of today.

The space between the two seasons at the fair was a turning point in urban spectatorship. On one side was the culmination of decades of speculative architecture that celebrated the play of the imagination, and on the other was the beginning of a realized city that left little to the imagination. The urban spectatorship cultivated throughout the 1920s and 1930s incorporated the potentialities of the invisible ether and the distant promise of the visible skyline into the very fabric of the city. The 1939 World's Fair brought that scale into focus for an American public eager to confront the problems of urban life. The idea of the future became an important weapon against the realities of the present. But this began to change with the 1940 World's Fair. As the war rendered the future unpredictable and menacing, the present began to take on a much more appealing face. The imaginative expanse of the American city as seen through the speculative medium of ether could no longer satisfy the insatiable American desire for possession and control.

THE OPERATIVE CITY

The Machine Intelligence of Urban Renewal

Los Angeles has now become an undifferentiated mass of houses, walled off into sectors by many-laned expressways, with ramps and viaducts that create special bottlenecks of their own. These expressways move but a small fraction of the traffic per hour once carried by public transportation, at a much lower rate of speed, in an environment befouled by smog, itself produced by the lethal exhausts of the technologically backward motor cars. More than a third of the Los Angeles area is consumed by these grotesque transportation facilities; two-thirds of central Los Angeles are occupied by streets, freeways, parking facilities, garages. This is space-eating with a vengeance. The last stage of the process already beckons truly progressive minds—to evict the remaining inhabitants and turn the entire area over to automatically propelled vehicles, completely emancipated from any rational human purpose.

LEWIS MUMFORD, *The City in History*

After World War II, the city was no longer at the center of America's optimistic future. Crumbling at its core because of diminishing middle class populations and tax dollars, the American city was increasingly understood as an antiquated form, one tied to the material and social restrictions of failed urban planning. By the 1950s, suburbs were growing at four times the speed of the typical downtown—and in many cases, downtowns were losing population. As a result of this rapid decentralization, the inner city became associated with an aging body—in popular news and political discourse the city itself was considered as diseased as the poor and underclass populations inhabiting it. Homer Hoyt, a real estate economist, proclaimed that America's cities were

FIGURE 5.1.
Bunker Hill at Olive and Second streets, showing parking lots mixed in with houses and apartment buildings in the Bunker Hill redevelopment area. Security Pacific Collection, Los Angeles Public Library. Leonard Nadel, Photographer

suffering from a dangerous disease. "Like a cancer, blight spread[s] through all the tissues of the urban body and the urban organism [is] unable to cure itself except by a major surgical operation" (1943). Far from the speculative musings of the 1930s, the postwar conversation about cities in America predominantly turned toward maintenance and correction. The cultural construction of the American city transformed as the literal and figurative position of the spectator shifted. No longer looking out at urban images from within the city, the urban spectator was outside looking in at the city. As more and more of the middle class packed up their urban apartments for suburban accommodations, for the first time since the nineteenth century, middle class spectators didn't want to be involved in urban presentation — they wanted the city to be made for them in a manageable, and contained, form. The longing to possess and assemble urban images, the inclination that characterized early modes of spectatorship, was largely absent from the postwar city. The new city was to be functional, self-sustaining, and predictable. The urban spectatorship of the postwar period was decidedly rational, a cognitive interconnection between the city and its theoretical user. As a result, the technocratic justification for wide-scale urban renewal closely paralleled the growing popular faith in rational systems and thinking machines.

This process comes into unique clarity in Los Angeles: the city Carey McWilliams characterized as the "first modern, widely decentralized, industrial city in America" (1949, 28). Just as soon as its downtown centralized, Los Angeles began the process of decentralization. By the end of World War II, while the city was still growing by about three thousand people a day, the downtown had lost much of its symbolic importance as the city's center. In 1953, only 15 percent of the population entered the downtown area on a typical workday; this was down from 41 percent in 1926. By the 1940s, some planners were talking about multinucleated urban growth patterns, downplaying the importance of a central business district for the life of the city. But when hundreds of downtown acres were deemed blighted in the 1950s, the city had to respond. The Bunker Hill renewal project in downtown Los Angeles was one of the largest and most dramatic in the country (Wagner 1960). While it covered a relatively small portion of the sprawling geography of Los Angeles, it was charged with the task of reordering Los Angeles's entire urban landscape. Urban renewal was as much psychological as physical. And in the case of Los Angeles, in order to be effective, the psychological effects of downtown renewal would have to spread far outside the physical limits of the development (see figure 5.1).

A report written to assist the Los Angeles Community Redevelopment Association in conceiving of the Bunker Hill project plainly described the psychological ramifications of renewal: "The impact of building forms, particularly when the buildings are tall, is felt far beyond their immediate surroundings. Through their silhouettes, such buildings speak to the entire city and create symbolic images which impress themselves powerfully upon the mind of even the most distant observer. The Design for Development, therefore, reflects our concern also that the distant image — the profile — of Bunker Hill should clearly express its dominant position at the heart of metropolitan

Los Angeles" (*Report on Bunker Hill* 1960, 6). Urban renewal was a corrective process. It was meant to destroy decades of ingrained experiences and perceptions of the city and replace them with a stable, reliable, distant image. The image of urbanism that planners and developers sought to construct in Los Angeles, and in many of America's downtowns, was different than those that had preceded it. It was an image that resembled what the mathematician Norbert Wiener described as operative: "Operative images, which perform the functions of their original, may or may not bear a pictorial likeness to it. Whether they do or not, they may replace the original in its action, and this is a much deeper similarity" (1964, 31). Indeed, the intention of the renewal of downtown Los Angeles was to replace the urban imagery of chaos and degradation with one of order and function. It didn't have to be beautiful; it didn't even have to correspond with the surrounding urban fabric. It was a departure from the speculative architecture of the past that was premised on the ability of a spectator to possess the spatially and temporally distant city from within its borders. The renewed city was an image of function. It was an operative city. With no particular reference to any existing urban form, Bunker Hill was designed to do what ideal cities do: to perform logical functions, without being limited to history, memory, and experience. Distinct from the spectatorship structured through the speculative architecture discussed in the previous chapter, the operative city was premised on a spectatorship whose origins were outside the city limits. And instead of producing a unified visual aesthetic through network connectivity, the spectatorship associated with the operative city produced a functional aesthetic through the assemblage of logically consistent mechanical parts. Possession was still important; only now, the city was constructed through a spectator's ability to possess and control its functionality.

The Road to Renewal

As early as 1942, California had initiated several large commissions to deliberate over urban reorganization after the war. The California Senate Interim Committee on Economic Planning observed that "California is at the crossroads in her economic program. She will either become a great industrial empire or she will become a ghost state—a casualty of the war" (Lotchin 1996, 320). There was widespread concern that the boom in California cities (the population of Los Angeles went from 1.5 million to 2 million in the 1940s), often described as the second gold rush, was sparked primarily by the war economy, and once the flood of economic resources dried up, so would the city. Bunker Hill was already experiencing dramatic declines in its economic and social infrastructure, so fear of the end of the booming war economy drastically heightened concerns for the symbolic value of the inner city.

The urgency of the situation in Los Angeles created a need for dramatic solutions. At the Los Angeles City Council meeting on April 15, 1948, the Community Redevelopment Agency (CRA) was established with the primary mission of "renewing" Bunker Hill. According to William T. Sesnon, Jr., the first chairman of the CRA, the plan was to "wipe out substandard housing on the hill and redevelop it in conformity with its highest use potential" (Reay 1960). This dramatic statement of purpose was a response to the impending passage of the U.S. Housing Act of 1949. Title I of the housing act would give cities the authority to clear slums from urban cores. If a particular site was required for civic development and the seller refused to accept the terms, the newly granted power of imminent domain allowed the city to condemn the building and take it from the owner at below-market rates.

Lawmakers understood this process as necessary in improving America's cities. Poverty, crime, and disease were rampant in inner cities, and until 1949, city governments had few resources to intervene. Landowners in the most impoverished areas were often unresponsive to civic desires for improvement. Because property values in residential areas immediately surrounding a city's financial district (called the loop, ring, or collar) were elevated because of the proximity to downtown, many building owners held on to property while providing little or no maintenance. And out of fear of losing tax revenue, most cities refused to reduce the assessed value of these properties. This ultimately led to a culture of profit-making neglect. Buildings just sat, unattended, for years. And the squalor with which tenants lived only became more extreme.

In its most positive light, the housing act was an intervention into a problem that had become much bigger than city government. Title I of the housing act aimed to provide "the realization as soon as feasible of the goal of a decent home and suitable living environment for every American family." It provided federal subsidies for two-thirds of the cost for municipalities to acquire land, relocate tenants, and demolish buildings in areas deemed "dilapidated." Practically, it paved the way for unprecedented slum clearance, but it dictated little in the way of rebuilding—a shortcoming that became immediately visible in New York City.

The first large-scale slum clearance prompted by Title I took place in New

York. In anticipation of the new bill, Mayor William O'Dwyer established the Committee on Slum Clearance in 1948. He appointed Robert Moses, then city construction coordinator, to chair the newly formed committee. His first task as chair was to identify nine thousand slumacres within the borders of New York City and earmark them for demolition. His second task was to find private partnerships to expedite the process. Moses was wary of leaving this process to the public alone. He believed it should be the city's job to propose sites for redevelopment. The city would then sell the land to a private developer at a reduced cost. The developer would be charged with the task of fulfilling the city's policy of slum clearance while still being able to make a profit for themselves (Garvin 1980).

But the public-private partnerships Moses demanded did little to provide "suitable living conditions" for people currently living in slums. It only mandated that impoverished areas be repurposed for middle-income residents as the private partner needed to return a profit on their investment. During Moses's tenure, he initiated twenty-three renewal projects which resulted in the construction of 37,000 new apartments (Garvin 1980), but he didn't necessarily house those whom he was responsible for dislocating. In the Lenox Terrace project in Harlem (1950–59), for instance, 1700 apartments were demolished and replaced with 6800 new units that rented at four times the existing price. As a result, the majority of the previous tenants were excluded from the new development. Moses showed little remorse for displacing residents. He understood it as a necessary casualty for the larger goal of civic renewal. He was well known for quoting Stalin: "you can't make an omelet without breaking eggs."

His hubris worked. Moses became known across the nation as the guy who was "getting things done." He knew how to manipulate local and state government and he rarely bothered with community input. Moses believed that communities couldn't know what was best for the city, as they were too concerned with their immediate circumstances. This approach caught on very rapidly. City officials from other municipalities looked to Moses to justify their overzealous approach to slum clearance. It became common practice to demolish and relocate whole blocks without first securing private partnership in redevelopment. In most cases, slum clearance took precedence over community development—as the federal funds were not contingent on the actual implementing of a plan. These early clearance projects were myopic strategies of removing a problem without first considering its cause or solution.

But in 1954, changes were made to the U.S. Housing Act to address this issue. While the original law permitted funding only for slum clearance, amendments expanded the law to include rehabilitation. The federal government was now encouraging the "improvement" of urban areas, not just their destruction. In short time, the rhetoric of redevelopment translated to the new rhetoric of "renewal." The idea (and this was especially boosted by the U.S. Housing Act of 1959) was that development projects would have a positive effect on the larger city. They wouldn't merely fix one problem; they would work to fix the much larger problem of urban obsolescence. In New York, this was first embodied in the West Side Urban Renewal Area, originally created in 1956. The new mayor, Robert Wagner, embarked on the city's largest renewal project with the goal of "saving" the entire West Side. Responding to the rapid exodus of middle-class residents from the city, the West Side Renewal project was a preemptive intervention into potential slums. The area was categorized as "blighted," which according to the Committee on Blighted Areas and Slums of the President's Conference on Home Building and Home Ownership, meant it was "an economic liability to the community," whereas a slum was a "social liability" (qtd. in Fogelson 2001, 347). This was an important distinction because it allowed for cities to claim imminent domain on much larger areas than they would otherwise be able to if they had to characterize all clearance zones as slums. This semantic distinction allowed cities to demolish "future slums" in the name of improving the entire city.

The premise behind urban renewal was that if a large enough parcel was cleared and built anew, natural urban processes would extend the positive effects of development outward. If the development area was too small, however, renewal efforts would not be successful. According to Edith Elmer Wood, a prominent backer of large-scale development in New York, no matter how well designed, "a single good building in a slum area is foredoomed to failure . . . [and] the development of a whole block is only slightly better. . . . A complete neighborhood unit, large enough to create and preserve its own atmosphere, should be the minimum size of a development" in a slum (qtd. in Fogelson 2001, 337).

In Los Angeles, the scale of the Bunker Hill development was conceived within this context. A very large area was earmarked for renewal so that its effects could properly reach out into the surrounding areas. "The site will be transformed into a modern acropolis of office buildings, hotels and parkways, forming a crown for the magnificent Los Angeles of tomorrow," the *Los Angeles Times* reported. And it would not stop there. Bunker Hill "represents an incalculable material asset to the community. Its beauty will inspire the creation around it of a splendid new metropolis" ("Bunker Hill Rebirth" 1959). The project would span the vicinity between Hill Street and the Harbor Freeway and from First Street to an irregular line between Fourth and Fifth Streets. One Los Angeles city-planning official commented that "Bunker Hill is almost a textbook case of what we have been preaching. Cities get run down and outdated just like anything else. But with modernization, you can improve living standards, cut crime and disease and produce the new tax revenue which every city in the country is looking for" ("Speed Urged" 1956).

So the battle of Bunker Hill began anew. With the charging orders of modernization and technological progress, Bunker Hill started the long process of erasure and renewal. It was to transform from a diseased urban body to a fully realized, self-sustaining image of urban function.

The Battle of Bunker Hill

In 1874, landowner and speculator Prudent Beaudry chose the name Bunker Hill Avenue for one of the streets in downtown Los Angeles, in recognition of the approaching 1875 centennial of the Battle of Bunker Hill in Boston. Thereafter, the name was applied to the entire hill. The name, as a reference to that famous battle against the British in 1775, connoted an against-all-odds American struggle. When Beaudry chose this affiliation, the similarities between the revolutionary battle and his dreams of seeing a first-class residential neighborhood in the second-class city of Los Angeles were certainly not without intention. The symbolic name was important during the area's heyday and continued to be through to its renewal. For half a century, in newspaper articles and reports, someone was fighting the battle of Bunker Hill—first the city of Los Angeles fighting against all odds to establish itself on the national scene and then the poor and elderly residents fighting to keep their homes against a city ordinance designed to erase them. In its short history, Bunker Hill embodied the extremes of Los Angeles: in the first decade of the twentieth century it was ranked one of the city's finest residential areas, but by the fourth decade, it was ranked its worst.

Beaudry defined Bunker Hill in an ad in 1874 as a "Fine, Dry, and Airy Location" with "Splendid View" (Chapman 1968, 24). He told stories of being able to see the Pacific Ocean from the hilltop and of women being able to see their sea captain husbands docking their ships at Wilmington. His boosterism worked: by the 1880s a slate of wealthy families were building Victorian mansions all along the hill. The Simona Bradbury house at the southwest corner of Court and Hill was built in 1888. In 1914 it had become home of the Roland Film Company, an early movie enterprise founded by Hal Roach and Dan Lithicum, where Harold Lloyd got his start. The Leonard J. Rose home at the southwest corner of Fourth and Grand was also built in 1888 and was one of the largest houses on the hill. And the Judge Anson Brunson home on the west side of Grand just north of Fourth, built around the same time, was a huge mansion with one drawing room sixty feet long.

The prosperity of the neighborhood continued its steady incline throughout the teens, after which things began to change. Many of the hill's most prominent residents were beginning to move away, likely for more spacious environs elsewhere. Because there weren't enough people with means who were interested in mansions on the hill, these single-family dwellings were converted into multiple-unit rental properties. Not surprisingly, all of the homes discussed above were demolished before the outbreak of World War II (Driscoll 1954). After 1930, despite the constant flow of immigrants, new construction ceased. But this did not stop people from moving in. During the Depression, the population exploded to rival the density of eastern cities, with immigrants from Mexico, Germany, Canada, Italy, and England flooding into the area. By 1955, 11,670 people were living in the half-mile-square district of Bunker Hill (Community Redevelopment Agency 1958).

As these statistics received press coverage, the hill was increasingly seen as a public health risk. The *Los Angeles Times* referred to Bunker Hill as "Los Angeles' No. 1 blighted area" ("The Redemption" 1958), repeatedly using words like "decaying" and "diseased" to describe the city's downtown. While maintaining the allure of being one of the city's oldest neighborhoods, it attracted a stigma for the same reason. The quaint old architecture, neglected and deteriorating, became the symbol of urban decay in Los Angeles. In his popular novel *The High Window* (1942), Raymond Chandler describes the hill as follows:

> Bunker Hill is old town, lost town, crook town. . . . In the tall rooms haggard landladies bicker with shifty tenants. On the wide cool front porches, reaching their cracked shadows into the sun, and staring at nothing, sit the old men with faces like lost battles. . . . Out of the apartment houses come

> women who should be young but have faces like stale beer; men with pulled-down hats and quick eyes that look the street over behind the cupped hand that shields the match flame . . . people who look like nothing in particular and know it, and once in a while even men that actually go to work. (60)

Chandler aligns the decaying urban landscape with the physical and mental state of the characters. Spilling out onto the cracked sidewalks, these decrepit figures are all products of the environment. In this and other novels, Bunker Hill came to symbolize confusion, corruption, convalescence, and the degradation of values. This was well illustrated in Joseph Losey's 1951 remake of Fritz Lang's *M* (1931), where the ordered streets of Berlin are replaced with the disorienting streets of Bunker Hill.

So when the Los Angeles Department of Building and Safety released several undoubtedly exaggerated reports by 1957, the public was eager to accept them. Sixty percent of the buildings were deemed "dangerous" while only 24 percent were "standard." Living conditions were considered to be 40 percent extreme, while only 18 percent acceptable. The crime rate in the area was reported to be twice the city's average and the arrest rate was almost ten times as great (Community Redevelopment Agency 1958). William Sesnon told the *Los Angeles Times* in 1956 that "the shocking figures on crime and juvenile delinquency alone support the decision to clear and redevelop Bunker Hill in the interests of safety, health and general welfare of the people" ("Bunker Hill Pictured" 1956).

But perhaps the most startling figure and that which garnered the most public vitriol was from a report by Patricia Adler in 1957: "The city tax revenue from Bunker Hill amounted to $106,120, while the estimated cost for fire, police and health services was $754,101" (Chapman 1968, 25). It was one thing for a slum to exist in a distant rotting core of the city, but when the CRA suggested that everyone in the city was paying dearly for the unprofitable district, Los Angeles residents grew increasingly concerned with their city's "rotting core."

Regardless of where the numbers were coming from and how the studies were being conducted, the results were incontrovertible. As the *Los Angeles Times* described, the change was spurred by "an influx of transients and derelicts, and overcrowding and neglect; in sum, blight" (Chapman 1968, 24). The rich history of the hill had been flattened by media coverage to become a simple tale of paradise lost. "What comes up must come down" coupled with an almost religious sense of progress had pushed through the changes in policy both locally and nationally. And the housing act provided a means for the city to intervene in its own decline. The public was becoming convinced that cities had just reached a natural downturn in their evolution. So for the first time in the history of the American city, the "city" itself had become a matter of public policy.

Evans Clark, the executive director of the Twentieth Century Fund, wrote that the "city has come to be thought of as a vast and complicated organism, each part interacting on every other, embracing elements both of growth and decay—but an organism, unlike most others, subject to human mastery and control" (Clark 1953, v). As I've described in previous chapters, since the end of the nineteenth century, the American city was desirable because it was composed through the practice of spectators. But as Clark clearly stated, by 1953, when the influential Twentieth Century Fund report was authored, the city was no longer seen within this constructivist context. It was presented as something that could be presented all at once—completely within the parameters of human understanding. Accordingly, if the city as a whole was "subject to human mastery and control," then the city could be produced from scratch. Whatever could be understood could be manufactured.

So when planners and financiers were confronted with the problem of Bunker Hill, demolition and reconstruction were the first and most viable options on the table. In 1954, $33 million was requested from the federal government to renew a thirty-block area, or 136 acres. Four firms were selected the following year to conduct a thorough survey: the architectural firms Pereira and Luckman and Welton, Becket and Associates and the engineering firms Donald R. Warren, Co., and Henry Babcock. The first public showing of graphic plans and drawings prepared by Pereira and Luckman was an elaborate scheme with three levels of plazas, with the upper devoted to business and commercial structures, the middle devoted to residential use, and the lower developed as a trade plaza including an auditorium, music hall, and convention headquarters (see figure 5.2). The Federal Government agreed to loan the CRA almost $60 million and to make an outright grant of almost $15 million (Community Redevelopment Agency 1958). It was estimated at the time that within five years, private investors would pour an additional $300 million into the project. William Zeckendorf, Sr., president of the New York finance company Webb & Knapp, Inc., said in reference to the plan: "There is no doubt that the regeneration of your downtown area is absolutely assured by this

project. Los Angeles is no exception to a trend in the nation's cities which is seeing them rot out at the core unless action is taken. The effect of the highly feasible project will be to cause your city to take form, instead of being fluid and going ahead in a pogo-stick jumping way, because you will have a care and a heart" ("Financiers Urge" 1958). Without a mind to the master plan, according to Zeckendorf, the urban future is given over to randomness. "The pogo-stick jumping way" of urban development not only implies the lack of understanding but it implies a lack of moral fortitude. Urban renewal took on a decidedly moralistic tone as planners and developers justified radical measures by promising to take responsibility for the failure of cities.

Miles Colean, the main author of the Twentieth Century Fund report, saw urban renewal as a moral imperative. "Like all creators, man creates in his own image, and, if he does not like the reflection he finds in his city, he has his own lack of interest, competence or foresight to blame. If his city is confused and disorderly, that is because he himself is confused or unmindful of disorder, or lacking in the means to achieve order. If the city is ugly, that is because he either does not care about beauty or is not able to produce it. If the city sinks into decay, it is because he has lost the wish or the vigor to maintain it" (1953, 9). The Twentieth Century Fund Report was influential in shifting the blame of urban decline from the poor to the middle class. It was everybody's responsibility to repair the cities with which they identified. The city was man's (read: the middle class's) creation, and therefore, it was man's responsibility to assure that it lives up to his expectations. In this case, the state of America's cities reflected poorly on the morality of men. With the technological and political sophistication to correct urban problems, there was little excuse not to act. Colean saw intervention, therefore, not as a social issue, but as a moral one.

(opposite)
FIGURE 5.2.
Charles Luckman Associates, supervising architectural firm for the Bunker Hill project, developed a master plan that divided the area into three separate sections, each built around plazas and connected to one another for foot traffic by a series of street overpasses, moving stairs, and moving sidewalks (1959). Herald Examiner Collection, Los Angeles Public Library

Throughout the 1950s, the morality of social intervention was encouraged by the changing rhetoric of the technological future. With the dramatic arrival of the nuclear and computer ages, there was a growing perception that the long speculated future had finally arrived. The perceived imminence of future technologies forced the concern of how best to integrate them into the physical and social world. The war demonstrated that technology could easily overwhelm the intentions of its creator. Left unchecked, progress could be dangerous. For this reason, technological displays turned away from speculation and toward control.

The Operative Image

This sentiment was most clearly articulated in Norbert Wiener's 1948 book, *Cybernetics*. As defined by Wiener, cybernetics was the study of messages, and in particular, the effective messages of control. It was the study of how systems communicate with themselves in order to maintain internal cohesion, and how they interact with other systems. According to Wiener, "Society can only be understood through a study of messages and the communication facilities which belong to it; and . . . in the future development of these messages and communication facilities, messages between man and machines, between machine and man, and between machine and machine, are destined to play an ever increasing part" (1950, 9). By placing the understanding of communication before the understanding of the bodies communicating, cybernetics aimed to remove the social actor from the study of society; everything meaningful could be gleaned from the patterns and flows of messages. And because communication patterns were alterable, it introduced the possibility that any system, properly understood, could be controlled. People, cities, and societies were no different than machines. "It is my thesis," says Wiener, "that the operation of the living individual and the operation of some of the newer communication machines are precisely parallel" (1950, 15).

Control is contingent on familiarity. Accordingly, Wiener argued that technology forced the need to rearrange our understanding of similarity. Similarity between communication systems did not merely suggest pictorial likeness; rather, it suggested operational likeness. While this process was described in Wiener's early work, it wasn't until his 1964 book, *God and Golem, Inc.*, that he actually gave it a name. In reference to God creating man in his own image, he called the result of any system's production of another system an *operative image*. Every system creates in its own image—God and man, man and machine. But systems, broadly understood, do not have to look like their creator. Their similarity is much deeper. They "replace the original in its action," Wiener says (31). The concept of the operative image, while Wiener coined it in reference to artificial intelligence, had implications for technological representation in general. In the age of modern technology, every system was an image of another. Every system had operational similarities to other systems. As a result, pictorial likeness was insufficient in understanding the depth of cultural reference and meaning.

In urban planning, this was indicated by an abstraction and dissemination of an ideal urban form. As cities throughout the nation replaced low-rise tenement buildings with high-rise office buildings, they relied on an operative image of city to instill the newly vertical core with meaning. According to the architectural critic Joseph Giovannini, "A group of high-rise buildings now under construction on or near Bunker Hill is rapidly Manhattanizing the skyline, making downtown look more like the center it has always been" (1975, 10). Giovannini implies that the "distant image" of high-rises was primarily intended to amplify the existing functionality of the city. He places little emphasis on the specific architectural references in each of the structures — only on their combined function as urban image. The operative image was the foundation of a Concept-city that sought to distance the spectator from his central position of aggregator by prioritizing urban function.

Characterizing the city as an image of its functionality was a common strategy in urban renewal. And it had significant implications for the role of the spectator in urban life. Martin Heidegger, in his essay "The Age of the World Picture," details the repercussions of such a spectatorial shift. In the age of modern technology, Heidegger argues, the world is increasingly grasped through scientific method. Modern science is determined by what Heidegger calls "ongoing activity" — or the transforming of knowledge and experience into a scientific process. The problem for Heidegger is not that science is too readily applied to the world, but that the world has taken on the character of science. This is how the modern world is knowable. The world is an image capable of existing alongside and not within experience. "Where the world becomes picture, what is, in its entirety, is juxtaposed as that for which man is prepared and which, correspondingly, he therefore intends to bring before himself and have before himself, and consequently intends in a decisive sense to set in place before himself. Hence world picture, when understood essentially, does not mean a picture of the world but the world conceived and grasped as picture" (1977, 129). The distinction is important. "The world conceived and grasped as picture" suggests that the change is in the spectator's approach, rather than in the quality of the image itself. Seen through the lens of modern technology, the spectator, Heidegger argues, engages the world as a series of types organized by operational similarities.

The recognition by the spectator of the world as picture allows the world to be convincingly reproduced and marketed as an image of itself. While the pictorial image, in Wiener's formulation, is the visual re-creation of something in the world, the operative image is its functional re-creation. An operative image needs no original. Accordingly, Bunker Hill was to be transformed into an operative image. It was to symbolize centralization, urbanism, cleanliness, and safety, without any specificity in its representation. And perhaps most strikingly, it was to learn from its functionality and spread outward. Giovannini asserts, "Though few of the high-rises will be architecturally distinguished, they will establish a convincingly urban downtown profile" (1975, 12). The question that arises from such a statement is how a city becomes "convincingly urban"? The answer rests in the emerging discourse of artificial intelligence. Just as machines were programmed to represent human thought, so were cities tasked with the challenge of representing urban function.

Machine Intelligence

On February 24, 1956, IBM 704, a machine that could play checkers, was demonstrated on live television (Samuel 1963).[1] That same year, the official plans for Bunker Hill were made public. In each case, the public was exposed to a blueprint for the future — machines capable of learning. There was a great deal of fanfare around this possibility, for once the code was cracked, the human mind and all of its creations would be an open book. Machine learning had supplanted simple mechanization as the central theme of the scientific future. The mere codification of reality didn't allow for change without constant human maintenance. But if machines were capable of thinking, the systems that they represented could be infinitely adaptable. As Allen Newell said of a particular thinking machine: "If one could devise a successful chess machine, one would seem to have penetrated into the core of human intellectual endeavor" (Newell, Shaw, and Simon 1963, 39).

If scientists cracked the code of human thought, the mind could be rendered a useful servant instead of a persistent antagonist. This was the promise of the thinking machine — the outward projection of the versatility and adaptability of the human mind within a finite environment. This way of thinking was not new to the computer age; understanding the world as a system of classifiable objects had been an accepted way of thinking since Descartes. He introduced an idea that was at the time quite radical. The Scholastics believed that objects emanated a "form" that directly penetrated into the mind and influenced perception, but Descartes believed that objects were totally contained in the outside world and known to the mind only through their representations. This idea was of course influential in the advancement of science, because it made it possible for the world to be classified and organized. It made it possible for the world to become picture.

This way of conceiving the world opened up possibilities for different ways of organizing the world — if objects are known to us only through their representations, then those representations could be abstracted even further into symbols. This is precisely the principle on which computation machines were built — a machine programmed to recognize and organize data through symbols. As one historian of artificial intelligence writes: "Internally, the mind operated not with reality directly but with representations that stood for or symbolized it; therefore, analogous operations performed on appropriate symbols of the same things ought to be capable of reproducing something comparable to what the mind did" (Hogan 1997, 15).

While a longtime preoccupation among scientists and philosophers, the principles of artificial intelligence couldn't truly be tested or even fully theorized until the advent of the digital computer in the early 1950s. Only at this point could thought adequately be reproduced in a manner that mimicked the function of the human mind. In 1956 Allen Newell and Herbert Simon announced at a Dartmouth conference: "Every aspect of learning or any other feature of intelligence can in principle be so precisely described that a machine can be made to simulate it" (Crevier 1993, 48). This became known as the physical symbol systems hypothesis.

Newell and Simon's announcement was indicative of a shift in the overall direction of machine intelligence. It was no longer a theoretical quandary: the digital computer had transformed thought from a philosophical concept to an empirical object. In Alan Turing's famous essay "Computing Machinery and Intelligence" (1963), he announced that we shouldn't get bogged down in the kind of philosophical and semantic quagmires that result from speculating about unobservables that go on inside people's heads. Instead, we should talk about how we would expect to know a thinking entity if we met one. This is the premise of the "Turing Test." By formulating the question in this way—not "what is thought?" but " 'how do you know thought when you see it?"—Turing effectively made the real possibilities of machine intelligence into a topic of broad concern. And just as Bunker Hill struggled to be "convincingly urban," Turing understood the thinking machine as convincingly human.

The test was composed of the following actions: a man, A, and a woman, B, answer the questions of an interrogator who is in contact via a teleprinter. The interrogator can ask any questions she chooses with the goal of determining which of the subjects is which. A's aim is to mislead the interrogator and B wants to be identified correctly. If B says, "I'm the woman, don't listen to him," A could just as easily say the same thing. But if a machine takes the place of A in the game, will the interrogator be wrong as often as in the first case? This was the crucial question for Turing. A machine passes the Turing test when the interrogator is unable to distinguish between it and the human; when the machine has become as artful as the human in displaying the *skills* needed to deceive another human. But what does it take, Turing wondered, for a thinking machine to pass for human?[2] The answer was versatility. Humans expect other humans to be versatile: have multiple interests, moods, and skills. The machine needed to represent those expectations. So while individual programs could play games, look up information, interpret data, and so on, it was another matter altogether for a single machine to represent all of those functions with equal clarity and find a natural language with which to discuss them. When this happens, Turing claimed, there would be little separating the average function of the machine from the average function of a human mind.

The general conception of a machine until this point was that of a "finite state automaton," essentially a machine capable of performing specific tasks, like a vending machine or a digital clock. Each of these machines is composed of a finite number of discrete, distinguishable states with no memory external to the system. These finite-state automata are not necessarily simple (a digital clock showing the month, date, and time down to seconds has 31 million states, each of which it visits once a year), but because they lack external memory, they are incapable of learning from situations imposed on the machine by external stimuli. But Turing was dissatisfied with the finite-state machine; he believed that machines were capable of much more. For this reason he proposed the Universal Machine. Essentially, the Universal Machine could redefine its parts to suit the requirements of the moment as it proceeds, instead of having to possess all kinds of different specialized parts with most of them, most of the time, doing nothing. This machine, in other words, could be programmed to recite a poem with the same parts that it used for arithmetic. It could respond to an external stimulus and adapt its parts to satisfy new requirements.

The question for many was whether or not the versatility described in the Universal Machine was equivalent to thinking. It may be a "different kind" of thinking, Turing admits, but why should that matter, considering human beings are also versatile in their thinking. After all, the point was not to perfect rational thought, but to replicate thought processes. Turing was convinced that with advancements in memory, speed, and programming, any subject taking the Turing Test would not have more than a 70 percent chance of guessing the right answer after five minutes of questioning. And this, for him, would be the greatest success imaginable—a machine smart enough and versatile enough to operate within the realm of humanity. In effect, the true test of machine intelligence was its ability to *lie* effectively.

Turing conceived of his test in reaction to what had become known as "Lady Lovelace's exception." Ada Byron (otherwise known as Lady Lovelace), was the assistant to the English mathematician and inventor, Charles Babbage. While serving in that capacity, she wrote the first critique of machine intelligence in 1842. In reference to Babbage's proposed computer, she wrote: "The Analytical Engine has no pretensions to *originate* anything. It can do *whatever we know how to order it* to perform" (qtd. in Norman 2005, 268). Byron concluded that machines could not surprise their creators. But Turing was convinced that this view was premised on a misinterpretation of machine intelligence. "The view that machines cannot give rise to surprises is due, I believe, to a fallacy to which philosophers and mathematicians are particularly subject. This is the assumption that as soon as a fact is presented to a mind all consequences of that fact spring into the mind simultaneously with it. It is a very useful assumption under many circumstances, but one too easily forgets that it is false. A natural consequence of doing so is that one then assumes that there is no virtue in the mere working out of consequences from data and general principles" (Turing 1963, 26). The surprise that comes from machines is not their ability to retrieve information, according to Turing, but their ability to combine information into unforeseen patterns and arrive at unpredictable conclusions. This is a process that Arthur Samuel, the IBM scientist who developed the checkers-playing IBM 704, called "generalization learning." The goal of generalization learning was to give the machine as little information as possible, such as the rules of a game, and have it successfully make decisions about specific situations. "Highly developed machine learning procedures," Samuel argues, "may greatly diminish the amount of information that must be given to a machine before it can work on a problem. At the moment it is easier to solve most social and economic problems without computers than it is to adjust a machine for their solution" (Osmundsen 1959). But Samuel figured that in very little time, machines could successfully intervene in most aspects of modern life.

Norbert Wiener questioned the usefulness of such an intervention. Operative images, he argued, do not equal the complete predictability of a system. Wiener put this into biblical terms. God created man (and by extension, the devil) in his own image. In reference to the devil, Wiener says, "[God] is actually engaged in a conflict with his creature in which he may very well lose the game. And yet, his creature is made by him according to his own free will, and would seem to derive all its possibility of action from God himself." But if a creature is programmed with all possible messages, how could the creator have a significant engagement with it? The creator would know exactly what it was capable of and therefore know exactly how to beat it. Wiener asks, "Can God play a significant game with his own creature? Can any creator, even a limited one, play a significant game with his own creature?" (1964, 17).

The answer is yes. In 1957, Samuel's machine lost to the New England checkers champion, Saul Weslow, in a public display of the machine's capability. Philip Morse, a physics professor at MIT, said that the machine played an impressive game, but Weslow's victory is a testament to the human brain's ability to adapt to situations ("Mechanical Brain" 1957). But in 1959, when IBM 704 publicly beat Samuel, the creator himself, in a game of checkers, the *New York Times* ran this headline: "I.B.M. Brain Beats the Hand That Fed it Data on Checkers." "There was a time," the article explained, "when [Samuel] could beat the machine without much trouble. But now the big 704 whips him at every game, each time a little more soundly" (Osmundsen 1959). The machine, so it seemed, was learning. It was able to more intelligently make decisions based on the limited information it had. In 1959, 704 played a "significant game" with its creator. The surprise, as Turing suggests, did not stem from its ability to store every possible checkers move; instead, the surprise was in the machine's ability to adapt to its environment and respond to a particular situation.

But this achievement was not without its threats. There were potentially frightening consequences of a machine besting its creator. Indeed, this is the *golem* in Wiener's title: an embryo Adam, a monster. *Golem* is a reference to a rabbinical story from sixteenth-century Prague. Rabbi Löw used his incantations to blow the "breath of life" into a clay statue. The statue came to life and became the rabbi's willing servant. Each night the rabbi would put a piece of paper into its mouth and the automaton would perform the task. Over time, however, the rabbi grew dissatisfied with the state of his machine because he wanted it to be more human. He programmed it to eat, think, study, all the things that differentiate humanity from its machines. Soon, the golem turned unpredictable and grew more powerful than its creator and the only solution was to destroy it and take heed of the dangers of playing God.

The golem story was a persistent counternarrative to the redemptive discourse of machine intelligence. It was a warning against mistaking the lie of machine intelligence with the truth of human intelligence. The golem only became dangerous when the rabbi began to believe in its human qualities, when it became a reflection of its creator. But as Turing describes, this reflection is always a lie. Man is not God; and a machine is not man. And yet the desire to possess the operative image is profound. Colean declared in the Twentieth Century Fund report that the city, produced in the image of man, illuminated the desires and passions of its inhabitants. The modern city should be able to pass Turing's test: it should be programmed to make its creators think that it is thinking. Through scientific planning it can solve urban problems and increase economic value far more efficiently than any human advisors. The goal of renewal was to produce an operative image—to play God, to instill the promise into distant spectators that they can, without getting too close, possess a functional reproduction of the city in urban form.

Outcome Prediction as Urban Design

Every element in the 136 acres of Bunker Hill was to be thought through. Each lot, every corridor was to be part of a master plan so efficient, so logical, that urban slums would be relegated to the pages of history books. Dr. Homer Hoyt, a CRA land economy consultant, said, "Bunker Hill would never redevelop by itself. Owners could not put a fine new building in an old area and expect to receive profitable rents. The whole atmosphere must be changed at one time" ("Bunker Hill" 1958). As urban renewal became official policy for city planners, the ideas of isolated developments or renewal through gentrification of existing neighborhoods became increasingly absurd. Interfaces need designers. Games need rules. It was widely understood that entering into an information stream with no parameters is counterproductive. Likewise, building a new development in the midst of a slum does not produce a predictable outcome. If urban planning had a mission in the 1950s, it could only be described as "outcome prediction."

The plans for Bunker Hill went through several stages. The initial documents previewed in 1956 by Pereira and Luckman were a schematic of its three major plots: residential, commercial, and cultural, all of which interacted with each other to create a centralized mechanism. The idea was that the city adopts a master plan from which developers could not deviate. Private investors could develop specific parcels of land but each development had to fit within the overall logic of the master plan.

Before the plans were officially unveiled, the media began to speculate about the awesome potential of the renewal project. As early as 1955, long before any construction had actually taken place, a series of articles was published in the *Los Angeles Examiner* in reference to an early rendition of the master plan. "If Los Angeles created a modern Acropolis, it might easily be an 'eighth wonder of the world.' At least it would give the 'Queen City' a dazzling new crown," reported one article in the series. The article continued to describe the best possible scenario, suggesting that the new landscape will become the city's destiny:

> Private investors will buy the cleared land, out of which the federal loan will be repaid. And on the land, if Los Angeles architects have their way, there will arise a great dream city built entirely by private capital. Tall, graceful buildings will be silhouetted against the sky. Beautiful plazas and malls for pedestrian use will surround them—in many instances built right over the street arteries which will be depressed 20 to 30 feet. Autos will move through the depressed streets into underground parking structures—where passengers will alight and move up stairways to the plaza areas. Never shall pedestrians and autos travel on the same levels. ("LA's Acropolis" 1955)

What's interesting about this description is that the utopian aspects of the "Acropolis" are described primarily as flow patterns. The movement of people and automobiles around plazas take precedence over the look and feel of the street. Little is said about the visual appeal of architecture. In the distant image of the buildings silhouetted against the sky, the Queen City's crown is operative. The author expresses a great hope that the city council will approve the plan "so that this major blighted area—one of the city's fifteen substandard areas—can be replaced with a new, sensationally conceived, yet practical acropolis." In most descriptions throughout the decade, the plan was hyperbolized in a fashion that highlighted its practicality—a practical acropolis seems a strange descriptor, but one that was unusually fitting for Bunker Hill. Its practicality, not its spectacular visuality, was what appealed to the city-worn population of Los Angeles. According to Mayor Norris Poulsen, the Bunker Hill urban renewal program would create a "new shot of life" for Los Angeles ("Bunker Hill Project" 1959).

In 1957, William Sesnon made plans for a pilot study in the two-block area that would become the new courthouse. Sesnon reported to Mayor Poulson and the city council that the pilot area would include three fifteen- to twenty-story office buildings, a pedestrian street, moving sidewalks and garages for sixteen hundred cars. He announced at this council meeting that certain streets would be widened and the moving sidewalks would make it easy for shoppers and office tenants to get to the heart of the business area. Moving sidewalks were a popular solution to pedestrian travel in the 1950s. One need only look at the large number of airports with moving sidewalks built during the decade to understand what a powerful utility they were. They not only served the function of faster pedestrian travel, they were also aligned with the promise of modern design and efficiency. Sesnon said that "[m]oving sidewalks will run from Hill St. to Olive St. parallel to the Third St. Tunnel, thus making it an easy matter for shoppers and office tenants to get to the heart of the business area" ("Bunker Hill Test" 1957). The moving sidewalks would replace the disorder of the street with an orderly machine, singular in function. Sidewalks were a means to an end—a means of funneling people into the business district. The renewal plan would assure that they never again fall into chaotic disarray.

While the moving sidewalks never made it into Bunker Hill, the very fact that they were highlighted in almost every report throughout the 1950s suggests what a powerful component they were to the overall success of the plan. Ultimately, the things that were never realized—the separation of pedestrians and vehicles, the moving sidewalks, and the large pedestrian plazas—were the things that were most important in establishing strong public support for the renewal. These were the things that highlighted function; they were the elements of the design that established the city as rational and aligned the discourse of urban renewal with that of machine learning.

Toward a Programmable System

This rational city stemmed from an urban planning discourse most notably initiated by Le Corbusier's *Radiant City* (1970). All activities were logically separated in Radiant City; leisure and commerce were physically removed from one another in order to assure order and easy maintenance of the urban plan. According to Le Corbusier, "On the day when contemporary society, at present so sick, has become properly aware that only architecture and city planning can provide the exact prescription for its ills, then the day will have come for the great *machine* to be put in motion" (1970, 143; italics added). While Le Corbusier aligns the utopian urban plan with the machine, and quite obviously influenced postwar urban plans in the United States, the utopian qualities he assigns to the machine are decidedly different than that described by Turing. Le Corbusier's Radiant City was a finite-state automaton, a machine that was programmed with all it would ever need to know. The godlike stature of the architect and planner (Le Corbusier himself) would dictate the city's every move.

In Bunker Hill, on the other hand, the machine was designed to be adaptable, capable of learning from its environment and changing its operations to fit the varying contexts. The machine could do the looking so the spectator wouldn't have to. Each of the elements of the city was conceived as a finite automaton programmed to respond to specific inputs from the environment. The master plan was conceived as a Universal Machine, organizing the outputs of each part and building an information structure based on their activities—all within the careful structure of a controlled environment. The operationalization of machine intelligence in the urban context was made explicit in Jay Forrester's *Urban Dynamics* (1969). Forrester's book, with a specific emphasis on Boston, characterized the city as a complex system whose behaviors could be modeled with computers. Stemming from his work on industrial systems, Forrester created a computer program intended to predict urban behaviors. Once the functional features of the operative city were coded in a computer, the behaviors of additional features, such as policy decisions or renewal projects, could be accurately mapped over a fifty-year span. These features demonstrated what he called "counterintuitive behaviors" that are common to all complex systems. Like all universal machines, the city integrates variables in unpredictable ways. Forrester's book demonstrated how the unpredictability of machine learning could be contained and mastered. It reinforced the integrity of the previous decade's renewal strategies by providing "computational proof" of their effectiveness.

Forrester's models had had little to do with the life of urban residents. As evidenced in the plans for Bunker Hill, most urban renewal projects characterized the city as an entity that could exist apart from those who lived there. The urban erasure central to the renewal of Bunker Hill was equally as focused on the disposal and reconstruction of the population as it was with the physical environment. While renewal efforts have always focused on the "improvement" of lives of urban residents, the creation and justification of the operative image was an abstraction of those lives into features of a programmable system. The city was a functional tool for the advancement of human society. Without having to rely on the whimsy of human behavior, the renewed city could forge humanity's steady progress into the future. But as Americans pushed headlong toward a technocratic urban future, some very vocal critics began to complicate the popular dialogue. Just as soon as the process of renewal was irreversible, serious questions about the operative city emerged. Norbert Wiener predicted these questions: "The world of the future will be an ever more demanding struggle against the limitations of our intelligence, not a comfortable hammock in which we can lie down to be waited upon by our robot slaves" (Wiener 1964, 69).

Re-placing the Spectator

After World War II, the image of the American city experienced a severe decline while the perceived health of the culture was on the rise. America had helped to win the war and had finally emerged as a world power. The proud state of national consciousness brought about by military victory was largely contradictory to the distressing state of the American city. The image of the city had departed from the image of the nation. Rife with poverty and malaise, the city seemed to contradict the American consciousness. Indeed, with improved communication and transportation systems to enable the expansion of the city's geographical purview, the centralized city was in danger of becoming anachronistic. Lewis Mumford lamented this technological push outward in his powerful attack against suburbia. "Each member of suburbia," he wrote, "becomes imprisoned by the very separation that he has prized. . . . He is fed through a narrow opening: a telephone line, a radio band, a television circuit. This is not, it goes without saying, the result of a conscious conspiracy by a cunning minority: it is an organic by-product of an economy that sacrifices human development to mechanical processing" (1989, 513). As the city was expanding outward in the name of scientific progress, planners were devising solutions to fortify the center using the same justification. The city as a thinking machine was considered a "progressive" position that ensured the parallel advancement of humanity and technology. Again, Mumford presented an opposing view: "Instead of bringing life into the city, so that its poorest inhabitant will have not merely sun and air but some chance to touch and feel and cultivate the earth, these naïve apostles of progress had rather bring sterility to the countryside and ultimately death to the city. Their 'city of the future' is one leveled down to the lowest possibility of active, autonomous, fully sentient life: just so much life as will conform to the requirements of the machine" (1989, 527).

The desired outcome of urban renewal, which steadfastly "conformed to the requirements of the machine," was to reduce the unpredictability of urban life. And yet as the bulldozers ravaged America's inner cities, some voices were heard from under the rubble. Many residents of Bunker Hill fought hard to keep their homes. In letter-writing campaigns and protests, they highlighted the lack of humanity in urban renewal. To an unreceptive public, they declared the importance of memory and community in urban life. In a letter to the *Los Angeles Examiner* in 1956, this resident wrote of his struggle against automation:

> At Christmas time in the olden days, there was suspension of lawsuits; moratoria on evictions and sentences to debtors prison, and even hangmen took a holiday.
>
> But today, the 600 to 800 of us living in a block-wide strip on Bunker Hill, must vacate the premises by January 1, 1957. We in this strip—which is to be used as a parking lot for the new courthouse—are not transients. Many of us have lived here for 20, 30, 40 years and longer.
>
> Is it that the Board of Supervisors, to quote Francis Bacon, "would leave the minds of a number of . . . poor shrunken things, full of melancholy and indisposition, and unpleasing to themselves?"
>
> Is it true that bureaucracy has no heart?
>
> —Bunker Hillite (Letter to the Editor 1956)

For all the utopian promise of this new intelligent city, the concept of heart was not programmed into it. Thousands of people were forced to vacate their homes. While there was some compensation for relocation, it was negligible and of course could not make recompense for emotional and social connections. Entire communities were demolished to make room for the distant image of the operative city.

In addition to Mumford's *The City in History* (1961), Jane Jacobs's *The Death and Life of Great American Cities* (1961) was strongly influential in the growing antagonism toward urban renewal. Jacobs argued for the vitality of the streets and for the continued importance of locating the spectator within them. While the city of machine intelligence was physically clean and orderly, it was spiritually dead, she argued. As an example, she explained how the renewed city reduces the "moving chaos" of the sidewalk and street to a finite function. Jacobs wrote that "streets in cities serve many purposes besides carrying vehicles, and city sidewalks—the pedestrian parts of the streets—serve many purposes besides carrying pedestrians. These uses are bound up with circulation but are not identical with it and in their own right they are at least as basic as circulation to the proper workings of cities" (1961, 29). The moving sidewalk, so popular in early plans for Bunker Hill, aimed to reduce the sidewalk to its singular function. Jacobs rejected every aspect of renewal that programmed functionality into the city, arguing that this level of planning effectively removed any possibility for serendipity, play, and chaos. The whole human actor is dissected within the city into instances of action, resulting in an actor that is hardly human.

While Jacobs and Mumford rejected urban renewal entirely, others sought to insert the human actor into the process. Kevin Lynch's *The Image of the City* (1960) suggested possibilities for human intervention into the operative city. Lynch attempted to bring the spectator back into a central role in the formation of the urban image: "He should have the power to change the image to fit changing needs. An environment which is ordered in precise and final detail may inhibit new patterns of activity" (1960, 6). For Lynch, it was not the urban machine itself that could transform the image; it was the human in the midst of the machine. Good urban design was about visual legibility or "the ease in which its parts [could] be organized into a coherent pattern" (1960, 7). While not completely abandoning the machine logic of the city, Lynch sought to recenter the human being in the formation of that order. The image might be machine produced, but it was the spectator who possessed and organized the image, not the machine.

Lynch offered the possibility that the spectator could continue to have a role even within the purportedly self-sufficient machine logic of the operative city. Lynch devised a mechanism he called "cognitive mapping" wherein solicited drawings of people's perceptions of the urban environment would factor into the planning process. By specifically appealing to spectatorship and its representation, Lynch made significant strides toward recombining human and machine logic in the city. He attempted to draw close what had, through years of urban renewal, become the distant and externalized image of the city.

Colin Rowe and Fred Koetter, in their book *Collage City* (1978), brought this argument into historical perspective. Their reaction against the utopianism of modern architecture was received in a number of different ways: as an apology for postmodern formalism, an apology for historicist architecture, and, quite distinctly, as a prescription for a deep respect for the urban fabric. These multiple interpretations were a result of the rather disparate implications of the book. While aiming to define a collage aesthetic for urban architecture, they also used collage to imply the depth of historical reference. Rowe and Koetter took issue with the historical flattening of modern architecture and proposed a future city that was both logical and experiential. The logical city, they argued, should always be tempered by the human city. The "city as science" should coexist with the "city as people." "Science will and should build the town," they said, "and, up to a point, so will and should collective opinion" (6). For Rowe and Koetter, to conceive of the city as an entirely rational object is to disregard the elements of the city that are necessarily irrational. They called their project one of "constructive dis-illusion . . . simultaneously an appeal for order and disorder, for the simple and the complex, for the joint existence of permanent reference and random happening, of the private and the public, of innovation and tradition, of both the retrospective and the prophetic gesture" (8). Reacting against the operative city, Rowe and Koetter argued that progress and logic cannot productively exist without memory and nostalgia. "For, if without prophecy there is no hope, then, without memory there can be no communication" (49).

All of these writers made it clear that the operative city was susceptible to interpretation; even practical urban spaces were potential sites of experience. The spectator, with her historical references and experiential desires, could never be fully removed from the city, and no amount of modernist planning could change this. Instead, as Jane Jacobs pointed out, urban problems should not be understood as issues of "simplicity" or "disorganized complexity," both of which characterized modern science. Instead, she argued, the city was a manifestation of *organized complexity*—a complex system quite distinct from Forrester's characterization. Organized complexity was not entirely predictable; it had order, but part of that order was its lack of predictability. The sidewalk was, by design, unpredictable.

But ultimately Jacobs and others were struggling against a popular culture that embraced the operative simplicity of machine intelligence. In this context, possession was a product of computation, but never a practice that required personal organization. The sidewalk (and the city more generally) was already organized and inflexibly poised for dissemination. As the promise of machine intelligence settled into American life, there was a question as to whether Americans would ever turn their back on absolute certainty; if possessive spectatorship would ever return to a process of personal assembly.

RERUN CITY

Nostalgia and Urban Narrative

By the 1960s, almost every major American city had been transformed by urban renewal. Slums and historical districts had been cleared, and function had replaced speculation as the organizing attribute of the city. But just as soon as planners and politicians finished reciting history's eulogy, those same planners and politicians began to lament its passing. According to a 1966 publication by the U.S. Congress of Mayors, *With Heritage So Rich* (1983), historical structures should be tasked with communicating the permanence of community and national values. Informed by this publication, Congress passed the National Historic Preservation Act in 1966, empowering the federal government to mitigate building efforts within the mandate of historic preservation. As a result of this act, the historic preservation movement began shifting its efforts away from singular rural locations to large-scale urban locations. Instead of Civil War battlefields and farmhouses, whole urban districts were deemed historical. Streets and signs, in addition to blocks and squares, were given landmark status as a means of resurrecting the historical city from near total demolition. Just as planners claimed that slum clearance needed large swaths of land to be effective, the preservationists made the same claim for historical renewal.

Historical permanence symbolized a cultural stagnation, more aligned with the old world of Europe than the progressive culture of the United States. But beginning in the 1960s, the historic preservation movement sought to change this perception. American cities had their own unique history worth preserving. And history was the only thing that could rescue the modern city from its reliance on machine intelligence. There was still meaning in the disappearing urban vernacular. Preservationists, according to historian Mitchell Schwarzer, "began to take interest in buildings that had previously received little attention: factories, commercial structures, and residences. They also looked to matters beyond history and architecture, crafting policies that took into account the interrelationships of buildings within the urbanized environment. Indeed, during the seventies and eighties, preservation efforts gradually shifted from an exclusive emphasis on individual buildings to historic districts, from part to whole, from landmark to street" (1994, 5). It was urban renewal that forced the Concept-city into public policy debates. But advocates of renewal treated the city as something to react against as opposed to something to protect. Preservationists reversed the terms of the debate—instead of the operative city being the simple solution to a complex problem, the historical city became the simple solution. The city of machine intelligence represented the transience and complexity of American culture; the city of historical significance resurrected a preindustrial urban past, a simpler time, a symbol of American unity and cultural permanence.

Historical preservation, despite the best intentions of its advocates, had its own biases. It required a decision as to what was worth preserving. As Peirce Lewis suggests, preservation necessitated the freezing of a "human landscape which, by its very definition, resulted from dynamic, changing events" (1975, 9). Certain parts of history had to be erased so that other parts could be highlighted. In the process of preservation, images of poverty and crime were removed from the historical record so that a nostalgic urban community could be preserved. Nostalgia, as David Lowenthal describes it, is "memory with the pain removed." It is the specific longing for an unspecific experience of the past (1985, 8). Indeed, the nostalgia for the city that emerged after renewal was a longing for what we had lost—regardless of how complex it was when we had it.

Like all iterations of possessive spectatorship in the United States, the spatial practices apparent in historic preservation cannot be seen in isolation. The 1960s witnessed the full integration of familiar repetition into popular viewing practices. For instance, reruns took hold on television, literally dominating the programming schedules of most stations. With all the rhetoric around progress, Americans fortified their taste for the familiar. On television, it was cheaper to run repeats than it was to produce first-run content, and as it turned out, the ratings were often just as high or higher. As stations throughout the country began relying on syndication to fill their programming schedules, it became clear that history was profitable. This was just as true in the postrenewal city as it was on television. Urban and televisual narratives were equally dependent on the consumption of the familiar through perpetual repetition. As middle-class Americans grew comfortable in their distanced view of the city, they discovered the sweet assurance of being reminded of what they already thought they knew. Whether re-viewing an episode of *I Love Lucy* on television or reexperiencing an episode of American history in the streets, they privileged the memory of viewing over all else. The "trauma" of renewal and historical / spatial displacement was met with a compulsion to relive, replay, and reexperience the lost object. But not in a way that necessitated the abandonment of the present. Historical preservation, once complimented by narrative through the design practices of New Urbanists and their predecessors, reframed the present city as a forum for the repetition of the past. This was formative of the "rerun" city—a city that comes into being through the compulsive repetition of familiar stories.

Heidegger's notion of repetition is instructive in this context (Heidegger 1962). As Calvin Schrag interprets Heidegger's conception, "Repetition is the handing-over and appropriation of possibilities. It is an appropriation through which the past is reclaimed as possibility. Repetition thus occasions a reopening of the past by translating that which has been into possibilities to be chosen time and again" (1970, 289). Heidegger understood repetition as essential for historical understanding: "Without repetition the past would simply be a collection of isolated facts and would remain without meaning or sense" (Schrag 1970, 289). Repetition allows the past to enter the present on the spectator's terms.

So while repetition is a natural part of being, the desire for it is dictated by social factors, specifically a perceived loss of history. The trauma of urban renewal and the resulting temporal and spatial displacement after the war might be seen in accordance with what Sigmund Freud called the "death drive." Freud noticed in analyzing World War I veterans that they were compelled to repeat or reenact traumatic events. Repetition, he argued, went beyond the pleasure principle—we don't always repeat to achieve pleasure, continuity, or wholeness; often repetition is a destructive practice that aims "to restore an earlier state of things" (Freud 1922, 36). But even when repetition is motivated by external forces, as Freud noticed, it would tend toward constructing the practices Heidegger described. The spectator is attracted to repetition as means of coping with historical loss, and he does so with a mind to assembling isolated facts for the purpose of opening up possibilities. While Freud argued that repetition is a normal response to trauma, Heidegger offered the option of seeing repetition as a necessary means of producing the present. The rerun was a cultural practice cultivated by industrial changes in television and in urban planning that allowed individual spectators to find comfort and promise in possessing the past without abandoning the present.

From Historic Preservation to Historical Repetition

While historic preservation took root in the 1960s throughout the country, it achieved a distinct urgency in America's "most historic" city. By 1964, large-scale urban renewal efforts in Boston had replaced the sinuous streets of the historic Scollay Square with the operative Government Center—a modern brutalist building designed by architects Kallman, McKinnell, and Knowles. With the perceived success of that development, as early as 1965, there were plans to renew the adjacent Waterfront and Faneuil Hall areas as part of another master plan to "revitalize a key portion of downtown Boston" (*Downtown Waterfront* 1964). But because the city placed "the highest" priority on Revolutionary War sites, there was interest in retaining the structures. Faneuil Hall was remembered for housing the meeting that led to the Boston Tea Party, and the surrounding markets were touted as the first buildings in the country expressly designed for public use (see figure 6.1). The cluster of buildings was therefore recognized as comprising important artifacts of the city's, and the nation's, history. But historical sites, when not bulldozed in the name of urban renewal, were often left unused after receiving a landmark designation. They were expensive to repair and any development required considerable red tape. "To preserve is imperative but it is not enough," the architects Benjamin and Jane Thompson wrote of the site. "It is only the first step, usually aimed at saving old buildings from the path of bulldozers—harbingers of dubious public or private 'progress.' In the case of Faneuil Hall Markets, saving the structures from mass clearance, scheduled for the new Government Center in the 1960s, was a fortuitous rescue" (1975).

They understood that simply rescuing a building didn't make it relevant. A historical building without narrative context would only reproduce the practices of looking that became dominant with the operative city. "Famous Faneuil Hall and its three block-long market annexes—Quincy, North, and South Markets—stand at the exact center of Boston's urban core. The Mayor looks down on the Markets from New City Hall; motorists look down from the Southeast Expressway; workers look up as they hurry from nearby Haymarket to State Street and Government Center." Spectators are still removed from the site. Either looking down on it from an office or highway, or up at it while walking from one place to another, the space is distant and without

FIGURE 6.1.
Faneuil Hall Market, ca. 1880. Meade, Dodge and Company, courtesy of The Bostonian Society / Boston Historical: Boston Streets Collection, ca. 1855–1999

immediate resonance. A successful development, they argue, would need to transform that distant object into something proximate and meaningful by integrating the story of its past into each act of looking. It would have to reinstill urban practices into the Concept-city. "Once the heart of harbor activity and the city's wholesale food industry," the Thompsons note, "the Markets have been called one of the principle ornaments of America's Athens—indeed, its Agora." The resurrection of Boston's Agora, they argue, would be accomplished not by turning it into a museum space, but rather by making the space livable—making its history unfold in the process of engagement. They turn to Ada Louise Huxtable, perhaps the greatest proponent of historical preservation, in arguing that preservation "is finding ways to keep those buildings that provide the city's character and continuity; and of incorporating them into its living mainstream — original buildings on original sites that remember, but do not re-enact, an earlier time and a different way of life" (qtd. in Thompson and Thompson 1975).

While the historical preservation movement was gaining popularity as a reaction against the operative image of urban renewal, the notion that preservation could be used to instill life in the city was an untested concept in the 1970s. Historic preservationists used narratives of urban experience to justify material preservation; the idea was to use material preservation to authenticate narratives of urban experience. A document prepared by the Boston Redevelopment Authority (BRA) stated the goals of the Faneuil Hall development as: "We envision the markets project as a way to restore not only the physical structures of these beautiful buildings, but also as a restoration of this area to the crossroads of commerce and urban activity it was when first developed by Mayor Quincy" (Kenney 1973).

This vision was motivated by the successful proposal from the James Rouse Company, which in 1973 was named the primary developer of the site. In partnership with architects Benjamin Thompson and Associates, they proposed to reestablish the once vibrant marketplace by creating conditions for a contemporary, pedestrian-centered market, entirely built within the existing structures, and premised on the narratives of those structures. Called a festival marketplace, this "renewed" shopping space was based on a rather simple concept: it was a regionally sensitive adaptation of an "ideal market form" combining indoor and outdoor space to create a context for social interaction, and the "re-integration of the city and the market" ("Roundtable on Rouse" 1981, 103). The space below the hall and the neighboring Quincy, North, and South Market buildings were to be filled with pushcart vendors, small storefront retail businesses, and restaurants to create a vibrant urban space — one that had history as its justification, but not as its content.

When the Faneuil Hall development opened in 1975, it surpassed expectations of success. It demonstrated that historical memory could be popular (see figure 6.2). While Americans might have been interested in extending spatial distance between themselves and their cities, the alienating realities of the operative city created an opportunity to return the city to a product of the spectator's assembling. This was done by overlaying a simple and familiar narrative onto the space — and instead of presenting the city as a finished

FIGURE 6.2.
Faneuil Hall Market, ca. 2009. Photograph by Eric Gordon

product, inviting the spectator to engage in its playback. Overlaying a clear narrative onto the space gave it an authenticity not possible otherwise. The historian Hayden White described this process: "The very distinction between real and imaginary events that is basic to modern discussions of both history and fiction presupposes a notion of reality in which 'the true' is identified with 'the real' only insofar as it can be shown to possess the character of narrativity" (1987, 6). Through an imposition of narrativity, Rouse sought to convert "the true" space of the Markets (the actual buildings) into a "real" space of history. This kind of preservation, as much as it was an effort to preserve the built environment, was effectively an effort to capitalize on the built environment to preserve a memory of it—and consequently, to make it seem "real." "We can comprehend the appeal of historical discourse," says White, "by recognizing the extent to which it makes the real desirable, makes the real into an object of desire, and does so by its imposition, upon events that are represented as real, of the formal coherency that stories possess" (1987, 21). As it turned out, the formal coherency of stories proved to be more important than even the structures that lent authority to the stories. This was made clear when the Rouse and Thompson team duplicated their success with the "festival mall" concept in Baltimore. The $22 million Harborplace project (1980) consisted of *new* buildings constructed to look like vintage markets. Harborplace brought millions of people into Baltimore's inner city that had little reason to come before it was built (Salmon 2001). The success of these developments, and later the team's South Street Seaport (1983) in New York City, motivated the journal *Planning* to refer to Rouse as the "Robin Hood of real estate," and sparked hundreds of replica projects throughout the country (Hannigan 1998, 53).

Rouse understood that stories could reconnect the spectator to the city. But not just any stories—stories that told our "collective" history. The Faneuil Hall Markets told the familiar story of American independence and commitment to democratic ideals. And the project did so through the even more familiar story of the marketplace. In accordance with the opening of the development, there was a parallel "multimedia" exhibition in the hall's rotunda that told the story of Faneuil Hall's role in paving the "road to revolution." But as it turned out, this wasn't necessary to appropriately communicate the desired spatial narrative. The act of shopping itself enabled the narrative to unfold. It didn't require reading wall text or listening to a docent—the newly iterated story of Faneuil Hall was, from the moment one arrived in its space, always already familiar. Like watching a repeat of your favorite sitcom from childhood—the space communicated no new information, but it reinforced the familiarity of the story and the memories of watching. Just as Lowenthal says of nostalgia, the memory evoked in this space was of "past thoughts rather than past things, a daydream in reverse, like thinking we loved the books of our youth, when all we love is the thought of ourselves young, reading them" (1985, 8). Faneuil Hall invoked the simple stories of American diligence, democracy, and free trade. The space addressed the spectator quite intimately not only by communicating the content of history, but even more importantly, by invoking the comfort of consuming familiar stories.

The Allure of the "Rerun"

By the end of the 1970s, the rerun would become the ideal product of U.S. commercial television. While television stations had, throughout the 1950s, made common practice of airing theatrical motion pictures and shorts (such as *Looney Toons* and *Our Gang*), and even repeating certain telefilm programs such as *Highway Patrol* and *I Led Three Lives*, it wasn't until the mid-1960s that local stations and networks began heavily relying on repeated content to fill their daytime schedules. First-run syndication, or the network production of original programs to be distributed to their affiliates, was very expensive. As an alternative, networks shifted their business model toward acquiring existing properties from independent production companies and distributing those. However, they still maintained an inordinate amount of power over content. According to a 1965 Federal Communications Commission (FCC) study, the networks controlled over ninety percent of the "independently produced" programs they aired. This near monopoly by the networks forced producers into unfavorable business relationships with them. The networks were able to call all the shots—often making content decisions that the producers were forced to abide by if they wanted their shows on the air. So in 1970, the FCC passed two pieces of controversial legislation to mitigate the big three networks' concentration of power. The first was the Prime-Time Access Rule (PTAR), which limited network control of prime time to only three hours, giving local affiliates the chance to produce original programming in the early evening. And the second was the Financial Interest and Syndication Rules (fin-syn), which prevented the big three television networks from owning the shows they aired during prime time. While these rules were intended to shift power away from the networks, Derek Kompare points out that "they fell short of taking down the network system in principle, ultimately sanctioning the growing reliance on repetition, and standardizing the continual reuse of past television as part of the American television experience" (2006, 85).

These rules brought the economic viability of repetition to the foreground. In the 1971–72 season, the first year PTAR was in effect, most network affiliates used the last half of the access period (the newly available slot of prime time between 7 and 8 P.M.) to program reruns of network series. However, because PTAR was set up to force affiliates to produce more local content, there were rules established against airing reruns during this valuable time slot. The FCC gave the affiliates a one-year grace period, but by the next season, the entire hour had to be filled with original programming. This often took the form of newsmagazines or game shows. But while the network affiliates were forced to follow these rules, the local independent stations were not. They began programming reruns to compete against the affiliates, and ultimately ended up on top. It was widely recognized in the industry that the ability to air reruns gave the Independents a stature they had never before enjoyed. According to a trade magazine, "in the ecology of television, the independents discovered endless recycling" (qtd. in Kompare 2006, 89).

The proven commodity of television repetition created a near frenzy around the acquisition of network series. In larger markets with several independent stations, there would often be bidding wars to win the rights to broadcast popular shows. As a result, network producers began selling syndication "futures" to independents. Local independent stations would pay for the right to air network shows years in the future so that they could have a leg up over their competitors. The networks began to realize that the value of a product extended well beyond its original run. In fact, they could often make more money on selling the syndication rights than they could in its first broadcast. By the mid-1970s, when acquiring any series, the networks would consider the potential value of syndication.

The surge in television repetition in the 1970s was the result of industrial and economic changes, but it needs to be seen in conjunction with the cultural transitions more generally. Reruns weren't forced on a viewing public—the viewing public wanted them. While repetition on television in the 1950s and '60s was met with mild disdain, by the 1970s, the shared experience of rehashed televisual memories became an important part of American culture. As Kompare points out, in the 1970s the "past had become as much a part of television as the present" (2006, 103). Television, only a few decades prior, was symbolic of the great American future; by the 1970s, that was still the case, only the great American future was composed largely of the past. John Leonard, the television critic for the *New York Times*, wrote in 1976: "By and large, our children not only watch the same new programs that we watch, but they are scholars of everything that went before, everything we have forgotten or never knew." Older generations no longer had a monopoly on memories. They had to cede control to those who were regularly studying those memories. Leonard compared television's endless replaying of its past to the function of home movies. Afternoon reruns, he says, are "TV's home movies." They are viewed not just for entertainment but also for the experience of recalling what it felt like to be entertained. Television began to breed a nostalgic pattern of viewing, one characterized not simply by a desire for television's past but by a desire for our own past as well, even if we didn't directly experience it. Familiar stories in comforting repetition became definitive of the medium. Kompare suggests that this was the kernel of a newly formed sense of a "television heritage"—one that he sees extending to the emergence of television fan cultures, television studies in academic departments, and perhaps most dramatically, the opening of the Museum of Television and Radio in New York City. The cultural scaffolding that surrounded the rerun served to authenticate the medium and to make its history a part of America's history.

When cable television entered the picture in the late 1970s, the scaffolding would be removed to expose the new permanent structure of syndicated viewing. Cable's many channels introduced thousands of programming hours to the existing broadcast spectrum. In 1979, ESPN was launched as a twenty-four-hour sports channel; in 1980, CNN followed suit with a twenty-four-hour news channel that inevitably relied on repetition; and in 1981, MTV introduced the repetition of short-format music videos. Most exceptionally, the children's cable station Nickelodeon (which was owned by Viacom) launched Nick at Nite in 1985. Nick at Nite was a programming block between the hours of 9 P.M. and 5 A.M. that showed nothing but reruns in order to capture the baby boomer parents of the station's primary demographic. The station capitalized on the growing nostalgia for the 1950s in everything from politics to prime time. With Ronald Reagan evoking his televisual and filmic recollections of the 1950s to promote family values, and prime time sitcoms such as *Happy Days* and *Laverne and Shirley* featuring "wholesome" teen problems, Viacom, with its immense television library, was in a unique position to take advantage of the cultural moment. Nick at Nite succeeded in turning that nostalgia into a mainstream aesthetic of the rerun. Through the repetition of "authentic" '50's sitcoms and by evoking familiar imagery, including '50s-era graphics and anachronistic slogans like "Hello out there from TV Land!" the late night programming block translated the viewing of reruns, which had become commonplace, into a self-reflexive practice. It played into the "scholar" mentality that Leonard described by offering quizzes and contests for viewers to prove their TV trivia acumen.

By the mid-1990s, Nick at Nite was carried by almost every cable company in the country. Viacom expanded on this popularity by launching TV Land in the spring of 1996. TV Land was a twenty-four-hour cable channel devoted exclusively to reruns. But instead of focusing on one particular era, TV Land was an all-purpose rerun clearinghouse, with shows from the 1950s to the 1980s. By this time, the culture of the rerun no longer required significant historical distance to be effective—repetition, in and of itself, began to frame contemporary spectatorship. The repetitive and archival presence of television's past informed each articulation of television's present and future.

The rerun had a profound resonance beyond television. The practice of urban spectatorship that emerged in the 1970s and '80s is consistent with viewing practices more generally. On the heels of the operative city, the rerun became an effective and safe means for the spectator to reengage with an urban landscape from which he had learned to be alienated. This was not the result of simply retreating into a fantastic urban past. However, many critics of historical preservation and neotraditional urban design argue for that position. M. Christine Boyer, in reference to South Street Seaport, claims that "not only is thematized history and geography used to sell everything from posters to fudge, but these consumer items end up as stand-ins for real-life travel and experience" (1992, 216). But by condemning these spaces as regressive ideological constructs, Boyer too readily blurs the logic of the rerun with the presentation of historical fact. The rerun allowed the spectator to reclaim past experiences for present ones, while the presentation of historical fact dictated precisely what those experiences could be. Boyer claims that South Street Seaport was a picture of the past that was so satisfying it dissuaded the spectator from wanting any other experiences. And yet, as far as I know, the repeated engagement with South Street Seaport never made a visitor decide to completely disengage with the present. More likely, it served to *reengage* spectators with the present by offering comforting analogies of past urban experience. Just as the rerun legitimized television by making its past always available, it legitimized the city in the same manner. It created, despite its simplistic terms, a platform for a very active engagement with the present. Indeed, the allure of the rerun was a matter of reclamation.

New Urbanism and the "Rerun" City

Throughout the 1980s, Rouse-style developments became very popular among architects and planners. The repetition of historical memory was profitable.

People flocked to renovated markets, warehouses, and docks to do their shopping and socializing. But it wasn't just any kind of shopping and socializing—these everyday activities were infused with historical justification. The practice of shopping in Faneuil Hall, for instance, was complimented by the familiar narratives of American history, thus transforming the act of shopping into the act of acquiring historical knowledge and reproducing that knowledge. The architectural historian Margaret Crawford describes this as the "principle of adjacent attraction," in which these developments attempted to blur the boundaries of commerce and culture (Crawford 1992, 14). Historical repetition, and by extension cultural articulation, was embedded in commerce. Buying a trinket from a pushcart vendor was a simple economic exchange infused with historic value.

But historical value wasn't enough to justify the costs. Within a decade, the Rouse-style "festival mall" proved to be unsustainable. They weren't the moneymakers they were thought to be. They cost three times as much as conventional shopping centers to build (on a square-foot basis) and they attracted one-third of the consumer spending (Hannigan 1998, 55). Consequently, the rapid growth of festival malls ended—only to be superseded by the suburban mall with its relatively inexpensive construction costs and ability and desire to attract high-paying, high-commitment national chain stores. Even though the festival mall lost favor with developers, the form proved that historical repetition was capable of bringing middle-class consumers back to the city. The desire for the rerun cultivated a new urban spectatorship that brought the viewer into close proximity with the city. Even from the perspective of the spatially separated suburb, spectators wanted to (re)claim the city from a temporally and spatially proximate space that was familiar and intimate. And perhaps most importantly, they wanted the assurance that those narratives were possessable and easily retrievable.

The urban rerun found its most significant expression in a design approach called the New Urbanism, characterized by its focus on walkable, centralized, and thus sustainable communities. One project from the late 1980s, called Seaside, Florida, came to symbolize the tenets of New Urbanism before the movement was officially established years later. Seaside was a completely manufactured community premised on the scale and lifestyle of a nineteenth century town. It was, as Philip Langdon described it in the *Atlantic Monthly*, a harbinger of the "new traditionalism": "By regulation, [it was] a place of wood-shingled, clapboard, and board-and-batten houses with deep front porches and shiny tin roofs like those on old houses in rural America" (1988). Langdon described Seaside as a development that taps into the interest in "vernacular architecture" characterized by Rouse's developments. Andres Duany, one of Seaside's architects, said at a Florida apartment developers conference in 1987, that "the newest idea in planning is the nineteenth-century town. That's what is really selling" (Langdon 1988). Seaside mandated certain architectural and planning elements to evoke the historical town, but it stopped short of re-creating lifestyles. There were no women walking to the general store in bonnets to sell their recently sheared wool, and there were no horses and carriages wandering the brick-laden streets. The historical presentation functioned on the theory that the built environment alone could recreate community behaviors: mixed-use buildings with housing atop storefronts, front porches to cultivate neighborly community, straight streets to foster visual continuity, and centralized resources within walking distance of all residents. The intention of the developer Robert S. Davis, and the husband and wife architectural team Andres Duany and Elizabeth Plater-Zyberk, was to maintain a little "messiness" in the historical presentation so that the town could resist transforming into a theme park or "living museum" of a bygone era. All the houses needed to be individually designed in a fashion Langdon described as "harmonious diversity." Consistency was important, but a distinct variety of styles would add to the space's historical authenticity. History in Seaside was not a finished commodity, the developers proposed; it was a recurring feeling that was manufactured through the process of engaging with everyday life.

This strategy was reproduced in a number of projects throughout the country, from Grand Harbor in Vero Beach, Florida, which was meant to be a Mediterranean village, to the Mashpee Commons on Cape Cod, Massachusetts, which was meant to evoke traditional elements of the New England town. These and other developments attempted to manufacture the memory of experiencing historical towns by guiding social practices through spatial design. They eventually coalesced into a movement in the early 1990s when several architects and planners met at the Ahwahnee Hotel in Yosemite National Park in California to draft a set of principles subsequently known as the Ahwahnee Principles. Authored by Duany and Plater-Zyberk, as well as Peter Calthorpe, Michael Corbett, Elizabeth Moule, and Stefanos Polyzoides, the list of principles established the groundwork for the new traditionalism. It cited the importance of mixed-use development, limiting the size of the community to the jobs and resources available, keeping activities within walking distance, establishing a diversity of housing, range of jobs, transit accessibility, and centralized design. In other words, the "new" in New Urbanism was the reclamation of the old. "It's a return to the notion of connection," said Brian Shea, one of the developers of the CityFront Project in Chicago. "People are looking at making parts of cities that will become extensions of what is familiar" (qtd. in Langdon 1988). There was a consensus among most New Urbanist developers that the proper response to sprawl, pollution, resource exhaustion, and social alienation was already articulated over a century ago. The old logic of town and urban development was capable of responding more effectively to the contemporary crisis than anything planners might concoct today. Todd Bressi explains that New Urbanism "revives principles about building communities that have been virtually ignored for half a century" (1994, xxv).

The New Urbanists evoked community as a naturalized concept, even though it had been in dispute for well over a century. Ferdinand Tönnies, the German sociologist, wrote in the late nineteenth century that community (*Gemeinschaft*) existed in opposition to modern society (*Gesellschaft*). Couched in a modernist nostalgia for premodern values, Tönnies's writing was responding to a profound shift in social life that was brought about by the industrial revolution. With industrialism came social separation, division of labor, and alienation — all contributing to the demise of the traditional agrarian community. The loss of *Gemeinschaft*, for Tönnies, was the inevitable result of a society forcibly jolted in space and time; it was the result of a social structure pushed from an agrarian economy to industrial capitalism. In essence, the New Urbanists were interested in producing a feeling of *Gemeinschaft* — a new urban space formed in opposition to the perceived alienation that accompanied advanced industrialism (1957). Community, in this sense, was a possibility, not an actuality. It was not something to which one could return, but by invoking its mythological origins, one could strive for it.

It is for this reason that the front porch plays so prominently in New Urban developments. Walking by someone's house and saying hello to them as they're sitting on their porch does not itself equal community. But this action is intended to have a metonymic relationship to that concept. In other words, saying hello to someone on a front porch could have meaning well beyond the single practice. It contains a myriad of cultural references that are recalled each time it occurs. By and large, this is how these spaces function. They provide a platform for spectators to *rerun* meaningful experiences (or cultural references) of urban culture. Paul Bray notes that the "binding element of the new urbanism is urban culture, which encompasses the story of human achievements that occurred in urban settings" (1993, 59). What Bray means by urban achievements is more vernacular than extraordinary. The binding elements are things like community engagement and public discourse. One of the central tenets of New Urbanism, as he sees it, is the ability to link new development with existing urban spaces. This can be accomplished by appropriating those spaces into the overall design.

He looks at the example of Lowell, Massachusetts. The entire downtown of this former industrial town—known as the "birthplace of the American industrial revolution"—was designated a state park. "Urban park planning," says Bray, "is the essence of city planning [as] the entire city is viewed through the lens of a park" (58). With a claim similar to those made about the White City, Bray contends that urban park planning "makes for a more legible and livable city." The old textile mills, canals, warehouse buildings, and the nondescript side streets that extend out from the industrial center were regarded as a singular planning unit which could enable a more cohesive engagement than if the city was addressed piecemeal. "When the city is regarded as a park that visibly celebrates urban culture, citizens can better see how the features of the city relate to each other . . . and how people and places fit in the continuum of time" (63). Bray makes the argument that urban park planning is specifically interested in producing a sense of the present, rather than a simplistic sense of the past. He sees the redevelopment of Lowell as being able to inform the contemporary city experience through the evocation of past urban culture.

This concept of urban culture informed the majority of projects built under the label of New Urbanism. However, despite the noble-sounding goals of replenishing public life, in actual practice, many neotraditional developments, including Seaside, came across as trite and simplistic and were therefore subject to intense scrutiny and criticism. They were often seen as nostalgic and inauthentic. Critics characterized the anachronistic solutions to modern problems as counterproductive for urban and community vibrancy as they served only to produce parallel fantasy spaces incapable of affecting larger urban and community trends. The architect and critic Amy Murphy puts it this way: "Instead of allowing tradition(s) to be emergent, simultaneous and contradictory, the New Urbanists seemingly intend to freeze these 'salvaged' purified pasts as safe havens where one can escape the tides of social progress. . . . Although the New Urbanists acknowledge change as an incremental 'process,' their strategies imply that there is a single History which is linear rather than dialectic and relative" (2000, 135). She compares New Urbanist strategies to the "salvage paradigm" in anthropology, where freezing an endangered culture's traditions and customs is seen as a means of saving it from historical erasure. New Urbanists, she claims, are doing the same thing for traditional Eurocentric history and social spaces. They are, with good and misguided intentions, intervening in the steady pace of progress to preserve what would soon be lost. However, just as salvage anthropologists framed traditional cultures within a colonial perspective, so are New Urbanists colonizing historical urbanism, and in effect, placing it behind glass to be consumed in a controlled manner. The dialectic and relative nature of history, she argues, is replaced by a single History that maintains its stability in order to sell real estate.

Murphy's apprehension about New Urbanist strategies addresses the danger of adopting simple solutions to complex problems. And her critique as applied to individual iterations is useful. However, the general trend toward neotraditional urban spaces that emerged in the 1970s, points to a larger phenomenon of the reassimilation of the city into contemporary culture. If understood in the context of the rerun, individual developments can be seen as complicating the general landscape of city presentations that had previously veered toward the distant and operative. Watching a rerun of *Leave it to Beaver*, for instance, doesn't convince the spectator that she is living in the 1950s, it instead provides a counternarrative to her actual historical placement. And most importantly, it situates the persistence of television's past as constitutive of viewing practices in the present. As Heidegger suggests, it opens up possibilities for meaning.

When Repetition Becomes Too Familiar

While not always progressive, the context of the rerun made it comfortable for middle-class spectators to reengage with the city. From the safe, distant perspective of historical repetition, the spectator could explore the possibilities of urban experience and culture that had been overshadowed by the rhetoric of function. The return not only to historical sites but to historical spatial practices and community conceptions revealed a more complex relationship to the city and urban life than had been in place for decades. Urban renewal removed active possession from the organization of the American city. New Urbanism, in the form of the rerun, put it back. Visitors to these developments were encouraged, in the way Leonard described young television viewers, to become "scholars" of the urban past. They could collect references to urban experience and use them to inform encounters with other spaces.

Consider what happened to the sitcom after decades of reruns. *The Simpsons*, in many respects, is a post-sitcom sitcom. The animated series, which debuted in 1989 on the new Fox network, is premised on the spectator having a fairly in-depth understanding of sitcom conventions. The dysfunction of the nuclear suburban family is placed in opposition to the families that had populated most sitcoms. The show also makes constant references to old movies and TV shows, making the knowledge of those references essential to the experience of the show. The sitcom landscape changed considerably in the 1990s, as the suburban family was replaced by different configurations that reflected both the changing society and the typical spectator's saturation with sitcom formats. This would come into remarkable clarity with the 1999 debut of *Family Guy*, also on Fox. The humor of *Family Guy* is largely premised on references to television. The narrative of each episode is interrupted with referential interludes that put the characters in the context of a reimagined televisual past. *Family Guy* is a database of television reruns that engenders an experience of contemporary television as a collection of references to television's past.

As New Urbanism grew in popularity throughout the 1990s, urban developments would begin to take on the character of television shows like *Family Guy*. In other words, the act of referencing became the most meaningful part of the reference. New Urbanism got caught in the middle of its own success. The growing resentment against these developments from scholars and commentators reflected a disdain for what appeared to be simplistic, self-conscious, and nostalgic representations. But the problem was not in the representations of the urban past; it was in the spectator's increased familiarity with them. Reruns so saturated the culture that they became meaningless outside of self-consciously referential tactics. The spectator in the rerun city comfortably possessed these images of the past. The challenge in the coming years for urban designers would be in keeping the city, now composed of proximate repetitions of history, interesting and desirable.

THE DATABASE CITY

The Digital Possessive and Hollywood Boulevard

The development of visual media in the 20th century made photography and movies the most important cultural means of framing urban space, at least until the 1970s. Since then, as the surrealism of King Kong *shifted to that of* Blade Runner *and redevelopment came to focus on consumption activities, the material landscape itself—the buildings, parks and streets—has become the city's most important visual representation.*

SHARON ZUKIN, *The Culture of Cities*

In the summer of 2000 I took a bus tour of Hollywood. I went into the experience with the assumption that the tour would primarily be about the media spaces that make up the city—"this film was shot here and that one was shot there." But what I did not realize was how much emphasis would be placed on photographing and reproducing those media spaces—"if you snap this picture, it'll be the exact scene from the movie," the tour guide repeatedly instructed. The trolley tour departed from the Grauman's (then Mann's) Chinese Theater on Hollywood Boulevard and headed north to Franklin, where we were instructed to photograph the steps of the Hollywood United Methodist Church, where the opening scene of *Sister Act* (1992) was shot. Next, we were taken to the top of Beachwood Canyon, otherwise known as the "best place in the city to photograph the Hollywood sign." The trolley pulled over to the side of the road and the guide instructed the passengers to take a picture. After a few minutes for the photo break, the tour continued. On the corner of Yucca and Ivar we found the "best perspective of the Capital Records building." And with the trolley blocking traffic on Melrose Avenue we were instructed to snap a picture of the Paramount Studios gate. Before arriving back where we started, we drove by the not-yet-finished Hollywood and Highland

FIGURE 7.1.
Babylon Square from D. W. Griffith's *Intolerance* (1916)

development, where we were told about the upcoming photo opportunities. "Right there," the guide said, "will be the place to take the ultimate picture of Hollywood." Interestingly, the guide didn't suggest that one would want to photograph the development; only that one would want to use the development as a staging ground for photographing Hollywood.

The Hollywood and Highland development, which opened in 2001, is an urban entertainment district (UED) built in the heart of Hollywood. It is composed of 635 acres of retail, dining, and entertainment spaces, all structured around a central courtyard, which is a reproduction of Babylon Square, the set

FIGURE 7.2.
The reproduction of the arch from Babylon Square in *Intolerance* is the centerpiece of the Hollywood and Highland development. Photograph by Eric Gordon

of D. W. Griffith's 1916 epic film, *Intolerance* (see figures 7.1 and 7.2). This stage set, both a historical referent and an access point to other historical referents, was designed to be the primary interface to the Concept-city of Hollywood. Looking from Babylon Square to the Hollywood sign "will be the postcard shot for millions of American tourists who flock to Hollywood each year," said David Malmuth, the project's lead developer. "Walking on the Boulevard today you see people craning their necks to find the sign and the best vantage point to photograph it. Hollywood and Highland will not only capture this moment, but create the *true* Hollywood memory" (Press Release 2000).

Of course, this truth is composed of fantasy. The urban sociologist John Hannigan suggests that consumer fantasy is the primary building block of the contemporary UED. They are developments that set out to create "a new kind of consumer who feels 'entitled' to a constant and technologically dazzling level of amusement" (1998, 70). He likens these spaces to what Sharon Zukin calls a theme park: seamless narratives spaces where the surrounding "authentic" urban fabric is downplayed, if not consciously repressed (1995). To be successful, themed spaces need to mask their boundaries by obfuscating the distinction between the fantasy city and the real city that contains it (Baudrillard 1998). For example, New York, New York on the Vegas strip or Hollywood Boulevard at Disney's California Adventure operate as self-sufficient

FIGURE 7.3. Hollywood and Highland courtyard from the reproduction arch. Photograph by Eric Gordon

representations, where all the essential interpretive components are contained within the structures.

But despite the surface level similarities to the theme park, Hollywood and Highland is different. Its narrative is composed by pointing the spectator's attention outside of the development's physical boundaries (see figures 7.3–7.5). It is a representation of Hollywood *in* Hollywood. The city's context defines its content—a point emphasized in the development's press material. Malmuth said that "Hollywood and Highland embodies the same glamour, excitement and emotion in an environment which goes beyond the seeing to the being there" (Press Release 2000). The Mann's Chinese Theater is now, once again, called the Grauman's Chinese Theater in an attempt to rekindle the glamour associated with that space in the 1920s. Even the reconstruction of the set of *Intolerance* is in reference to the historical space of the city—the set existed in Hollywood as a tourist attraction for more than a decade after the film's opening. The spaces of Hollywood and Highland all link outside the development into a database of Hollywood imagery. The difference between a simulacrum like Hollywood Boulevard in Disney's California Adventure and a database space like Hollywood and Highland is that the former claims to be a perfect simulation of the city, while the latter claims to avail its referents to spectators. The former denies access, while the latter grants it.

This is the *database city*—a city with no content other than to grant access to content. Hollywood and Highland, despite its vulgarity, resists the singularity of narrative repetition by providing a platform for spectators to assemble their own narratives. It was built for a spectator who wants to reconnect with the city, but doesn't want to be told precisely how that connection is to take place. This is the same spectator steeped in the language of digital networks and databases who desires a city he can possess and organize into a personalized urban narrative. I call this mode of spectatorship the *digital possessive*—an appropriation of possessive spectatorship that corresponds to everyday navigation patterns of digital landscapes. Possessive spectatorship becomes quite literal in the *digital* possessive as the practices of networked media encourage, if not mandate, the possession of thoughts, actions, and memories in personal folders, accounts, and devices. Just as information online is assembled and ordered in digital aggregators, in the city, material structures, physical spaces, narratives, imagery, and other people are assembled and ordered in urban aggregators—physical spaces built to construct a sense of possession and control over urban experience and history. The example of

HOLLYWOOD
CIGARS
LUCKY STRIKE
LANES

Hollywood and Highland, while extraordinary in some respects, is an archetype of an urban development built to accommodate this spectatorship. What follows is a reflection on the parallel developments of urban and digital spaces — and how the corresponding practices that emerge from each are becoming increasingly difficult to distinguish.

Toward a Digital Possessive

In 2006, *Time* magazine named "You" the person of the year. As part of what the magazine called a "revolution" in networking technology, it described how the new Web is ushering in a culture of participation where users are just as likely to produce as they are to consume. This technological and cultural phenomenon first found a name in 2004 when Tim O'Reilly organized a conference called "Web 2.0." The term has since become the most recognizable designation of new trends. While it remains controversial to many critics (Scholz 2008; Zimmer 2008; Lanier 2006), it has had unquestionable influence in solidifying economic investment in the post-dotcom network landscape. Americans are contributing to wikis, keeping their own blogs, writing reviews for Amazon, keeping their photo albums on Flickr, and making movies to post on YouTube. They are entrusting their most intimate thoughts and records to corporate servers and services. And yet in what *Time* called the "new digital democracy," the consumer holds the power. "You control the media now," reads a headline, "and the world will never be the same" (Grossman 2006, 242). This is a rather strong declaration, especially coming from a major media company with a lot at stake in continuing to control the media.

(opposite)
FIGURE 7.4.
View of the Hollywood sign from the arch. Photograph by Eric Gordon

Time was not alone in this apparent capitulation to the power of the people. In January 2007, CBS announced that users could clip, share, and "mash-up" television content. Companies that once clutched to the control of content with all their might are now saying they want users to "make it their own." Leslie Moonves, the chief executive at CBS, announced his support for this strategy because it gives the network the ability to tap into the passion of dedicated viewers. "If somebody spends the time to take 20 clips from *CSI Miami*, I think that's wonderful," Moonves said, "That only makes him more involved with my show and want to come to CBS on Monday night and watch my show" ("CBS to Let Viewers" 2007). Moonves, along with many other top executives at networks and production companies, are realizing that the rules of the game have changed. There are different tactics involved in being a successful gatekeeper of content. Now, many companies are adopting the

beard papa

strategy of hiding the gate and giving everyone the key. In other words, they're giving users the perception of control while blurring the boundaries between control and consumption.

This transition has been years in the making. After the dotcom bubble burst, the commercialization of the Web continued, but in a more cautious and orderly fashion. The flood of money into new ventures all but dried up as venture capitalists sat back and watched users populate cyberspace. This time, however, they weren't coming for programmed content, as everyone thought they would only a few years earlier; they were coming to do things—chat, hang out, share "cool stuff" (Weinberger 2002). Digital networks were taking on a different character. In 2002, the social networking site Friendster was an overnight success. And with the popularity of MySpace in 2003, Facebook in 2004, and Google's IPO also in 2004, the consumer Web was making a comeback. Of course, when the video sharing site, YouTube, went from start-up in February 2005 to commanding a $1.65 billion purchase price from Google in November 2006, it became quite clear that there was big money in no longer "controlling" the media.

(opposite)
FIGURE 7.5.
Entrance to Hollywood and Highland from Hollywood Boulevard. Photograph by Eric Gordon

While the reverberations of these deals extend to every sector of the American population, they have been most notable with teenagers. According to a study by the Pew Internet and American Life Project, 55 percent of American youth between the ages of twelve and seventeen use online social networking sites (Lenhart and Madden 2007). Because of this trend, companies are focusing on this demographic to demonstrate and alter the norms of online interaction. According to Chris DeWolfe, one of the founders of MySpace, "The Internet generation has grown up, and there are just a lot more people who are comfortable putting their lives online, conversing on the Internet and writing blogs" (Cassidy 2006, 57). The comfort level that users have in putting their lives online is not a natural product of the Internet. Companies like MySpace have normalized the expanding perception of privacy in online public spaces. By giving users personalized access to networks, they have perpetuated the impression of stability and control. Certainly, this phenomenon is much bigger than MySpace alone; most social media platforms employ at least a few possessive adjectives to identify user access points (i.e., *my* page, *my* box, *my* favorites, etc.).

The personalization of online spaces produces user behaviors where marketable details of personal data are exchanged for the convenience of network interaction and consumption. It's not that users are being deceived, but rather that they perceive the conveniences of online acquisition, personalized product suggestions, and the pleasure of "just hanging out" as outweighing the potential threats of data harvesting and surveillance. In the United States, it is much easier for corporations to collect and use personal information than it is for the government. The consumer data collection industry in the United States spends millions lobbying against more restrictive data policies so that the imbalance doesn't change (Dash 2005). This friendly climate toward personal data collection by corporations suggests a willingness to be monitored as long as it results in the convenience and perceived control of consumerism. For instance, just as most major retail outlets monitor consumer habits for future marketing campaigns, consumers have come to expect the resulting convenience of that surveillance. If you want to return something purchased at a different store, you expect the data to be networked; if you lose a receipt, you hope that the store has kept your records. Regardless of the threats that accompany this compromised privacy, the payoffs are much more immediate.

Most users understand that digital actions are recorded and archived. But few have an understanding of the life of those actions. Daniel Solove suggests that privacy concerns that emerge in contemporary digital culture are not simply a matter of total surveillance by a malevolent overseer; instead, they are a matter of data disclosure to "objective" machines. Each user builds for herself a "digital dossier," personal data connected to an IP address or user name that can easily be recalled by a machine. For instance, Amazon's "recommend" feature, or YouTube's personal statistics or private channels, or even automatic forms, are silently customized through everyday use. Microsoft is working on software that could predict the gender, age, occupation, and location of a user by analyzing search histories (Marks 2007). In essence, the machine is watching our every move, recording it, and then playing it back for us. Solove argues that instead of looking to Orwell's *1984* as a descriptive metaphor for digital surveillance, it is more accurate to look to Kafka's *The Trial*. We are being watched, but by whom and for what reason is unclear, even for those doing the watching (2004).

So why are users comfortable with this kind of uncertainty? The answer rests in the suggested transparency of many networked interactions. Personal data, even those with little practical application, are made available to users. For example, Google gives users access to their personal search histories. Even though the same information is shared with marketers, the ability to see it within one's personal (and personalized) interfaces suggests the ability to control it. Through the process of personalization, the conception of one's computer as private receptacle of personal data is extending to the larger network. As Vito Acconci explains, "the electronic age redefines public as a composite of privates" (1990, 914). As a result, users have come to expect access to personal data from multiple computers and multiple devices. Freeing information from spatial constraints has become associated with personal freedom and mobility. Private space is no longer limited to a singular physical location; rather, private space in networks is wherever we happen to be. And network privacy is the manageability of complex information environments through the personalization and adaptability of those environments.

Consider Microsoft's 2007 advertising campaign for its Internet Explorer 7 browser. In the video ad, a man runs through his daily routine: brushing his teeth, buttering toast, and feeding the cat. But instead of using a toothbrush, a knife, and a can opener, his bare hands take on these tasks. He steps outside in his bathrobe to take out the trash and sees a very attractive female mail carrier approaching on a bike. He uses his hands to transform his bathrobe into an ironically "stylish" seersucker suit. He then frames the woman with his hands, snaps an imaginary photograph and pulls a Polaroid from his wrists. The commercial concludes with the caption: "Everyday tasks made easier." Within the always-on culture of network communication, users have become dependent on the technology that enables their access to people and things. Accordingly, Microsoft is not only selling access to the network, it is selling freedom from the anxiety that goes along with being detached from the network. And ultimately, it is selling access to the roving private spaces users have come to expect.

And this goes way beyond Microsoft. As digital networks are being accessed with smaller devices and simpler interfaces, the notion of ubiquitous private space is becoming even more naturalized. Apple's iPhone is a nice illustration of this. The announcement in January 2007 of the multifunction device that operates as a phone, camera, and music player, with all the functionality of the Mac OS, prompted declarations of a paradigm shift from industry leaders. Paul Saffo, a Silicon Valley technology forecaster, commented that "[c]yberspace was a wonderful thing, but the only place you could enter cyberspace from was your desktop. . . . [The iPhone] isn't the next computer. *This is the next home for the mind*. Computers have had a nice long run, and laptops will always play at least some role. But the center of gravity is now slowly shifting from the desk to the device in your pocket" (Calore 2007; italics added). Indeed, as minds move into networks, possessive spectatorship is made quite literal. This is the digital possessive. It implies a different kind of access to the sensations and experiences that compose the world. What once were the invisible traces of social life—browsing, consuming, and talking—have become visible building blocks of digital environments, on par with buildings, streets, and nature. The connective tissue between objects, the searches and networks that assimilate data into meaningful organizations, has itself become the object of engagement. Therefore, the relations between things, those that justified the "radical" in radical empiricism, are no longer radical. Relations have become empirical in the traditional sense. They are fully visible and accessible phenomena for the spectator to assemble in the process of composing her experience of networks.

In describing radical empiricism, the philosopher Richard Mosier suggests that "We have transcended the immediately experienced qualities of things and passed to their relations; and this we can only do if we assume that we are not mere passive spectators separated from reality by a screen of phenomena, but are ourselves active participants in the process itself" (1952, 413). Mosier, writing over fifty years ago, seems to be describing the business model for Web 2.0. The user becomes an active participant in cultural consumption and content, or "the immediately experienced quality of things" is transformed into "relations," or the shared, commented on, and mashed up. Content within networks is never outside of its relations. From movies on YouTube, to pictures on Flickr, to news stories that get posted and analyzed on multiple blogs, to friends in a MySpace network, relations provide the necessary scaffolding for traditional content. Consider the life of a typical news story. The *New York Times* publishes an article: it gets bookmarked, blogged, and clipped, and in no time, a context of interpretation is built around it. In many cases, users encounter reactions before they encounter the catalyst. Mosier explains that cultural discourse has long followed this pattern: "the world as directly experienced becomes a qualitatively unique and plural world of things in interaction" (1952, 414). But digital networks increase the extent to which this plurality is observable.

The digital possessive is the network manifestation of radical empiricism. It can be described in two parts. It is the transformation of relation into observable and lasting objects: in digital networks, relations are material. And it is the ordering of those objects within personal interfaces. For example, at any given moment, a MySpace page is the externalization of the subjectivity of the user (boyd 2006). It is where objects, broadly conceived, are organized into comprehensible experiences. To be clear, this externalization does not replace the experiencing subject; it only extends the processes of experience into networks.

Indeed, the need to order relations should be considered a product of modernity, rather than a product of the Internet. As I have been arguing throughout this book, the impulse to order and possess has been central to urban spectatorship since the end of the nineteenth century. But thus far, outside of setting crowds at a distance from the individual, urban spectatorship has largely been concerned with ordering and possessing the appearances of the built environment. Digital social media have extended that process to include other individuals, in a way similar to how Marcel Proust describes the social personality:

> Even in the most insignificant details of our daily life, none of us can be said to constitute a material whole, which is identical for everyone, and need only be turned up like a page in an account-book or the record of a will; our social personality is a creation of the thoughts of other people. Even the simple act which we describe as 'seeing someone we know' is to some extent an intellectual process. We pack the physical outline of the person we see with all the notions we have already formed about him, and in the total picture of him which we compose in our minds those notions have certainly the principal place. (1989, 20)

Well before the Internet made it possible to plot one's personal thoughts and physical navigations, the social need to order was apparent. Speaking of a social personality that is composed of tiny bits of information stored in the minds of the multitude of people we come across, Proust asserts that an objective self is impossible. It does not exist; it is assembled again and again in every context. Thus, "seeing someone we know" is a complex process whereby we aggregate memories and impressions into a singular experience. Imagine if those impressions, for Proust merely relegated to the minds of observers, were externalized and uniformly available. Imagine if one's private thoughts as well as public actions could compose the impressions on which others relied to assemble your social personality.

Digital social networking is ostensibly transforming the social personality as such. Instead of relying on the whimsy of others, users can manufacture their own data to be ordered by others, and likewise, they can obtain greater control in ordering the data of people and places with which they come into contact. But these external processes require maintenance. As every personal action leaves a data trace, what once was only a fleeting sensation to be immediately experienced by another subject is now materialized into the network to be ordered by human and machine. From reading to driving to dating, data, even if not always accessed, is always accessible. As a result, the ordering of the "plural world of things in interaction" has become the primary task of network spectatorship. This is reminiscent of Martin Heidegger's understanding of modern technology, where instrumental ordering converts the objects and activities of experience into what he calls "standing reserve," a process through which "everywhere everything is ordered to stand by to be immediately on hand, indeed to stand there just so that it may be on call for a further ordering" (1993, 220). My-oriented spaces, ready to hand and organized to suit the spectator's needs, constitute an entry point to this "standing reserve." Within these spaces, data, including personal data, is "on call" and can be ordered and reordered in line with emerging interests and needs. Now that personal search histories are ready to hand, it is just as much a part of one's orderable world as a favorite movie or favorite song. Heidegger makes clear that this process of converting experience into data implies a double loss: (formerly) stable subjects not only become alienated from objects in the world —which are being converted into "objects-for-personal-use"—they also become alienated from themselves. The human subject, according to Heidegger, "in the midst of objectlessness is nothing but the orderer of the standing reserve. . . . [H]e comes to the point where he himself will have to be taken as standing-reserve" (1993, 220).

Heidegger's rather bleak formulation of technological subjectivity would seem to be manifested in every act of network consumption, "producing not docile subjects," argues Drew Hemment, "so much as better consumers" (2004). Each act of consumption is premised on the ability to access a seemingly infinite dataset of images and references, while having the impression of being able to assemble that dataset to meet the immediate needs of experience. And as digital social media have effectively blended the details of user experiences with the details of urban history, the complex composition of urban space, once relegated to individual interpretation, is now both collectively composed and composed from the data traces of the collective.

The Database City

As people enter Hollywood and Highland from Hollywood Boulevard, the first thing they see is the Hollywood Walk of Fame—a renewal effort in its own right that started in 1960.[1] With over two thousand names etched into the city's sidewalk, a walk down the boulevard is already an interactive experience. One is literally reading the street and making connections between it and familiar cultural texts. The already established walk of fame functions as a kind of gateway into the complex. Unlike a mall, Hollywood and Highland has an expansive and quite dramatic connection to the boulevard — a large, spectacular staircase spans the distance from the courtyard to the street, encouraging visual and physical connection to the surrounding city.

Once the walk of fame ends at the limit of the boulevard's sidewalk, another sidewalk text immediately begins. This one is a public art project by the satirist Erika Rothenberg entitled *The Road to Hollywood* (see figure 7.6). The artwork contains forty-nine stories of how different people in the entertainment business came to Hollywood. Gathered from interviews, books, oral histories, and articles, Rothenberg assembled brief sound bites from Hollywood actors, directors, musicians, and others, and sprinkled them within a red road that spirals throughout the complex. To enhance the mystique of the quotes, they are all anonymous. One of them reads as follows:

> I parked my car in front of each movie studio, posed, and waited to be discovered. That never happened, but eventually I got a manager. He turned me into a movie star.
>
> — Actor

And another:

> I drove out from Missouri with my luggage piled up to the back of my head and all the way to the top on the passenger side. I couldn't see behind me, but I was heading west, and that's all I needed to see.
>
> — Movie Star

The road ends on Highland Boulevard at an oversized chaise lounge made of glass-reinforced concrete over a steel frame. Visitors can sit on the lounge and take their pictures with the Hollywood sign in the background.

Rothenberg's piece can be read in a number of different ways. For many of the tourists who visit the site, the road is read as a straight, rather sincere documentation of the Hollywood dream. They seem to consume the individual stories with an ardent excitement and conclude their experience with what seems an unironic photo opportunity in front of the Hollywood sign. However, it is not difficult to imagine that the piece can also be read as a satire — a

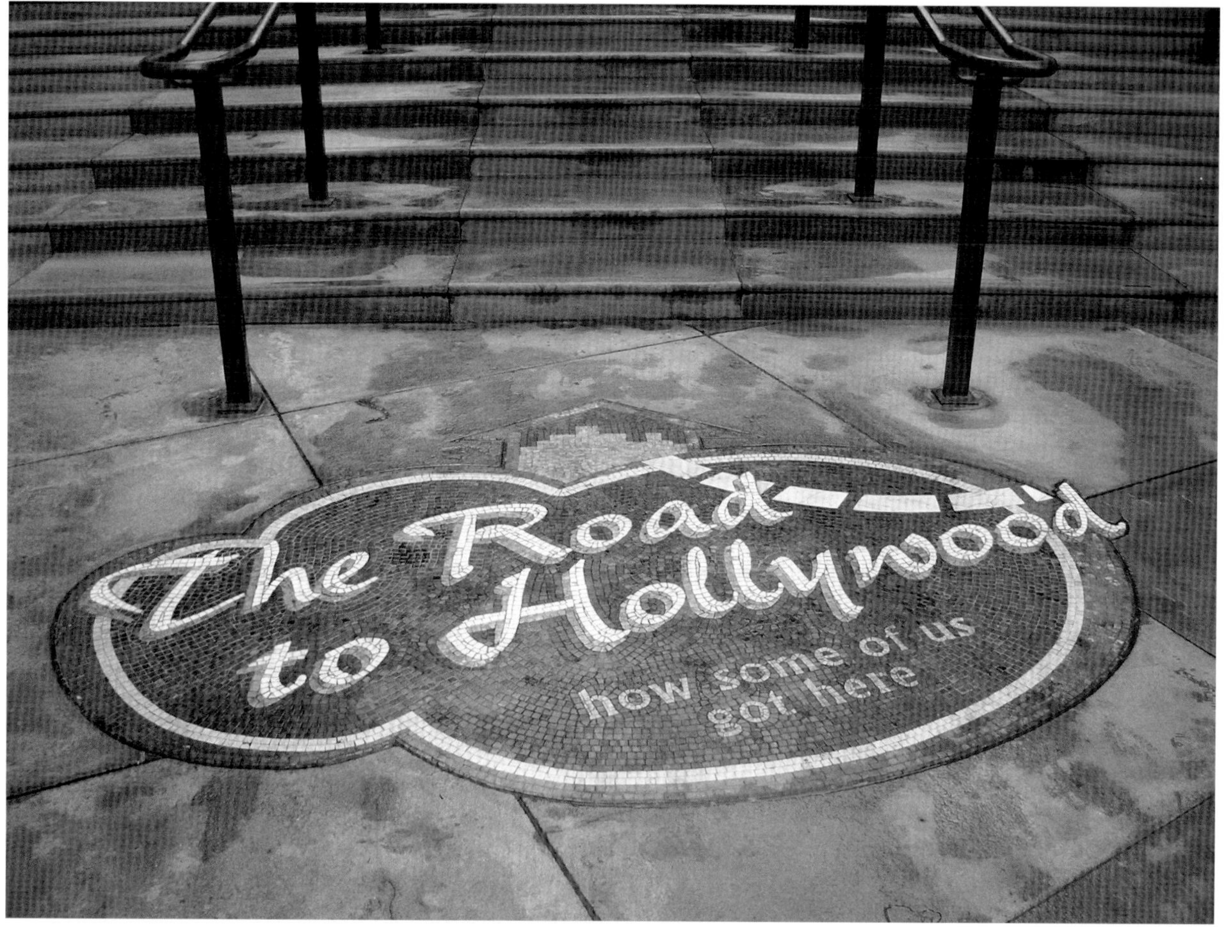

FIGURE 7.6.
Erika Rothenberg, *The Road to Hollywood*, 2001; this "road" winds through the Babylon Square in Hollywood and Highland. Photograph by Eric Gordon

series of understated stories from anonymous people spread along a red carpet to a big glass casting couch. In other words, along the road to success, there is only fantasy with the inevitable result of exploitation. In either case, the road serves as an interactive narrative of the stereotypes and mythologies of Hollywood. Whether one reads it ironically or sincerely (or both), the text passages are search strings within the broader database of the city.

Once one arrives in the central courtyard, it is impossible to miss the replica of the set of D. W. Griffith's *Intolerance*. The set piece, as I mentioned earlier, is significant to the city's history on a number of levels. For quite a while it held the distinction of being the largest, most expensive set ever built. In addition, the stage set remained in Hollywood on the corner of Hollywood and Sunset and served as a tourist attraction for years after the film had wrapped. Its connection to both the soft city of the cinema and the hard city of architecture make it an apt metaphor for the new Hollywood. Whether or not one is knowledgeable of these histories does not preempt a user from experiencing the space in the intended way, because the possibilities of its interpretation are built into the database.

Interacting with the Database

If in the middle of the twentieth century, the promise of machine intelligence was the self-sufficiency of the machine and its ability to interact with the world of humans, interactivity, as it is now understood, is more aligned with the user's ability to interact with the world through machines. While this might not seem like such a dramatic departure, it has wide-reaching rhetorical effects: interactivity now represents our ability to transcend the machine—to use it to enhance human experience, as opposed to using human experience to enhance the machine.

Interactivity has become a defining feature of digital media. And yet there is no agreement as to the meaning of that feature. Many theorists and artists have invoked interactivity as the liberator of consciousness from linear narrative and passive consumerism (Landow 1991), while many corporations have appropriated interactivity as a means of focusing narrative and enhancing commodity consumption. Interactivity, therefore, does not necessarily equal a greater degree of freedom in narrative interpretation—it does, however, equal an enhanced perception of this freedom. Janet H. Murray, in her book *Hamlet on the Holodeck*, suggests that two complementary forces define interactivity: procedure and participation (1997, 72). "Authorship in electronic media is procedural," she says. "Procedural authorship means writing the rules by which the text appears as well as writing the text themselves" (1997, 152). In other words, a sense of authorship, or participation, in digital media is not simply premised on the creation of content but on the way in which that content presents itself. Participation, according to Murray, is the ability for a user to at least have the impression of having an effect on the text.

Murray focuses on the beginning of the interactive computer game phenomenon, with "role playing" adventures like *Zork* that were designed in the 1980s. In this realm, she admits, all that could be expected was an *interactivity-effect*, as the technology was not yet available for "high latency" interaction in which the user could actually change the programmed environment (Meadows 2003). Today, interactivity has become the chief motivator for media spectatorship. For instance, many graphical Web ads require some interaction from the user. An ad for Classmates.com prods the user to complete the sentence, "I graduated in:" by clicking on one of many options. Each takes the user to the same page, but the invitation to interact opens the visual representation to new possibilities. Or consider the near ubiquitous Google AdSense (and its imitators): an advertising model where messages are delivered in accordance with Internet search. So when I do a search for "Hollywood," I receive ads for everything from Queen Latifah to the Renaissance Hollywood Hotel and Spa. Tied into context, these ads born of database interaction are more relevant (at least in perception) to my immediate desires. But it doesn't stop with advertisements. News sites such as CNN.com consistently feature opinion polls about the news of the day as a means of inviting participation. And most market sites such as Amazon.com and Target.com appropriate user reviews into their format. The benefit to these companies is less the value of the content provided by users and more the seduction of interactivity to compel users to stay.

As the Web has changed the audience's ability to interact with content, the "old" media are trying to adapt (Bolter and Grusin 1999). Most new television game shows have an "audience version" where people can call or text in to "play at home." *American Idol* has perhaps been the most successful at this, giving the television audience an opportunity to vote for the winner by dialing a phone number. Websites for television narratives offer episode recaps, discussion forums, and games to extend the text beyond the allotted broadcast time. Movies, too, commonly offer games, forums, character profiles, and other small content areas with which users can interact. While these sites extend existing content, the content is not their most important attribute. Interaction has, itself, become the content of the media — a self-perpetuating system, as each interaction expands the size of the database.

Database Narrative

To further explore what I mean by the database city, I turn to a discussion of a DVD-ROM produced by the Labyrinth Project, entitled *Bleeding Through: Layers of Los Angeles, 1920–1986* (Klein 2003). This visual piece uniquely illustrates the complex interactions between urban practices and the Concept-city in a database environment (see figure 7.7). Appropriately, the producer, Marsha Kinder, characterizes the project as a database narrative — something she defines as a narrative, "whose structure exposes or thematizes the dual processes of selection and combination that lie at the heart of all stories and that are crucial to language: the selection of particular data (characters, images, sounds, events) from a series of databases or paradigms, which are then combined to form specific tales" (2002, 6). Every aspect of the narrative's unfolding is theorized within this framework. It explores the story of a real-life woman named Molly and her memory of sixty-six years of life in Los Angeles. It's a murder mystery, or rather a mystery about things that disappear, whether it is a human being or the city around her. But ultimately the things that go missing are all the inevitable casualties of narrative.

Bleeding Through is a work of fiction. It's also a work of urban documentary. Each bleeds through to the other, leaving only a database of information and images. Conceived as story and archive, the inner workings of the database illuminate the dual processes of narrative and cultural context. The narrative is divided into three tiers. In the first tier of the project, the cultural critic Norman Klein, positioned in a little window in the upper right portion of the screen, recites Molly's story. The story is divided into seven chapters, each representing a major time period in her life. The user can move about these chapters in any order she chooses, effectively constructing the sequence of the narrative. But as becomes clear within the first moments of engaging with the project, the story itself, like all stories, is just the beginning. While Klein talks, the user glides through a number of sequences of images, all loosely related to the narrative, but none directly so. The images—some of old buildings from Bunker Hill, some of now defunct Los Angeles nightclubs, and others of domestic interiors—are related memories. They don't fill in the gaps left by the narrative; they don't complete a thing, but instead supply the context for storytelling. As Molly's story is reduced to a linear narrative through Klein's narration, her life—all the things that might have composed her perceptions and memories—is brought to the front. We quickly realize the limitations of biography as we search through its details—entranced by all those scraggly components unwilling to get into narrative line. The images hang onto the story, but because we have freedom to peruse them at our own pace, they take on a life of their own; they form a narrative of their own.

Some of the images are clips from movies, further fictionalizing the details that compose Molly's past. Still others are what the producers call "bleed throughs." These image compositions are archival pictures of downtown Los Angeles coupled with modern pictures taken from the exact same location. A

FIGURE 7.7.
Composite image of *Bleeding Through: Layers of Los Angeles.* Courtesy of the Labyrinth Project

slide bar beneath the image allows the user to move from old to new and back again, fully illustrating the city's erasures and the sometimes dire manipulations of personal memory. These compositions expose the process of remembering, sometimes filled with sadness as we realize what's no longer there, and sometimes with comfort as we authenticate the past with our gaze. In these images, the workings of the database are unveiled; as the past bleeds through to the present, we are given the impression of access; the archive promises to flesh out experience.

These images can, by themselves, support some kind of narrative structure. Molly's story, as told by Klein, is by no means the central aspect of the experience. The user can actually choose to turn off the commentary and just navigate the database, further highlighting the tenuous nature of narrative within the DVD. In the novella that accompanies the DVD, Klein writes Molly's story in a linear fashion, but questions his own position as narrator. He distances himself from the novella's authorship by citing his own name in the third person and suggesting that the narrator, in fact, doesn't exist.

> Of course, first, I must tell you that I do not quite exist—that is, in the a priori sense. I am contingent, an invention of Norman Klein. He and I mostly coexist on the page, but once you close the book, not much of me will be following you into the DVD-ROM. I am the opening act, so to speak. But I have been doing my homework. I believe I have found a program that allows me to function as a ghost inside the DVD-ROM. . . . So if while operating the DVD-ROM you sense another presence breathing down your neck, it will most likely be me. (Klein 2003, 42)

Klein is here referring to the first person perspective of the novella as narrative itself. In the DVD, he implies, there is no linear narrative to guide the user through. She will inevitably construct the narrative through the materials given to her, but it will not be an overwhelming presence. *Bleeding Through* deemphasizes the master narrative within the overall experience. The user moves through the DVD in expectation of narrative moments, but learns quickly not to rely on them. What might be "breathing down your neck" while navigating the DVD is that glimmer of narrative, a fulfilled expectation that is quickly taken away and replaced by the equally compelling drive to search and interact.

In the project's two additional tiers, the story, and Molly's life, grows deeper. The second and third tiers bring together archival material both related and unrelated to Molly. In the second tier, we are given access to the process of historical writing, seeing for ourselves how documents turn into plot and movies turn into flourishes. Klein delivers a bit more background on Molly, but for the most part, the user gets the opportunity to backwards engineer her story. The third tier is composed of all the things Molly never mentions, but are influential nonetheless: politics, the bevy of movie murders committed in her general vicinity, even maps. Interviews with Japanese Americans talking about internment, Los Angeles residents talking about race relations, and clippings from newspapers are just some of the materials to navigate through. Taken alone, they construct elements of a narrative, that hook on to which we always latch, the second we feel it "breathing down our neck."

Bleeding Through provides a means to visualize that tension between personal control and narrative structure that exists in the city. But the question remains: what is the motivation for users to interact with this text when it requires such sustained engagement? Espen Aarseth provides some insight into this by defining these sorts of texts as *ergodic*. The term is borrowed from physics and is derived from the two words *ergon* and *hodos*, meaning "work" and "path." Aarseth argues for the distinction between traditional texts and what he calls cybertexts, which for our purposes here can be correlated to the database narrative. In a cybertext, he argues, narrative meaning is constructed through the "work" of the user. Whereas in a traditional text, the "reader, however strongly engaged in the unfolding of a narrative, is powerless. Like a spectator at a soccer game, he may speculate, conjecture, extrapolate, even shout abuse, but he is not a player" (1997, 4). The reader of a cybertext, conversely, is a player—with all the problems that accompany that distinction. On this topic, it is useful to quote Aarseth in length:

> The cybertext puts its would-be reader at risk: the risk of rejection. The effort and energy demanded by the cybertext of its reader raise the stakes of interpretation to those of intervention. Trying to know a cybertext is an investment of personal improvisation that can result in either intimacy or failure. The tensions at work in a cybertext, while not incompatible with those of narrative desire, are also something more: a struggle not merely for interpretative insight but also for narrative control: "I want this text to tell my story; the story that could not be without me." In some cases this is literally true. In other cases, perhaps most, the sense of individual outcome is illusory, but nevertheless the aspect of coercion and manipulation is real. (1997, 4)

As one engages in urban practices within the database city, the presence of the database provides incentive to interact—it makes the spectator a player. A successful development communicates from the outset that outcomes of walking through the space are never entirely predetermined—they are dependent upon the user's engagement with references and her willingness to control the

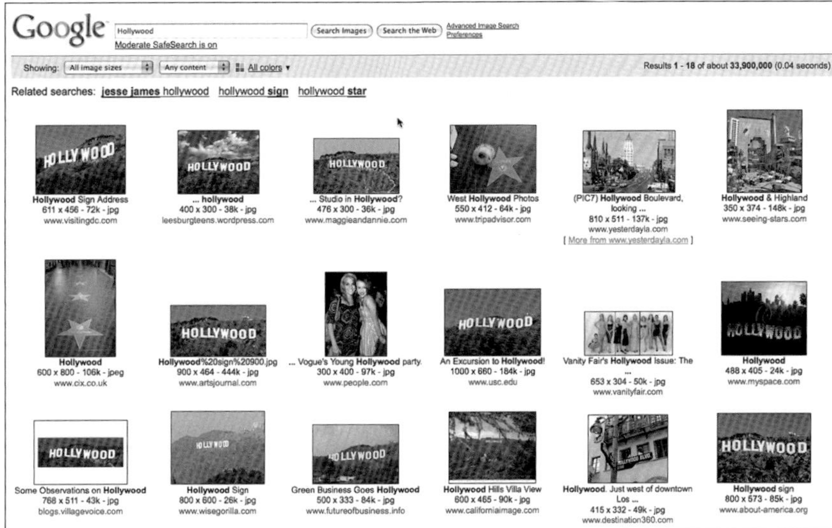

FIGURE 7.8.
Google image search for "Hollywood," February 14, 2008.

space's unfolding narrative to accommodate immediate desires. While "individual outcome" is almost certainly illusory, the impression of that outcome is one of the main rhetorical goals of the database city.

Composing the Database

It we accept that the presence of the database influences urban practices, it is important to scrutinize just how the database is composed and ultimately integrated into the city. To this end, I look to the most common database interaction—Internet search. When I type the word "Hollywood" in Google's image search, a seemingly endless stream of pictures is retrieved (see figure 7.8): everything from the Hollywood sign to that famous picture of William Faulkner lounging poolside to a postcard shot of the Capitol Records building. These pictures have an obvious connection to the city. They each represent a Hollywood icon. With some of the results, however, the connection isn't so clear. An image of a dog named Hollywood and a roadside diner in the Midwest graces page 19 of the search. A studio executive and a drawing of dinosaurs are on page 26. While these images don't seem to be immediately relevant, their inclusion in the list is determined most likely by something to which they're linked. Google crawls through every available website and retrieves relevant images based on the frequency and quality of links to and from the image. The set of images is not displayed in alphabetical order; rather, it is

displayed in the order of their PageRank, which is an algorithm designed to determine the relevancy of the results. Essentially, it determines how well a particular link is cited throughout the Web; the logic is that a page hyperlinked to many other pages is probably worth looking at. Put another way, PageRank is the probability that a random surfer will visit a particular page. Regardless of the relative obscurity of some of the 1.5 million pictures that constitute the results of my search, taken as a whole, these pictures mark the existence of an important representational device: *the database image*.

In using Google, the user is able to transform any word or phrase into a collection of images. At the time of this writing, "Los Angeles" is rendered in 48.8 million image files and "New York" in 61.1 million image files. While it is difficult to imagine a situation in which one would view all of these images simultaneously or take them all to compose a particular meaning, the very existence of these datasets, constantly expanding with the scale of the Internet (these numbers have grown threefold in the course of a single year), produces a particular relationship between the user and the image. When I perform a Google search, the single image with which I interact is always in the context of all similarly classified images online. This relationship might be described as paradigmatic. In Ferdinand de Saussure's view, words are always situated within two simultaneous contexts: the syntagmatic and the paradigmatic (1986). The syntagmatic is the relationship between words in any given sentence and the paradigmatic is the relationship between words in abstract categories: like nouns, verbs, adjectives, and so on. In this sense, just as my use of a noun in a sentence is informed by its status as a noun, my engagement with any given image online is informed by the set in which it is found. It exists within a database image—an image that is the whole of any particular paradigm.

But according to media theorist Lev Manovich, new media have forced a change in de Saussure's linguistic model. For de Saussure, the syntagm implies presence, in that words are brought together either verbally or textually; and the paradigm, appropriately, implies absence, in that relations exist only within the minds of the speaker or writer. Film theorists, like Christian Metz (1974), have taken up this model to explain the semiotics of narrative—an approach that became the foundation of structural film theory. But Manovich suggests that new media have reversed these semiological categories. "Database (the paradigm) is given material existence, while narrative (the syntagm) is dematerialized. Paradigm is privileged, syntagm is downplayed. Paradigm is real; syntagm, virtual" (2001, 231). The dataset, not the narrative, according to Manovich, is the primary means through which meaning is made in contemporary new media. He goes on to say that "regardless of whether new media objects present themselves as linear narratives, interactive narratives, databases or something else, underneath, on the level of material organization, they are all databases" (2001, 228).

Underneath every representation is a database image—the correlated search results to any particular query. "Hollywood" provides a database image; "Love" provides another. These too-big-to-be-comprehended images are the assumed backbone of every representation. Each act of possession or organization within digital networks presumes an interaction with a database image. David Weinberger (2007) refers to the possibility of this interaction as the third order of order. While the first is the organization of things themselves, and the second is the organization of things into categories (the Dewey decimal system, for instance), the third, enabled by digital media and without physical restrictions, makes it possible for each bit of datum to serve multiple functions and occupy multiple places. A table is a type of furniture; it is also a wood product, perhaps a chair (if it's low), an object for lamps to sit on, and a place to eat dinner. The table does not have to exist in only a single category because of the limitations of library subject headings, or traditional encyclopedias; in the third order of order the table can be all of those things at once. In Weinberger's language, it is miscellaneous. It doesn't need to be limited to a single category, because it can (and should) occupy multiple categories. The same is true with the database image: each of the 1.5 million images that form my Hollywood image search can just as easily be found in other searches.

The flexibility of the database image is the founding principle of the digital possessive. Spectators have come to rely on this apparent freedom of personal and social consumption. To elaborate on that point, I turn to the microblogging service Twitter. The concept is simple: users have a maximum 140 characters to continually answer the question "what are you doing?" The answers, which originate as text messages or Web entries, range from the ordinary ("feeding the cat") to the extraordinary ("just witnessed a mugging on Market Street"). Or, on May 15, 2007, at 9:04 A.M. EDT, I wrote: "writing about Twitter." In essence, Twitter is a platform for the accumulation of life annotations, for personal, community, and public consumption. It allows users to choose their broadcast range—making annotations available only to those they've designated as Twitter friends, or to the world via the public timeline (which is a constantly refreshed stream from every user who opts in). The result is a pile of miscellaneous information made visible so that it might be ordered for meaningful consumption. As such, it provides new incentive to publicize personal ordering. When you're wandering down the street and happen upon a café to which you've never been but would love to try some time, while once it was only possible to pull out a piece of paper from your pocket, which you would undoubtedly lose, and write it down, now it is possible to send a text message to Twitter.com, which will immediately notify your friends (and perhaps the general public) about your discovery. The scrap of paper as a tool for impulsive annotations is quickly losing its place in the hierarchy of personal ordering tools. Consider the impression that if something doesn't exist on the Web it doesn't exist, or if a restaurant doesn't have a website, it might not be worth trying. Those assumptions, which have long been accepted for the world out there, are becoming more accepted in the personal realm. If a thought isn't documented, or if the note about that café doesn't make it to a computer or social network, it might fall outside the realm of possibilities. Ironically, the more complete the ordering process becomes, the more data that gets lost. As search results are thought to contain everything relevant; users are less likely to pursue things that fall outside of them. How many people, after doing a couple of searches on Google, go to the phone book to make sure they didn't miss anything?

In this regard, because Twitter traffics in the quotidian, it creates the impression of presence. These are not just the fantastic moments of someone's life, or the weighty thoughts of a blogger, this is the everyday, and it would appear that little is left out. Reading updates from "friends" is not like talking to them, but more like hanging out with them as they take notes about their life. Like a voice-mail away message, Twitter allows people to communicate only that they are doing or thinking something at some point. The motivation to participate in such a thing is a mutual reassurance of presence — it allows users to communicate that they are communicating.

Meaningful interactions within Twitter are only possible through aggregation. Individual users do this by "following" people or groups. Integrated with other platforms like Facebook, one can even follow multiple streams at once, aggregating the everyday lives of other people into the personally assembled interface of their own. Or the database can be assembled using other search strings all together. When Twitter is connected to a Google map, like on Twittervision (http://twittervision.com), the individual "tweets" (as they are called by users), are ordered by their location. The view of this map of the world automatically moves to follow the live stream of individual tweets as they appear in their location of origin. For example, on May 16, 2007, at 4:20 EDT the following tweets appeared. "Testing out this new Twitter Widget that came with the Wordpress update," from Indianapolis. "Lunch was good . . . but now everything on or around me stinks of garlic. I can't wash the garlic off! I need more wet wipes! Ahhhhhh!" from Redmond, Washington. "E non vi racconta . . . ma ci son delle sorprese :P; aggiunge Black, Twitter glielo ha permesso, non è andato down," from Sicily, Italy. "Train + Rain = :(" from Baltimore. It is a touristic experience, where the "standing reserve" of networked individuals comes to represent geographic space.

FIGURE 7.9.
Downtown Boston in Google Earth, February 14, 2008.

While Twittervision provides a global perspective, Twittermap (http://twittermap.com), another Google mash-up with Twitter, localizes that perspective to the city level. With the ability to search by place, users can visualize a city as a collection of recent tweets. One May afternoon in Boston, I came across the following notations: "As a tall person, it annoys me when, given the choice between high and low, a short person chooses the high urinal," and "when did it get this hot . . . I've been trapped inside an old federal building all day with AC that blows." These comments have nothing in common except that they came from Boston. And, in the third order of order, they compose the database image of the city. Like an away message for the city of Boston, these comments, aggregated by a Google map, present the city as the ongoing activity of the people who live within it. The mundane thoughts of users, when associated by location, become meaningful by virtue of their categorization.

Geobrowsers, like Google Earth or Microsoft's Virtual Earth, highlight this point (see figure 7.9). Providing more flexibility than Web-based mapping applications, these tools provide users an impressive ability to manipulate and fly through the planet from a global view to a street perspective. They are geographically oriented visual search engines. What Google calls "placemarks" are user-generated points that include textual information, pictures, and weblinks. Place-specific wikipedia entries are plotted on the map (as they are in the Web-based Google Maps as well), and three-dimensional models created by Google's Sketch-up software can also be displayed. All annotations are displayed in conjunction with user searches: for instance, if I search for coffee and Boston, the camera automatically zooms down to the city level and populates my view with literally hundreds of dots, representing everything from Starbucks to local coffee shops. All elements can be toggled on and off; the city is manufactured in an instant, organized around very specific search criteria. Google Earth is part of that company's strategy to make the world searchable. It provides the framework for visualization, and users create the content. It is well understood among user communities that the use value of any network is directly proportional to the data available for aggregation. Google Earth provides such an engaging platform that users have invested time and energy into populating it, thus producing the most comprehensive geographical aggregator to date.

Google Earth, along with Twitter and other similar systems, is symptomatic of an emerging spectatorship that gives unprecedented leeway to the user to determine the parameters of the city. And as most digital social networking is accessible via mobile phone, these parameters can be set while physically located in the urban context. Pictures from a mobile phone can be immediately uploaded to Google Earth or Flickr, complete with geographic data; blog entries can be sent via SMS messages, and of course Twitter can be updated that way as well. The city is framework, never subject; scaffolding, never structure; digital mapping and mobile networking use the city as an interface through which data can be accessed. And as data proliferates and is accessible from wherever we are, ordering that data into meaningful categories to inform encounters with people, places, and things has come to define the city. The sheer amount of data that needs to be ordered and the number of users now doing the ordering has considerably altered how spectators interact with the Concept-city. The city can be assembled at any time, and in any context, to construct an impression or narrative. And while one can still engage in unmediated physical space, the city presents itself as data excess, bursting its bonds with dialogue, notes, opportunities, historical references, and other people.

Selling the Database

So how does this play out in the physical space of the city? While not explicitly stated, it is commonly understood among developers that providing access to the above-described excess is what makes the city sustainable. This means that the two most important pieces of any urban production are the mechanism to produce a constant supply of data and a platform from which the spectator can access it. With these pieces comes an understanding that the crowd is data, the landscape is data: if the city is a database, then all of its components must become datasets. And the function of an urban development must be directed toward granting access to that data. The reason that Hollywood and Highland is such an intriguing example of the database city is that, even before the proliferation of Web 2.0 technologies, it was built with this functionality. It is both media producer and aggregator. With every movie premiere, every broadcast, every representation of the city, the database image, or the material to which the hyperlinks connect, expands.

Consider the Kodak Theater. Located within the Hollywood and Highland complex, the 136,000 square-foot, 3,300 seat theater is the new permanent home of the Academy Awards. It is equipped with accommodations for a 1,500-person press corps, setting for the Governors' Ball in the adjacent five-star hotel, and a staging area to choreograph the gala arrival of the guests. The grand design of the theater is based on the structure's media accessibility. As evidenced in the theater's "media cockpit," the space is designed for broadcast. The media cockpit is an enclosed platform on a moveable lift directly above the orchestra pit. During live broadcasts, it is the technical heart of the production, containing Steadicams and specially constructed small crane-mounted cameras, so as to make every corner of the complex photographable. The entire theater is wired throughout to handle multiple transmissions and is flexible enough to be adapted for future technological advances.

The theater is literally a media space, conceived with the intention of its representation. According to the theater's press release, "it will tell the story of the legend and lore of Hollywood while looking forward to the future" (*Live Broadcast Theater* 2000). This story will be told not in the traditional architectural sense, but as an edited and interactive space. The theater is essentially the producer of new images that eventually filter back into the overall space of Hollywood and Highland. It's like an in-house content provider for the constantly expanding database of Hollywood imagery. And with each broadcast of the Academy Awards—"live from Hollywood and Highland"—more imagery filters directly into the historical foundation of the city.

The database image is complex. Likewise, the database city is not a pastiche or a schizophrenic collection of unrelated surfaces. As Frederic Jameson declares in his essay on postmodernism, "depth is replaced by surface, or by multiple surfaces (what is often called intertextuality is in that sense no longer a matter of depth)" (2001, 559). In the database city, the user is not lost to an avalanche of signifiers; she is given the authority, motivation, and framework to filter them. So while the database becomes surface, the interaction with the database becomes depth. The individual representations in the structure are not directly correlated to a specific meaning, but instead grant access to a

DEPARTMENT
OF
WATER
AND
POWER
LACityTours.com

multitude of representations and meanings. Representations are transformed from objects into tools. So what's to be learned from the commercial manifestation of the contemporary city is not some perfect image of urbanism to be emulated, but a significant structural transformation in the Concept-city. Despite the fact that Hollywood and Highland began as a commercial disappointment, with Trizec unloading the property to the CIM Group at a significant loss for $201 million in March 2004, the development continues to be relevant in the rapid transformation of Hollywood. Hollywood and Highland has functioned as a catalyst for development throughout Hollywood, not simply by bringing economic opportunity to the area but by granting access to the long dormant database.

(opposite)
FIGURE 7.10.
View of Hollywood and downtown from the top floor of Hollywood and Highland. Photograph by Eric Gordon

Toward a Database Urbanism

Since Hollywood and Highland opened, the surrounding area has gone through significant changes. There are five major commercial/retail projects and over twenty-five residential and mixed-use projects currently completed or under construction within a two-mile radius. The majority of these developments are conceived around the renovation of historical structures. The Hollywood Passage project on the 5500 block of Hollywood Boulevard includes the rehabilitation of two existing buildings, including the Louis B. Mayer Building and the Bricker Building. There is a large event space and over 250 residential units. The Metropolitan Hotel on Sunset and Van Ness has been converted to creative office space. And the Sunset + Vine development, which takes up an entire city block, includes the art deco facade of the former TAV Celebrity Theater (home of ABC Radio and the Merv Griffin Theater). "The times are right for this kind of project," said William Roschen, one of the design architects for the development. "There is a genuine love of our cities, and that empowers designers and urbanists to go out there and be a part of that" (Stein 2001). The Sunset + Vine development was an explicit effort to connect the city's future with its past. "Sunset and Vine will restore its immediate neighborhood in a style that ties back to Hollywood's glory days and heralds the return of a new, cool Hollywood urbanism," said Larry Bond, cofounder of Bond Capital Ltd., the project's principal developer (Aragon 2004). One of the main features of the development, which opened in 2004, was the reproduction of the storied Schwab's Drugstore (the original, which closed in 1983, was on the corner of Sunset and Crescent Heights, about two miles west of the new development). Whether in the historical place of Schwab's or the present space of the condominium lobby, the spectator is encouraged to move freely between past, present, and future, between impersonal spaces and meaningful places. But while many of these developments are anchored by at least one historical building, material structure is not the only method of granting access to the database.

Hollywood and Vine is a $500 million mixed-use project on five acres. While it did not renovate any historical structures, the new buildings remediate traditional urban forms. The buildings are framed by the sidewalks of two major boulevards with the aim of bringing the urban context into the development. The W Hotel, 375 luxury rental units, 150 luxury condominium units, and over 60,000 square feet of retail, is available from street level. The development looks outward to the street so that it can use the database of the storied corner as its content. There are hopes that the development will function as a content generator for the surrounding streets. According to Leron Gubler of the Hollywood Chamber of Commerce, "It will be the catalytic project for the rest of the Hollywood and Vine area" ("City Council Approves" 2006).

This and all of the developments presently under way in Hollywood are dependent upon the current high market value of "urban experience" for their success. The people buying urban condominiums or traveling into the city to do their shopping are not interested only in the convenience of the location; they want to "be" in the city, they want to access its history, and they want to have new, yet familiar experiences of urban space. They do not, however, want those experiences to be hand-fed to them. They want to feel as through they have been personally obtained, worked for, and adapted. This is the nature of the digital possessive—where personal agency is as important as narrative cohesiveness in the formation of urban experience. The database city necessitates the re-membering (the opposite of dis-membering), or the putting back together, of experience (Dewey 1929, 99). As it is in the active process of re-membering where perceptions of community and tradition are formed, this process is built into the structure of new urban developments. By referencing nostalgic urban forms, including grand vistas and spectacular sidewalk displays, new developments consistently prompt spectators to assemble ideal urban narratives. The experience of the present is communicated as a reframing of the past—not in the form of a static representation, but as an interactive re-membering. In Dean MacCannell's view, spectators understand the reframing of the past as more authentic than any original display. "[Walter] Benjamin believed that the reproductions of the work of art are produced because the work has a socially based 'aura' about it, the 'aura' being a residue of its origin in a primordial ritual. He should have reversed his terms. The work becomes 'authentic' only after the first copy of it is produced. The reproductions are the aura, and the ritual, far from being a point of origin, *derives* from the relationship between the original object and its socially constructed importance" (1976, 48). This important reversal of Benjamin's terms explains the logic of the database city. The ritual of urban experience, as MacCannell explains it, is dependent upon the context that is built around the material structures of the city. The corner of Hollywood and Vine is unimportant outside of its representations, Schwab's Drugstore is just another restaurant outside of its representations, and the larger flows of the city are only important in that they represent a "golden age." The assemblage of auratic urban reproductions has become the primary goal for developers, and the process of unpacking those references has come to define urban spectatorship. One cannot directly experience the database image; one can, however, experience the process of interacting with it.

While the developments in Hollywood are spectacular, they are by no means unique. Urban developments throughout the country are appropriating the rhetorical strategies of the database city. By capitalizing on historical images and narratives and by referencing previous iterations of spectatorship, new developments are primarily concerned with producing a legible city by enabling spectators to possess or aggregate only the data they choose. As the housing and office booms of the twenty-first century's first decade produced an influx of construction into almost every major American city, each new condominium and office tower project has been marketed as a conduit to the perpetual stream of urban data. Urban developments don't need to communicate with one another; each can be a self-sufficient search engine, granting access to a unique set of urban data. The database city is soft and portable, fully contained within the conduit of the database image. While it looks out onto the surrounding urban fabric, it actually depends less on the materiality of that fabric than ever before.

CONCLUSION

The ordered world is not the world order.
MARTIN BUBER, *I and Thou*

What becomes of the city when individual urban developments compete to define it? Over a hundred years ago, the White City introduced the rather novel practice of possessive spectatorship, where the Concept-city could be assembled by individual spectators through the possession and combination of unique impressions. Possessive spectatorship became a means of managing the scale of the city; it granted access to a social, cultural, and architectural formation that was either inaccessible because of its size, or undesirable because of its unformulated narrative. With each new mediating technology, the process by which an individual could possess a meaningful concept of the city continued to change. From the intimacy of the snapshotter to the alienation of computation, what has remained constant throughout the twentieth century is the cultural framing of the American city as a product of individual spectatorship.

And as we move further into the twenty-first century, individual spectatorship is just as likely to be informed by content on Flickr, YouTube, Google, MySpace, and Twitter as it is by official tourist guides or even architecture. What's more, the artifacts of this spectatorship are likely to be recorded and contributed to the standing reserve of data about the city. Data grows exponentially as viewing and producing become two sides of the same activity. In the words of one commentator, a successful presence on the Internet is determined by who can be the "most meta" (Lanier 2006). Users flock to news aggregators, RSS (Really Simple Syndication) readers, and search engines because individual bits of data are fleeting. Planners and architects are just beginning to understand the importance of data management, as it becomes increasingly clear that producing and managing a city's image requires aggregating various forms of data and making them accessible to people where they happen to be. Simply announcing new development plans is no longer sufficient for shaping the image of the city, as quiet thoughts and backroom conversations are now integral to a city's popular construction. The best position for a city to adopt is that of aggregator. While Charles Dudley Arnold struggled to produce the official image of the White City by carefully framing the city in photographs and censoring the amateur, today, managing an "official image" requires providing a dynamic platform for the mounting data of spectators.

Urban planners typically seek to maintain contiguous relationships and establish smooth flows for physical movement, but it is just as important that they disentangle established relationships, enable the individual ordering of user-created data, and acknowledge that, as David Weinberger says, everything is miscellaneous (2007). Even in 1893, as the amateur was beginning to win influence in the White City, user-generated content was emerging. The active gaze of the urban spectator was key to the production of the American city. And while the form of the city and the nature of spectatorship have changed throughout the century, the centrality of possessive spectatorship has remained relatively constant. The spectator was denied engagement with the operative city; however, she was strategically reengaged by the rerun city. In the midst of its deep-seated inequalities, violence, elitism, and triumph, the American city has largely maintained its populist ideology of open access to experience through cognitive (and literal) possession. Whether the spectator has been collecting images of the White City, gleaning snapshots of nature, speculating through the guiding metaphor of radio waves, reexperiencing the past through the episodic repetition of history, assembling from a database of images, or aggregating from the collective impressions of individual users, the American city, if not always accessible, has always had the allure of accessibility.

The digital possessive only reinforces that allure. The ideology of digital media—as evidenced in the phrases "participatory media" and "user-generated content"—is accessibility. Digital media directly align the rhetoric of progress with the rhetoric of populism. And while this is certainly not just an American phenomenon, it is in direct alignment with the history of American urban spectatorship. The digital possessive externalizes the internal practices of possessive spectatorship exercised in American cities throughout the last century. Essentially, it makes explicit what has only been implied—that anyone, regardless of social position, can participate in the ordering of city experience. But what's unique about the digital possessive is that it makes the products of individuals available to the network. And it makes the network a part of the product of individuals.

The built environment has already adapted to these new practices. Most major American cities are implementing some kind of citywide wi-fi; new developments are stocked with interactive billboards and information kiosks; and city information is becoming more accessible on the Web and mobile devices. But there are many more changes in store. Whether through integrating technology into the urban landscape via global-positioning system (GPS) or radio frequency identification (RFID), or creating parallel informationscapes to amend the production and consumption of the city, the digital possessive will be formative of American urbanism in the foreseeable future. The real challenge will be in the more subtle changes that the digital possessive implies. Spectatorship is not only the result of direct interaction with technology. "Kodak thinking," for instance, was a way of seeing as if one was carrying a camera. In most cases, technology has served primarily as a structuring metaphor for urban looking. The digital possessive will begin to alter how spectators interact with each other, with or without network connection. It will begin to alter how they interact with the built environment, with or without technology. It is imperative for designers, planners, and architects not to mistake spectatorship for the technology that helps shape it. If mismanaged, digital technology poses significant threats to urbanism—with its capacity for surveillance, the digital possessive can lead to the erosion of public space. But if considered appropriately, it poses unique possibilities for renewed public space through collaborative engagement and civic participation. As the digital possessive settles into the structures of the database city, the city's material will become immense. And as users produce and aggregate this material in almost every aspect of their daily lives, we can imagine a newly invigorated context for urban experiences and communication or a highly controlled platform where the city is merely mobilized by corporations as a brand no different than Coke or Pepsi. The extent to which architects, planners and city leaders choose to recognize the digital possessive as formative to the cultural construction of the American city will determine how urban spaces shape twenty-first century American life.

NOTES

Chapter 1. More Than the Sum of Its Parts

1 While some commentators, including William Wilson, disagree that the White City was a predecessor to the City Beautiful Movement because of the exposition's lack of functionality (Wilson 1989), there seems sufficient evidence to see the two as connected. The White City's emphasis on urban unity and pictorialism, despite its temporary structures, served as a test case for the aesthetic practices of the latter movement.

2 For some, the emphasis on communicating the singular phenomenon of the city was assuredly regressive. Protesting the way in which the grand exhibition sparked a neoclassical revival that proved contrary to the bourgeoning modernisms in Europe, some contemporaries and historians disparaged its single-mindedness and snobbishness. In his *Autobiography of an Idea* (1924), Louis Sullivan expressed his dislike for the White City (despite the fact he designed the "great golden archway" of the Transportation Building), calling it an "appalling calamity" and "virus" that would cause at least fifty years of damage to American architecture. Sullivan, who popularized the phrase "form follows function," was critical of lavish facades and ornamentation of any kind. Burnham's pictorialism and reliance on the Beaux Arts architectural style was an assault to Sullivan's vision of modernism.

Chapter 2. Picture Thinking

1 Archival research was conducted at the International Museum of Photography and Film in August 2006.

Chapter 3. City in Motion

1 Deleuze takes his conception of the image from Henri Bergson. Bergson understood all the world as the interrelation of images. "Every image is within certain images and without others," Bergson claimed, "but of the aggregate of images we cannot say that it is within us or without us, since interiority and exteriority are only relations among images" (1998, 13).

Chapter 4. Scaling Up

1 It took the invention of steel-reinforced frames and the electronic elevator for buildings to rise above a certain number of stories.

2 The move to decentralize radio was by no means universal. A point of comparison is the Soviet Union, where a centralized radio better met the ideological needs of the government. In 1928, the Soviet commissar for education, Anatoli Lunacharsky, said

of radio, "We must gradually conquer the radio waves both inside and outside our country to promote our goal of creating a new arena in which our voice must resound and our truths ring out, and where a heightened class struggle will take place. We support and proclaim the principle of class struggle across the radio waves."

3 Revised after 1961 and retitled "Architectural Rendering" (rev. 14th ed.).

4 At the project's beginnings, Hugh Ferriss, along with John Wenrich, worked on creating its renderings. However, Ferriss left the project early on, so his immediate influence on the final design is not obvious.

5 The property was leased for 90 million dollars for twenty-four years, or a yearly rental of 3.75 million dollars, with a privilege of three renewals of twenty-four years each.

6 Twenty percent of the rentable area in the entire development was leased to the National Broadcasting Company, the Radio Corporation of America, and affiliated interests.

7 At the time of the theater's opening, the famous dancing girl troupe was actually called the "Roxyettes." The name was shortened soon after opening night at the Music Hall.

Chapter 5. The Operative City

1 This was code for the IBM 704 completed in 1955.

2 The following is taken from the dialogue Turing wrote to illustrate his test.

> Q: Will X please tell me the length of his or her hair?
> A: My hair is shingled, and the longest strands are about nine inches long.
> Q: Please write me a sonnet on the subject of the Forth Bridge.
> A: Count me out on this one. I never could write poetry.
> Q: Add 34957 to 70764.
> A: (After about thirty seconds) 105721.
> Q: Do you play chess?
> A: Yes.
> Q: I have K at my K1 and no other pieces. You have only K at K6 and R at R1. It is your move. What do you play?
> A: (After a pause of fifteen seconds) R-R8 mate. (11)

Chapter 7. The Database City

1 The stars stretch for eighteen blocks (east-west) along both sides of Hollywood Boulevard, from Gower Street (on the east) to La Brea Avenue (on the west). The Walk of Fame also runs for three blocks (north-south) along Vine Street, beginning at Sunset Boulevard (on the south), crossing Hollywood Boulevard, and extending up to Yucca Street (on the north).

REFERENCES

Aarseth, Espen. 1997. *Cybertext: Perspectives on Ergodic Literature.* Baltimore: Johns Hopkins University Press.

Acconci, Vito. 1990. "Public Space in Private Time." *Critical Inquiry* 16(4):900–918.

Allen, John. 2000. "On Georg Simmel: Proximity Distance and Movement." In *Thinking Space*, edited by M. Crang and N. Thrift. London: Routledge.

Applebaum, Stanley. 1980. *The Chicago World's Fair of 1893: A Photographic Record.* New York: Dover.

Aragon, Greg. 2004. "The Next Act in the New Hollywood." *California Construction*, August 1, 12.

"Architects Picked to Plan Rockefeller Center, Which May Have Opera House as a Nucleus." 1929. *New York Times*, October 29, 1.

"Architectural Design Show." 1932. *New York Times*, February 7, N4.

Arnold, Charles Dudley, and H. D. Higinbotham. 1893. *Official Views of the World's Columbian Exposition Issued by the Department of Photography.* Chicago: Photo-Gravure Co.

The Artistic Guide to Chicago and the World's Columbian Exhibition. 1892. Chicago: Columbian Art.

Barnouw, Erik. 1990. *Tube of Plenty: The Evolution of American Television.* New York: Oxford University Press.

Baudrillard, Jean. 1998. "Procession of Simulacrum." In *Cultural Theory and Popular Culture: A Reader*, edited by J. Storey. Athens: University of Georgia Press.

Bel Geddes, Norman. 1940. *Magic Motorways.* New York: American Book-Stratford Press.

Benjamin, Walter. 1985. "On Some Motifs in Baudelaire." In *Illuminations*, edited by H. Arendt. New York: Schocken.

———. 1986. "The Work of Art in the Age of Mechanical Reproduction." In *Illuminations*, edited by H. Arendt. New York: Schocken.

Bergson, Henri. 1988. *Matter and Memory.* New York: Zone. Original edition, 1911.

———. 1998. *Creative Evolution.* Mineola, N.Y.: Dover. Original edition, 1911.

Berman, Marshall. 1988. *All That Is Solid Melts into Air.* New York: Penguin.

Bolter, Jay David, and Richard Grusin. 1999. *Remediation: Understanding New Media.* Cambridge: MIT Press.

Bottomore, Stephen. 1999. "The Panicky Audience? Early Cinema and the 'Train Effect.'" *Historical Journal of Film, Radio, and Television* 19(2):177–216.

boyd, danah. 2006. "Profiles as Conversation: Networked Identity Performance on

Friendster." Paper read at Hawai'i International Conference on System Sciences, January 4–7, at Kauai, Hawai'i.

Boyer, M. Christine. 1992. "Cities for Sale: Merchandising History at South Street Seaport." In *Variations on a Theme Park: The New American City and the End of Public Space*, edited by M. Sorkin. New York: Wang and Hill.

———. 1996. *The City of Collective Memory: Its Historical Imagery and Architectural Entertainments*. Cambridge: MIT Press.

Boyesen, Hjalmar Hjorth. 1893. "A New World Fable." *Cosmopolitan* 16(2):173–186.

Bramen, Carrie Tirado. 2000. "William Dean Howells and the Failure of the Urban Picturesque." *New England Quarterly* 73(1):82–99.

Bray, Paul M. 1993. "The New Urbanism: Celebrating the City." *Places* 8(4):56–65.

Bressi, Todd W. 1994. "Planning the American Dream." In *The New Urbanism: Toward an Architecture of Community*, edited by P. Katz. New York: McGraw-Hill.

Bruno, Giuliana. 1997. "Site-Seeing: Architecture and the Moving Image." *Wide Angle* 19(4):8–24.

Buel, C. C. 1893. "Preliminary Glimpses of the Fair." *Century Illustrated Magazine*, February, 615–625.

Bukatman, Scott. 2003. Matters of Gravity: Special Effects and Supermen in the Twentieth Century. Durham: Duke University Press.

"Bunker Hill." 1958. *Los Angeles Examiner*, September 6, A1.

"Bunker Hill Pictured as Crime Haunt." 1956. *Los Angeles Times*, July 5, 1.

"Bunker Hill Project Approved by Council." 1959. *Los Angeles Times*, April 1, 1.

"Bunker Hill Test Project Plan Set." 1957. *Los Angeles Times*, April 16, 1.

"Bunker Hill Rebirth Is Secured." 1959. *Los Angeles Times*, April 1, B4.

Burnham, Daniel H. 1902. "White City and Capital City." *Century Illustrated Magazine*, February, 619–620.

"By Night as by Day, That Section of the Great City Adjacent to Times Square Is a Scene of Constant Activity: The Centre of the Amusement and Transient Life of this Great Metropolis." 1905. *New York Times*, January 8, SM2.

Calore, Michael. 2007. "iPhone: Calling the Future." In Wired News. http://www.wired.com/news/technology/gizmos/0,72477-0.html?tw=rss.index.

Cassidy, John. 2006. "Me Media." *New Yorker*, May 15, 50–62.

"CBS to Let Viewers Use, Post Clips from Shows on the Web." 2007. *Boston Globe*, January 10. Retrieved January 15, 2008, http://www.boston.com/business/technology/articles/2007/01/10/cbs_to_let_viewers_use_post_clips_from_shows_on_the_web/

Chandler, Raymond. 1942. *The High Window*. New York: Knopf.

Chapman, John L. 1968. "Bunker Hill." *Los Angeles Times WEST Magazine*, November 3, 18–19, 23–24, 26.

Charney, Leo, and Vanessa R. Schwartz, eds. 1995. *Cinema and the Invention of Modern Life*. Berkeley: University of California Press.

"City Council Approves Development at Hollywood and Vine." 2006. NBC4, Los Angeles. Retrieved November 6 from http://www.nbc4.tv/news/4551212/detail.html

Clark, Evans. 1953. Foreword. In *Renewing Our Cities* by Miles L. Colean. New York: Twentieth Century Fund.
Cocks, Catherine. 2001. *Doing the Town: The Rise of Urban Tourism in the United States, 1850–1915*. Berkeley: University of California Press.
Colean, Miles L. 1953. *Renewing Our Cities*. New York: Twentieth Century Fund.
Community Redevelopment Agency. 1958. Box A, Bunker Hill Development Project. Regional History Collection, University of Southern California. Los Angeles.
Corliss et al. v. E. W. Walker Co. et al. 1894. Circuit Court, D. Massachusetts. November 19.
Crane, F. W. 1895. "Recent Amateur Photography." *American Journal of Photography* 18(208):457–464.
Crawford, Margaret. 1992. "The World in a Shopping Mall." In *Variations on a Theme Park: The New American City and the End of Public Space*, edited by M. Sorkin. New York: Hill & Wang.
Crevier, Daniel. 1993. *AI: The Tumultuous History of the Search for Artificial Intelligence*. New York: Basic Books.
Dash, E. 2005. "Europe Zips Lips; U.S. Sells ZIPs." *New York Times*, August 7, 1, 5.
Davis, W. S. 1908. "Photography's Worst Enemy." *American Photography*, March, 139–141.
Debord, Guy. 1994. *Society of the Spectacle*, translated by D. Nicholson-Smith. New York: Zone.
"Debut of a City." 1933. *Fortune*, January, 66.
de Certeau, Michel. 2002. "Walking in the City." In *The Practice of Everyday Life*, translated by Steven Rendall. Berkeley: University of California Press.
Deleuze, Gilles. 1986. *Cinema 1: The Movement-Image*, translated by Hugh Tomlinson and Barbara Habberjam. Minneapolis: University of Minnesota Press.
Derrida, Jacques. 1979. *Spurs: Nietzche's Styles*, translated by B. Harlow. Chicago: University of Chicago Press.
de Saussure, Ferdinand. 1986. *Course in General Linguistics*, translated by Roy Harris. New York: Open Court.
Dewey, John. 1930. *The Quest for Certainty: A Study of the Relation of Knowledge and Action*. New York: G. Allen & Unwin.
Douglas, Susan. 1986. "Amateur Operators and American Broadcasting: Shaping the Future of Radio." In *Imagining Tomorrow: History, Technology and the American Future*, edited by J. Corn. Cambridge: MIT Press.
Downtown Waterfront—Faneuil Hall Urban Renewal Plan. 1964. Boston: Boston Redevelopment Authority.
Driscoll, Marjorie. 1954. "Past Glories Told of Bunker Hill." *Los Angeles Examiner*, August 22, 12.
Duffus, R. L. 1928. "Charting the New York of the Future." *New York Times*, December 16, XX3.
——. 1929. "The Metropolis of the Future: Mr. Ferriss Considers the Problem Created by the Skyscraper." *New York Times Book Review*, December 8, 10.

"Editor's Note." 1899. *American Amateur Photographer*, September, 398.
"Fair Visitors 'Fly' Over U.S. of 1960." 1939. *New York Times*, April 19, 17.
Featherstone, Mike. 1998. "The Flaneur, the City and Virtual Public Life." *Urban Studies* 35(5–6):909–925.
Ferriss, Hugh. [1929] 1986. *The Metropolis of Tomorrow*. New York: Princeton Architectural Press. Reprint. Mineloa, N.Y.: Dover, 2005.
Fielding, Raymond. 1970. "Hale's Tours: Ultrarealism in the Pre-1910 Motion Picture." *Cinema Journal* 10(1):34–47.
"Financiers Urge Bunker Hill OK." 1958. *Los Angeles Examiner*, July 16, A3.
"Floating Sphere to Dominate Fair." 1937. *New York Times*, March 16, 25.
Fogelson, Robert M. 2001. *Downtown: Its Rise and Fall, 1880–1950*. New Haven: Yale University Press.
Fojas, Camilla. 2005. "American Cosmopolis: The World's Columbian Exposition and Chicago across the Americas." *Comparative Literature Studies* 42(2):264–287.
Forrester, Jay Wright. 1969. *Urban Dynamics*. Cambridge: MIT Press.
Frampton, Kenneth. 1992. *Modern Architecture: A Critical History*. London: Thames and Hudson.
Francastel, Pierre. 2000. *Art and Technology in the Nineteenth and Twentieth Centuries*, translated by R. Cherry. New York: Zone.
Frederick, Christine. 1926. "Radio Makes Isolated Lives Happy." *Radio News*, April, 1398.
Freud, Sigmund. 1922. *Beyond the Pleasure Principle*, translated by C. J. M. Hubback. London: International Psycho-Analytic Press.
Friedberg, Anne. 2006. *The Virtual Window: From Alberti to Microsoft*. Cambridge: MIT Press.
Garvin, Alexander. 1980. "Recycling New York." *Perspecta* 16:73–85.
Gelernter, David Hillel. 1995. *1939, the Lost World of the Fair*. New York: Free Press.
Gibson, W. Hamilton. 1893. "Foreground and Vista at the Fair." *Scribner's*, July, 29–37.
Giovannini, Joseph. 1975. "The Manhattanization of Bunker Hill." (Los Angeles) *Herald Examiner Magazine*, May 11, 10–14.
Grant, Robert. 1893. "People Who Did Not Go to the Fair." *Cosmopolitan*, December, 158–164.
Grossman, Lev. 2006. "Power to the People." *Time*, December 25, 42.
Guerard, Albert. 1930. "Tomorrow Seen by Today." (New York) *Herald Tribune Books*, January 19, 1.
Gunning, Tom. 1990. "The Cinema of Attractions: Early Film, Its Spectator and the Avant-Garde." In *Early Cinema: Space, Frame, Narrative*, edited by T. Elsaesser. London: BFI.
Hales, Peter Bacon. 2005. *Silver Cities: Photographing American Urbanization, 1839–1939*. Revised and expanded ed. Albuquerque: University of New Mexico Press.
Hall, Mordaunt. 1930. "A Clever Film Fantasy." *New York Times*, November 30, X5.
Hamilton, R. 1902. "The Degradation of Photography." *American Amateur Photographer*, August, 341–342.

Hammack, David C. 1991. "Developing for Commercial Culture." In *Inventing Times Square: Commerce and Culture at the Crossroads of the World*, edited by W. R. Taylor. New York: Russell Sage Foundation.

Hannigan, John. 1998. *Fantasy City: Pleasure and Profit in the Postmodern Metropolis*. London: Routledge.

Harwood, W. S. 1893. "Amateur Photography of To-Day." *Cosmopolitan*, December, 249–258.

Heidegger, Martin. 1962. *Being and Time*, translated by Joan Stambaugh. New York: Harper.

———. 1977. "The Age of the World Picture." In *The Question Concerning Technology and Other Essays*. New York: Harper & Row.

———. 1984. *The Metaphysical Foundations of Logic*, translated by M. Heim. Bloomington: Indiana University Press.

———. 1993. "The Question Concerning Technology." In *Basic Writings*, edited and translated by D. F. Krell. San Francisco: Harper Collins.

Helm, Edward. 1902. "Life Pictures in the Streets of a Great City." *American Amateur Photographer*, March, 107–111.

Hemment, Drew. 2004. "Locative Dystopia." Available at http://www.drewhemment.com/2004/locative_dystopia_2.html

Henkin, David. 1998. *City Reading: Written Words and Public Spaces in Antebellum New York*. New York: Columbia University Press.

Hogan, James P. 1997. *Mind Matters: Exploring the World of Artificial Intelligence*. New York: Del Rey.

Hood, Raymond. 1929. "A City under a Single Roof." Interview with Raymond Hood by F. S. Tisdale. *Nation's Business* 17(12):19–20, 206–208.

———. 1932. "The Design of Rockefeller City." *Architectural Forum* 56(1):1–12.

Howells, William Dean. 1909. *Impressions and Experiences*. New York: Harper & Brothers. Original edition, 1896.

———. 1994. *A Hazard of New Fortunes*. New York: Meridian. Original edition, 1890.

Hoyt, Homer. 1943. "Rebuilding American Cities after the War." *Journal of Land and Public Utility Economics* August:366.

Huizinga, Johan. 1950. *Homo Ludens: A Study of the Play Element in Culture*. Boston: Beacon.

"Impressions of a Scotsman and an Australian Artist during a Stroll up New York's Unique Thoroughfare from Fourteenth Street to the New Times Building: Its Wonderfully Cosmopolitan Atmosphere." 1904. *New York Times*, Dec. 11, SM5.

Ito, M., and D. Okabe. 2006. "Everyday Contexts of Camera Phone Use: Steps towards Techno-social Ethnographic Frameworks." In *Mobile Communication in Everyday Life: An Ethnographic View*, edited by Joachim R. Höflich and Maren Hartmann. Berlin: Frank & Timme.

Jacobs, Jane. 1961. *The Death and Life of Great American Cities*. New York: Random House.

James, William. 1908. *Pragmatism: A New Name for Some Old Ways of Thinking—Popular Lectures on Philosophy*. New ed. New York: Longmans, Green.
——. 1950. *The Principles of Psychology*. Volume 2. New York: Dover.
——. 1996. *Essays in Radical Empiricism*. Lincoln: University of Nebraska Press.
Jameson, Frederic. 2001. "Postmodernism, or the Cultural Logic of Late Capitalism." In *Media and Cultural Studies: Keyworks*, edited by M. G. Durham and D. Kellner. Malden, Mass.: Blackwell.
Jay, Martin. 2005. *Songs of Experience: Modern American and European Variations on a Universal Theme*. Berkeley: University of California Press.
Johnston, Hubert McBean. 1902. "Photography as an Educator." *Photo Era*, August, 65–69.
Jollie, Eleanor M. 1902. "How One Teacher Made Use of a Camera." *Photo Era*, November, 193–196.
Jones, Francis Arthur. 1911. "The Most Wonderful Electric Sign in the World: And How It Worked." *Strand Magazine*, October, 443–448.
Kaplan, Amy. 1988. *The Social Construction of American Realism*. Chicago: University of Chicago Press.
Karp, Walter. 1982. *The Center: A History and Guide to Rockefeller Center*. New York: American Heritage.
Kenney, Robert T. 1973. *Faneuil Hall*. Boston: Boston Redevelopment Authority.
Kern, Stephen. 1983. *The Culture of Time and Space, 1880–1919*. Cambridge: Harvard University Press.
Kinder, Marsha. 2002. "Hot Spots, Avatars, and Narrative Fields Forever: Bunuel's Legacy for New Digital Media and Interactive Database Narrative." *Film Quarterly* 55(3):2–15.
Kirby, Lynne. 1996. *Parallel Tracks: The Railroad and Silent Cinema*. Durham: Duke University Press.
Klein, Norman. 2003. *Bleeding Through*. Booklet accompanying the DVD-ROM *Bleeding Through: Layers of Los Angeles, 1920–1986*. ZKM Center for Art and Media and the Labyrinth Project at the Annenberg Center for Communication of the University of Southern California, Los Angeles.
Kompare, Derek. 2006. *Rerun Nation: How Repeats Invented American Television*. New York: Routledge.
Koolhaas, Rem. 1978. *Delirious New York: A Retroactive Manifesto for Manhattan*. New York: Oxford University Press.
Kracauer, Siegfried. 1995a. "The Mass Ornament." In *The Mass Ornament: Weimar Essays*, edited by T. Y. Levin. Cambridge: Harvard University Press.
——. 1995b. "Photography." In *The Mass Ornament: Weimar Essays*, edited by T. Y. Levin. Cambridge: Harvard University Press.
Krieger, Alex. 1987. "The American City: Ideal and Mythic Aspects of a Reinvented Urbanism." *Assemblage* (3):38–59.
Krinsky, Carol. 1978. *Rockefeller Center*. New York: Oxford University Press.

Landow, George. 1991. *Hypertext: The Convergence of Contemporary Critical Theory and Technology*. Baltimore: Johns Hopkins University Press.

Langdon, Philip. 1988. "A Good Place to Live." *Atlantic Monthly* 261(3):39–60. Available at http://www.theatlantic.com/issues/96sep/kunstler/langdon.htm

Lanier, Jaron. 2006. "Digital Maoism: The Hazards of the New Online Collectivism." *Edge*. http://edge.org/3rd_culture/lanier06/lanier06_index.html.

Larson, Erik. 2003. *The Devil in the White City: Murder, Magic, and Madness at the Fair That Changed America*. New York: Crown.

"LA's Acropolis." 1955. *Los Angeles Examiner*, November 28, A2.

The Last Rivet. 1940. New York: Columbia University Press.

Lazarsfeld, Paul F., and Patricia L. Kendall. 1948. *Radio Listening in America: The People Look at Radio—Again*. New York: Prentice-Hall.

Leach, William. 1991. "Introductory Essay." In *Inventing Times Square: Commerce and Culture at the Crossroads of the World*, edited by W. R. Taylor. New York: Russell Sage Foundation.

Le Corbusier. 1929. *The City of Tomorrow and Its Planning*. London: John Rodker.

——. 1947. *When the Cathedrals Were White: A Journey to the Country of Timid People*, translated by Francis Edwin Hyslop. New York: Reynal & Hitchcock.

——. 1970. *The Radiant City*. New York: Viking Press.

Lee, Gerald Stanley. 1914. *Crowds: A Moving Picture of Democracy*. New York: Doubleday, Page.

Leeuwen, Thomas van. 1986. *The Skyward Trend of Thought*. Cambridge: MIT Press.

Leich, Jean Ferriss. 1980. *Architectural Visions: The Drawings of Hugh Ferriss*. New York: Whitney Library of Design.

Lenhart, Amanda, and Mary Madden. 2007. *Social Networking Websites and Teens: An Overview*. Washington, D.C.: Pew Internet and American Life Project.

Leonard, John. 1976. "Old Sitcoms and Young Minds." *New York Times*, March 28, 91.

"Letter to the Editor." 1956. *Los Angeles Examiner*, December 19, B15.

Lewis, Peirce. 1975. "The Future of the Past: Our Clouded Vision of Historic Preservation." *Pioneer America* 7(2):1–20.

Lewis, Wyndham. 1986. "How the Fact of Style Obstructs." In *The Caliph's Design: Architects! Where is Your Vortex?* edited by P. Edwards. Santa Barbara: Black Sparrow Press.

The Life of a City: Early Films of New York, 1898–1906. 1999. Washington, D.C.: Library of Congress. Available at http://memory.loc.gov/ammem/papr/nychome.html

"Lighting 'The Great White Way.'" 1907. *New York Times*, Apr. 7, SM2.

Lindsay, Vachel. 1915. *The Art of the Moving Picture*. Norwood, Mass.: Norwood Press.

Live Broadcast Theater: Oscar's New Home. 2000. Los Angeles: Rockwell Group.

"Local Manipulation." 1920. *American Photographer*, August, 487.

Lotchin, Roger W. 1996. "World War II and Urban California: City Planning and the Transformation Hypothesis." In *Planning the Twentieth-Century American City*, edited by M. C. Sies and C. Silver. Baltimore: Johns Hopkins University Press.

Lovell, Margaretta. 1996. "Picturing 'a City for a Single Summer': Paintings of the World's Columbian Exposition." *Art Bulletin* 78(1):40–55.

Low, W. H. 1893. "The Art of the White City." *Scribner's Magazine* 14(4):504–512.

Lowenthal, David. 1985. *The Past Is a Foreign Country*. Cambridge: Cambridge University Press.

Lunacharsky, Anatoli. 1928. Untitled radio address. Accessed at http://www.nic.funet.fi/pub/culture/russian/voices/realaudio/

Lynch, Kevin. 1960. *The Image of the City*. Cambridge: MIT Press.

MacCannell, Dean. 1976. The Tourist: A New Theory of the Leisure Class. New York: Schocken.

"Magic Carpet to Take Visitors into the World of Tomorrow." 1938. *New York Times*, July 27, 12.

Manovich, Lev. 2001. *The Language of New Media*. Cambridge: MIT Press.

Markley, Horace. 1894. "Amateur Photography at the World's Fair." *American Journal of Photography* 15(170):61–68.

Marks, Paul. 2007. "New Software Can Identify You from Your Online Habits." *New Scientist*, May 16, 32.

McWilliams, Carey. 1949. "Look What's Happened to California." *Harper's*, October, 21–29.

Meadows, Mark Stephen. 2003. *Pause and Effect: The Art of Interactive Narrative*. Indianapolis: New Riders.

"Mechanical Brain Good at Checkers." 1957. *New York Times*, June 23, 167.

Mensel, Robert E. 1991. "Kodakers Lying in Wait: Amateur Photography and the Right of Privacy." *American Quarterly* 43(1):24–45.

Metz, Christian. 1974. *Language and cinema*. Approaches to Semiotics, 26. The Hague: Mouton.

Miller, E. M. 1900. "Why Not Photography?" *American Amateur Photographer*, July, 308–309.

Mitchell, J. A. 1893. "Types and People at the Fair." *Scribner's Monthly*, August, 186–193.

Morris, Lloyd. 1950. *William James: The Message of a Modern Man*. New York: Scribner's.

Mosier, Richard. 1952. "The Logic of Experience." *Journal of Philosophy* 49(12):411–415.

Mumford, Lewis. 1938. *The Culture of Cities*. New York: Harcourt.

———. 1989. *The City in History: Its Origins, Its Transformations, and Its Prospects*. San Diego: Harcourt. Original edition, 1961.

Murphy, Amy. 2000. "Past/Present: New Urbanism and the Salvage Paradigm." *Traditional Dwellings and Settlements Working Paper Series* 140:130–146.

Presented at the International Association for the Study of Traditional Environments conference in Trani, Italy, October.

Murray, Janet Horowitz. 1997. *Hamlet on the Holodeck: The Future of Narrative in Cyberspace*. New York: Free Press.

Musser, Charles. 1990. *The Emergence of Cinema: The American Screen to 1907*. Berkeley: University of California Press.

Naylor, David. 1981. *American Picture Palaces: The Architecture of Fantasy*. New York: Prentice Hall.

Negroponte, Nicholas. 1995. *Being Digital*. New York: Knopf.

Newcomb, E. N. 1900. "Why So Fast?" *Camera and Darkroom*, September, 7–10.

Newell, Allen, J. C. Shaw, and H. A. Simon. 1963. "Chess-Playing Programs and the Problem of Complexity." In *Computers and Thought*, edited by E. Feigenbaum and J. Feldman. New York: McGraw-Hill.

Newman, Philip H. 1890. "Some Relations between Fine Art and Photography." *Photographic News*, March 7, 179–181.

Nolen, John. 1909. "City Making." *American City*, September, 15–19.

Norman, Jeremy. 2005. *From Gutenberg to the Internet: A Sourcebook on the History of Information Technology*. Novato, Calif.: Historyofscience.com.

Nye, David. 1994. *American Technological Sublime*. Cambridge: MIT Press.

An Observer. 1901. "The Waning of the Popularity of the Camera." *American Amateur Photographer*, September, 394–399.

Okrent, Daniel. 2003. *Great Fortune: The Epic of Rockefeller Center*. New York: Viking.

Oppenheimer, Wm. Geo. 1897. "The Law of Privacy." *American Amateur Photographer*, January, 5–7.

Osmundsen, John A. 1959. "I.B.M. Brain Beats the Hand That Fed It Data on Checkers." *New York Times*, July 20, 27.

Photographs of the World's Fair: an Elaborate Collection of Photographs of the Buildings, Grounds and Exhibits of the World's Columbian Exposition, with a Special Description of the Famous Midway Plaisance. 1894. New York: W. W. Wilson.

Poore, C. G. 1930. "Greatest Skyscraper Rises on a Clockwork Schedule." *New York Times*, July 27, 114.

Pound, Ezra. 1950. *Patria Mia*. Chicago: Fletcher. Original edition, 1913.

"Press Release for Hollywood and Highland." 2000. Los Angeles: TrizecHahn.

Proust, Marcel. 1989. *Swann's Way: Remembrance of Things Past*, translated by C. K. S. Moncrieff and T. Kilmartin. New York: Vintage. Original edition, 1913.

Rand, McNally & Co.'s Pictorial Chicago and Illustrated World's Columbian Exposition: Containing Views of Principal Buildings, Residences, Streets, Parks, Monuments, etc. 1893. New York: Rand, MacNally & Co.

Reay, Neville. 1960. "Bunker Hill Job Due in '61." *Los Angeles Herald*, June 29.

"The Redemption of Bunker Hill." 1958. *Los Angeles Times*, June 28, 1.

Renssalaer, M. G. 1893. "At the Fair." *Century Magazine*, May, 3–13.

Report on Bunker Hill. 1960. Los Angeles: Design for Development.
Rockefeller Center. 1932. New York: Rockefeller Center.
"Rockefeller City Adds French Unit." 1932. *New York Times*, March 31, 23.
"Rockefeller Name for Radio City Units." 1932. *New York Times*, February 24, 23.
Ross, James. 1899. "Where Are We?" *American Amateur Photographer*, August, 324.
"Roundtable on Rouse." 1981. *Progressive Architecture* 7:100–106.
Rowe, Colin, and Fred Koetter. 1978. *Collage City*. Cambridge: MIT Press.
Sachse, Julius F. 1895. "Wheel versus Camera." *American Journal of Photography* 16(190):435–437.
Salmon, Scott. 2001. "Imagineering the Inner City? Landscapes of Pleasure and the Commodification of Cultural Spectacle in the Postmodern City." In *Popular Culture: Production and Consumption*, edited by C. L. Harrington and D. D. Bielby. Malden, Mass.: Blackwell.
Samuel, A. L. 1963. "Some Studies in Machine Learning Using the Game of Checkers." In *Computers and Thought*, edited by E. Feigenbaum and J. Feldman. New York: McGraw-Hill.
Sanders, James. 2001. *Celluloid Skyline: New York and the Movies*. New York: Knopf; distributed by Random House.
Santomasso, Eugene A. 1980. "The Design of Reason: Architecture and Planning at the 1939/40 New York World's Fair." In *Dawn of a New Day: The New York World's Fair*, edited by H. A. Harrison. New York: New York University Press.
Sartre, Jean Paul. 1955. "American Cities." In *Literary and Philosophical Essays*, translated by Annette Michelson. London: Rider.
Scholz, Trebor. 2008. "Market Ideology and the Myths of Web 2.0." *First Monday* 13(3). Available at http://firstmonday.org/htbin/cgiwrap/bin/ojs/index.php/fm/article/view/2138/1945.
Schrag, Calvin O. 1970. "Heidegger on Repetition and Historical Understanding." *Philosophy East and West* 20(3):287–295.
Schwarzer, Mitchell. 1994. "Myths of Permanence and Transience in the Discourse on Historic Preservation in the United States." *Journal of Architectural Education* 48(1):2–11.
"Sees City Traffic All Underground." 1925. *New York Times*, April 23, 16.
Simmel, Georg. 1971. "The Metropolis and Mental Life." In *On Individuality and Social Forms: Selected Writings*, translated by Donald N. Levine. Chicago: University of Chicago Press.
"Skyscraper City of Future Shown." 1926. *New York Times*, December 2, 29.
Smith, F. Hopkinson. 1893. "A White Umbrella at the Fair." *Cosmopolitan*, December, 150–156.
Smulyan, Susan. 1994. *Selling Radio: The Commercialization of American Broadcasting, 1920–1934*. Washington, D.C.: Smithsonian Institute Press.
Snappschotte, J. Focus. 1896. "The Age of the Bicycle." *American Journal of Photography* 17(202):448–453.
Snowden, Bayard Breese. 1916. "Picture-Thinking." *Kodakery*, April, 8–12.

Solove, Daniel. 2004. *The Digital Person: Technology and Privacy in the Information Age*. New York: New York University Press.

"Speed Urged on Bunker Hill Project." 1956. *Los Angeles Times*, April 8, 8.

Starr, Tama, and Edward Hayman. 1998. *Signs and Wonders: The Spectacular Marketing of America*. New York: Doubleday.

Stein, Jeannine. 2001. "In New Urban Villages, City Living Becomes Trendy." *Los Angeles Times*, November 19, A1.

Street, Julian. 1914. *Abroad at Home: American Ramblings, Observations and Adventures of Julian Street*. New York: Century.

Sullivan, Louis H. 1924. *The Autobiography of an Idea*. New York: Press of the American Institute of Architects.

Susman, Warren I. 1980. "The People's Fair: Cultural Contradictions of a Consumer Culture." In *Dawn of a New Day: The New York World's Fair, 1939/40*, edited by H. A. Harrison. New York: New York University Press.

Taylor, George L. 1899. "The Hand Camera." *American Amateur Photographer*, February, 55–58.

Thompson, Benjamin, and Jane McC. Thompson. 1975. *Reviving Boston's Marketplace*. Boston: Boston Redevelopment Authority.

Thompson, James. 1911. "Trips A-Field." *American Amateur Photographer*, August, 516–521.

Todd, F. Dundas. 1893. "Hand-Camera Guide to the World's Fair." *American Amateur Photographer*, April, 166–167.

Tönnies, Ferdinand. 1957. *Community and Society*, translated by C. P. Loomis. East Lansing: Michigan State University Press.

Trachtenberg, Alan, and Eric Foner. 1982. The Incorporation of America: Culture and Society in the Gilded Age. 1st ed, American Century Series. New York: Hill and Wang.

Turing, Alan. 1963. "Computing Machinery and Intelligence." In *Computers and Thought*, edited by E. Feigenbaum and J. Feldman. New York: McGraw-Hill.

Underwood, Loring. 1910. "The City Beautiful the Ideal to Aim At." *American City* 2(3):214–218.

Uricchio, William. 1982. "Ruttman's Berlin and the City Film to 1930." Ph.D. diss., New York University.

U.S. Conference of Mayors. 1983. *With Heritage So Rich*. Washington, D.C.: Preservation Press.

U.S. House Committee on Foreign Affairs. 1937. *New York World's Fair 1939*: Hearings before the Committee on Foreign Affairs. 75th Cong., 1st sess. March 23. Washington, D.C.: GPO.

Vaughan, Dai. 1990. "Let There be Lumiere." In *Early Cinema: Space, Frame, Narrative*, edited by T. Elsaesser. London: BFI.

Voitier, François. 1904. "Photographic Ennui." *Camera and Darkroom*, September, 276.

Wagner, Les. 1960. "Rejuvenation of Bunker Hill to Start Oct. 1." (Los Angeles) *Mirror News*, June 22, 8–9.

Waugh, F. A. 1902. "Photography and Education." *Photo Era*, May, 403–406.

Weinberger, David. 2002. *Small Pieces Loosely Joined: A Unified Theory of the Web*. Cambridge, Mass.: Perseus.

———. 2007. *Everything Is Miscellaneous: The Power of the New Digital Disorder*. New York: Times.

Welford, Walter D. 1897. *The Hand Camera and How to Use It*. London: Liffe, Sons, & Sturmey. Original edition, 1892.

Wellman, B., and C. A. Haythornthwaite. 2002. *The Internet in Everyday Life*. Malden, Mass.: Blackwell.

West, Nancy Martha. 2000. *Kodak and the Lens of Nostalgia*. Charlottesville: University Press of Virginia.

"What Is to Be Done About the Camera Fiend?" 1906. *American Amateur Photographer*, March, 103–104.

White, Hayden. 1987. *The Content of the Form: Discourse and Historical Representation*. Baltimore: Johns Hopkins University Press.

Wiener, Norbert. 1948. *Cybernetics: Or, Control and Communications in the Animal and the Machine*. New York: Hermann.

———. 1950. *The Human Use of Human Beings: Cybernetics and Society*. London: Eyre and Spottiswoode.

———. 1964. *God & Golem, Inc.: A Comment on Certain Points Where Cybernetics Impinges on Religion*. Cambridge: MIT Press.

Willis, Carol. 1986. "Drawing towards Metropolis." In *The Metropolis of Tomorrow* by Hugh Ferriss. New York: Princeton Architectural Press.

Wilson, William H. 1989. *The City Beautiful Movement: Creating the North American Landscape*. Baltimore: Johns Hopkins University Press.

"The World's Fair and Landscape-Gardening." 1893. *Century Magazine*, April, 953.

Zimmer, Michael. 2008. "Critical Perspectives on Web 2.0." *First Monday* 13(3). Available at http://firstmonday.org/htbin/cgiwrap/bin/ojs/index.php/fm/article/view/2137/1943

Zueblin, Charles. 1903. " 'The White City' and After." *Chautauquan*, December, 373–384.

Zukin, Sharon. 1995. *The Culture of Cities*. London: Blackwell.

INDEX